For Katherine,

Don

Studies in Marxism and Social Theory

History, power, ideology

Studies in Marxism and Social Theory

Edited by G. A. COHEN, JON ELSTER AND JOHN ROEMER

The series is jointly published by the Cambridge University Press and the Editions de la Maison des Sciences de l'Homme, as part of the joint publishing agreement established in 1977 between the Fondation de la Maison des Sciences de l'Homme and the Syndics of the Cambridge University Press.

The books in the series are intended to exemplify a new paradigm in the study of Marxist social theory. They will not be dogmatic or purely exegetical in approach. Rather, they will examine and develop the theory pioneered by Marx, in the light of the intervening history, and with the tools of non-Marxist social science and philosophy. It is hoped that Marxist thought will thereby be freed from the increasingly discredited methods and presuppositions which are still widely regarded as essential to it, and that what is true and important in Marxism will be more firmly established.

Also in the series

JON ELSTER   *Making Sense of Marx*
ADAM PRZEWORSKI   *Capitalism and Social Democracy*
JOHN ROEMER (ed.)   *Analytical Marxism*
JOHN R. BOWMAN   *Capitalist Collective Action*
JON ELSTER AND CARL MOENE (eds.)   *Alternatives to Capitalism*
MICHAEL TAYLOR (ed.)   *Rationality and Revolution*

History, power, ideology

Central issues in Marxism and anthropology

Donald L. Donham

The right of the
University of Cambridge
to print and sell
all manner of books
was granted by
Henry VIII in 1534.
The University has printed
and published continuously
since 1584.

Cambridge University Press
Cambridge
New York   Port Chester   Melbourne   Sydney

Editions de la Maison des Sciences de l'Homme
Paris

Published by the Press Syndicate of the University of Cambridge
The Pitt Building, Trumpington Street, Cambridge CB2 1RP
40 West 20th Street, New York, NY 10011, USA
10 Stamford Road, Oakleigh, Melbourne 3166, Australia

First published 1990

Printed in the United States of America

Library of Congress Cataloging-in-Publication Data
Donham, Donald L. (Donald Lewis)
    History, power, ideology : central issues in Marxism and
anthropology / Donald L. Donham.
        p.   cm. – (Studies in Marxism and social theory)
    Includes bibliographical references.
    ISBN 0-521-34663-0
    1. Communism and anthropology.   I. Title.   II. Series.
HX550.A56D66   1990
306–dc20   89-20984
                                                    CIP

For Nancy

Contents

A Klee painting named "Angelus Novus" shows an angel looking as though he is about to move away from something he is fixedly contemplating. His eyes are staring, his mouth is open, his wings are spread. This is how one pictures the angel of history. His face is turned toward the past. Where we perceive a chain of events, he sees one single catastrophe which keeps piling wreckage upon wreckage and hurls it in front of his feet. The angel would like to stay, awaken the dead, and make whole what has been smashed. But a storm is blowing from Paradise; it has got caught in his wings with such violence that the angel can no longer close them. This storm irresistibly propels him into the future to which his back is turned, while the pile of debris before him grows skyward. This storm is what we call progress.

Walter Benjamin, *Theses on the Philosophy of History*

Preface

According to Benjamin, to articulate the past means "to seize hold of a memory as it flashes up at a moment of danger." This book had its beginning in such a moment. Bridget O'Laughlin introduced me to Marxism when I was a graduate student at Stanford in the early 1970s. At that point, the upheavals of the '60s were still too immediate to constitute a memory. In 1968, 14,589 of my generation had died in battle – along with an estimated 180,000 Vietnamese. The same year, the Reserve Officer Training Corps Building at Stanford had been burned in protest. And not long afterward, a similar fire at the Center for Advanced Study in the Behavioral Sciences destroyed the anthropological fieldnotes of M. N. Srinivas, who happened then to be a Fellow.

Science did not proceed unaffected by these events, and the movements of the '60s, whatever their miscalculations or excesses, eventually opened North American universities to radical thought in a new way. This was the case in social and cultural anthropology at least. Anthropologists like Eric Wolf and Marshall Sahlins helped to organize the first teach-ins in the '60s, and by the early 1970s, a self-consciously Marxist anthropology – much of it influenced by the French philosopher Louis Althusser – was beginning to leave its mark on the discipline. I well remember its disquieting effect on me, its peculiar combination of the most traditional academic opaqueness with the promise of somehow totally remaking anthropology.

It has taken me some time to come to what I consider a provisional understanding of Marxism. As a critical theory – a theory aimed at both empirical knowledge and human emancipation – Marxism is an order of magnitude more ambitious than those theories that have dominated anthropology, whether interpretive and hermeneutic or analytical and social scientific. In Herbert Marcuse's bold language, "All materialist concepts contain an accusation and an imperative." Understanding, in the context of analyzing a society not one's own, exactly where the accusation should lie – not to mention the imperative – is difficult three times over. I do not claim to have accomplished this task. I hope to have clarified some aspects of it.

While I have pondered Marxism into the '80s, much has changed. As part of becoming an anthropologist, I have at various times lived among the Maale of southern Ethiopia for almost three years now – beginning in 1974, just before the Ethiopian revolution, and continuing afterward, through 1984. The revolution in Ethiopia was a top-down, socialist-influenced transformation of a very special sort. I do not treat its changes here, but observing the ironies of recent history in the lives of people I know well has made me wary of accepting too simplified a version of Marxism's metanarrative of historical progress.

If Ethiopia has seen a revolution, the center of gravity in international Marxist discussion has also shifted: The influence of Althusser has dramatically declined while (in social theory more generally) problems of culture, agency, and historicity have begun to receive as much attention as those of structure and organization. In the process, Great Britain and North America have become much more active centers of debate. And new social movements – many centered on sex and gender – have put into doubt old versions of Marxism that do not comprehend the plasticity of power.

As far as I can see, the late 1970s were something of a turning point. In 1976, Marshall Sahlins published *Culture and Practical Reason;* in 1977, Pierre Bourdieu's *Outline of a Theory of Practice* was translated into English; and in 1978, G. A. Cohen published *Karl Marx's Theory of History,* and E. P. Thompson, *The Poverty of Theory.* In both positive and negative ways, these works have influenced what follows.

Over the past twenty years, Marshall Sahlins has shown a remarkable ability to initiate the next wave of thinking in anthropological theory. Even if one believes, as I do, that he has gotten it wrong, Sahlins's work has set the terms of debate within anthropology. Philosopher G. A. Cohen's careful interrogation of Marxist concepts I have found more useful, and the following chapters build upon some of his insights. Elliptically put, what I attempt to do might be described as an anthropological critique of Cohen – one that gives the final say to historian E. P. Thompson, though not in the way that Thompson himself advocated.

In 1985, I published my Ph.D. dissertation, *Work and Power in Maale, Ethiopia.* Here, I use parts of the data reported in that work, supplemented by materials from subsequent field trips in 1982–1984. The present work supersedes, then, some of the empirical arguments of my earlier work. But the objective of this book is not just to convey information about Maale. My choice of data in the following chapters is motivated, in the last instance, by the goal of clarifying issues in social theory. *Work and Power* contains information not presented here, and the reader interested primarily in Maale ethnography may prefer to consult it, rather than the present work.

Writing this book, like any form of production, has been a socially conditioned process, both enabled and constrained by its particular context. I am grateful to a network of teachers and students, colleagues and friends – many tied in one way or another to the Department of Anthropology at Stanford – who have done much to help me improve my arguments: Phil Ansell, Frank Cancian, George Collier, Jane Collier, Akhil Gupta, Donald Moore, Bridget O'Laughlin, Lisa Rofel, Renato Rosaldo, Bill Skinner, Carol Smith, Katherine Verdery, and Sylvia Yanagisako. I would also like to thank new colleagues at Emory: Wally Adamson, Peggy Barlett, Peter Brown, Betsy Fox-Genovese, Bruce Knauft, Bobby Paul, Judy Rohrer, Buck Schieffelin, and Carol Worthman.

Toward the final stages of finishing this book, Helen Siu and Bill Kelly invited me to discuss the manuscript in their seminar on culture and political economy at Yale. That exercise helped me to clarify central themes of the book. Finally, I would like to acknowledge the role of G. A. Cohen. As it stands, this book has many weaknesses, but it would have had many more without his incisive reactions to successive drafts.

Fieldwork in Ethiopia was made possible by National Science Foundation grants BNS 81–21547 and GS–41672 and by the sponsorship of the Institute of Ethiopian Studies and the Institute of Development Studies at Addis Ababa University.

Previous versions of Chapters 1 and 4 have appeared respectively in *Man* in 1981 ("Beyond the Domestic Mode of Production," vol. 16, pp. 515–41), and in the *American Ethnologist* in 1985 ("History at One Point in Time: 'Working Together' in Maale, 1975," vol. 12, pp. 262–84). I thank Iowa State University Press for permission to reprint figures 8 and 9, table 10, and map 6 from my book, *Work and Power in Maale, Ethiopia;* Malaby Press, for permission to reprint a version of figure 10 in Jonathan Friedman's article "Tribes, States, and Transformations," in Maurice Bloch, ed., *Marxist Analyses and Social Anthropology;* the Frobenius-Institut, Frankfurt, Federal Republic of Germany, for permission to reproduce the photograph on p. 93 of this book; the Museum of Modern Art, New York, for permission to reproduce photographs of works by Man Ray and Meret Oppenheim.

This book is dedicated to Nancy Donham, whose critical intelligence was the that-without-which.

Center for Advanced Study
in the Behavioral Sciences   January 1990

Entrance to a Maale chief's compound

Introduction

> *What, after all, is one to make of savages? . . . For the anthropologist,
> whose profession it is to study other cultures, the puzzle is always
> with him. His personal relationship to his object of study is, perhaps
> more than for any other scientist, inevitably problematic. Know what
> he thinks a savage is and you have the key to his work. You know
> what he thinks he himself is and, knowing what he thinks he himself
> is you know in general what sort of thing he is going to say about
> whatever tribe he happens to be studying. All ethnography is part
> philosophy, and a good deal of the rest is confession.*
>
> Clifford Geertz

This book does not fit accepted categories of writing. For instance, what
follows does not constitute ethnography – yet in the course of presenting my arguments, I return repeatedly to the details of social life in a
remote area of southern Ethiopia called Maale. Similarly, this is not a
work in abstract social theory – yet I attempt throughout to pose and to
resolve conceptual issues of broad relevance. Neither simply ethnography nor social theory, the chapters that follow are both.

Trespassing the accepted boundary between fields involves some risk.
Social theorists of the purist sort, those dedicated to what has been called
the "detachable conclusion," may well grow impatient with my Maale
detail. After all, why should anyone but an anthropologist be interested
in an out-of-the-way people? At the same time, ethnographers, many of
whom are distrustful of wider-scale discussions, may tire of my didactic
return to "general" issues. In the end, doesn't abstract discussion dis-
tract from a proper appreciation of Maale society and culture?

The risks that these questions imply seem to me to be worth taking.
A number of years ago, Robert K. Merton noted the persistent gap in
academic sociology between grand theory and empirical analysis. A gap
no less great nor any less debilitating exists in many Marxist discussions.
More than sociology, Marxism has an inherent interest in closing this
gap. Therefore, one goal of what follows is to trace out, as precisely as
possible, the connections between abstract theory – in particular, Marxism – and embedded empirical analysis – in this case, of Maale political
economy. Otherwise put, my problem is to translate megawords like

history, power, and ideology into micropractices like dabo, lali ekane, and wolla soofane.[1]

The choice of where to situate myself relative to established discourses has, however, been motivated by more than a preference for the middle range. Located between ethnography and social theory, this book seeks to combine anthropology and Marxism so that the critical edge of one can be used to sharpen issues in the other. My master questions are: Can the critical moment in anthropology be used to transform aspects of Marxism? Can the critical aspect of Marxism be used to recast anthropology?

That anthropology indeed has a critical moment has often been overlooked of late. More attention has been devoted to ways in which the discipline – in the context of colonialism and the world capitalist system – has distorted the depiction of its subjects, suppressed inconvenient realities, and contributed, if only unwittingly, to extant forms of domination.[2] All of these are aspects of the subject as it has been practiced.

But social and cultural anthropology has another side, one from which writers have used portraits of other cultures to reflect upon our own practices – to disrupt our common sense, to disorient our moral certainties, and, in general, to place in doubt much of what we have always assumed as simply given. Anthropologists attempting to accomplish these ends have had to construct other cultural worlds – that is, write ethnography – in enough density and detail to overcome the initial resistances set up by our own cultural conditioning.[3]

Thus one of my concerns below in interpreting Maale political economy: By attempting to make a radically different way of living "real," I hope to be able to place the analysis of my own, capitalist society in a different light.

---

[1] These Maale phrases refer respectively to a particular kind of communal work arrangement, marrying a woman, and working together. They form the main empirical themes of Chapters 1, 3, and 4. Because I want other cultural notions ultimately to be accepted on the same basis as our own, I have not italized foreign words.

[2] Dell Hymes, ed., *Reinventing Anthropology* (New York: Pantheon, 1969); Talal Asad, ed., *Anthropology and the Colonial Encounter* (London: Ithaca Press, 1973); Gérard Leclerc, *Anthropologie et colonialisme* (Paris: Fayard, 1972). See also Edward Said, *Orientalism* (New York: Pantheon, 1978).

[3] A recent statement of this theme is George E. Marcus and Michael M. J. Fischer, *Anthropology as Cultural Critique: An Experimental Moment in the Human Sciences* (Chicago: University of Chicago Press, 1986). James Clifford's "On Ethnographic Surrealism," *The Predicament of Culture: Twentieth-Century Ethnography, Literature, and Art* (Cambridge: Harvard University Press, 1988), pp. 117–51, is an excellent study of the critical spirit of French anthropology between the wars.

If the critical aspect of anthropology (like history or literature) works in a positive way by expanding one's sense of human possibilities, the critical moment within Marxism works negatively. It seeks most fundamentally to remove, to lift away, those forms of consciousness, those partially self-imposed ideologies, that limit and deform people's lives. Such ideologies, according to Marxism, arise and function at particular social sites: namely, in relationships based on systematic differences in materially grounded power.

These relations may be as different, in different societies, as those between Maale commoners and chiefs, South African black workers and international capitalists, or – at closer range – middle-class American housewives and their husbands. Whatever the case, the critical assumption of Marxism is that such relationships, and indeed all others in which one group has the power to suppress the interests of another, are inevitably problematic. Ideologies naturalize power differences; they do social work. But according to Marxism, ideologies can be only partially successful for the fundamental reason that people suffer under such conditions. Not only do people suffer, they see, or in principle can be brought to see, the causes of their suffering.[4]

It is just in this context that Marxism takes on its critical aspect: of promoting the process of bringing people to see, of removing the veil of ideology, and by so doing, opening up the range of human possibilities.

These two notions of critique – anthropological and Marxist – are quite different. Characteristically, they exhibit opposite strengths and weaknesses. At its best, anthropology has stressed an unceasing respect for cultural differences, has maintained a genuine attempt to see the world from other, often despised, points of view. But at its worst, the anthropological project has descended into a kind of wearied relativism, a distanced and aestheticized practice, with very little critical purchase.

Marxism at its best has placed problems of human oppression at the center of attention and has stubbornly deconstructed ideologies that have perpetuated social inequalities. But at its corresponding worst, the tradition begun by Marx has degenerated into an iconoclastic disregard for other ways of living, a contempt for people who do not see the point of "liberation," a contempt that has increased the fund of human suffering.[5]

---

[4]For a closely reasoned discussion of the peculiar complexities of critical theory, see Raymond Geuss, *The Idea of a Critical Theory: Habermas and the Frankfurt School* (Cambridge: Cambridge University Press, 1981.)

[5]Stephen Lukes, *Marxism and Morality* (Oxford: Oxford University Press, 1985) cites Rosa Luxemburg's paradigmatic critique of the Russian revolution. Lenin's elimination of democracy was, according to Luxemburg in 1918, "worse than the disease it is supposed to

Precisely because of these differences, something may be gained by attempting to hold anthropology and Marxism together – in tension. Such is the initial assumption, at any rate, of the chapters that follow.

Over the century since Marx's death, anthropology and Marxism – these two bodies of theory and knowledge with such different social contexts and political aims – have gotten along better than one might have expected. At least, committed Marxism has often appeared satisfied with bourgeois anthropology.[6] To overstate the case, it is almost as if two critical theories, brought together, cancelled each other out. The result has often been a strangely quiet theory of so-called precapitalist modes of production, irrelevant to the present except as a completed past. Marxism for capitalism. Anthropology for everything "before."[7]

This pattern of thought began with Marx himself. Toward the end of his life, Marx read extensively in anthropology, and he used anthropological materials, as Maurice Bloch has shown, in two ways. The first was to construct the broad outlines of history that led up to capitalism: ". . . to show how capitalism and its institutions have been produced by history and how it will therefore be destroyed by history."[8] Related

---

cure; for it stops up the very living source from which alone can come the correction for all the innate shortcomings of social institutions. That source is the active, untrammeled, energetic political life of the broadest masses of the people" (p. 104).

[6] How academic anthropology received Marxism is another matter. So far, we have no historian's account of this question. See, however, James W. Wessman, *Anthropology and Marxism* (Cambridge: Schenkman, 1981), and Maurice Bloch, *Marxism and Anthropology: The History of a Relationship* (Oxford: Oxford University Press, 1985). According to Sidney Mintz, "While [we] Americans reconstructed a seamless past and resolutely avoided the present in dealing with our internal natives, the British studied a bounded present, and resolutely avoided the past in dealing with their external natives. I believe that it is in the context of these orientations that the absence of almost any reference to the work of Marx and the Marxists in the anthropology of the first half of the twentieth century is to be explained. " See Mintz's "American Anthropology in the Marxist Tradition," in Sidney W. Mintz et al., *On Marxian Perspectives in Anthropology: Essays in Honor of Harry Hoijer, 1981* (Malibu: Undena Publications, 1984), p. 16; Eric R. Wolf, "American Anthropologists and American Society," in Dell Hymes, ed., *Reinventing Anthropology;* Joan Vincent, "Anthropology and Marxism: Past and Present," *American Ethnologist* 12 (1985): 137–47; Hanna Lessinger and David Hakken, "Introduction," in David Hakken and Hanna Lessinger, eds., *Perspectives in U.S. Marxist Anthropology* (Boulder: Westview Press, 1987), pp. 1–23.

[7] Johannes Fabian's *Time and the Other: How Anthropology Makes its Object* (New York: Columbia University Press, 1983) is an insightful study of a persistent tendency within anthropology to distance the presentation of other cultures by, in various ways, denying coevality. This tendency is evident in the Marxist terminology that opposes *pre*capitalist to capitalist societies. The simple negative term, *non*capitalist, is not much better, for it raises other problems: a supposedly homogeneous type of society set off against capitalism. Although not satisfied with these terms, I have been unable to avoid them entirely.

[8] Bloch, *Marxism and Anthropology*, p. 27.

to this concern for the past was a second, more political, aim. Early anthropologists provided Marx with materials to undermine and to question the widespread assumption that capitalist norms offered the only possible way for human beings to live. If the Iroquois got along perfectly well without private property, the possibility of socialism seemed all the more real.

The combination of these uses of anthropology led finally to Marx's notion of primitive communism. In the 1870s, a number of early anthropological thinkers, from Lewis Henry Morgan to Henry S. Maine, were constructing a model of an original communal, egalitarian society, and by the 1880s, this notion proved too rhetorically convenient for Marx and Engels to resist. Whereas earlier in *The German Ideology*, Marx and Engels had written of the "latent slavery" contained within the family in so-called primitive societies, by the time that Engels wrote *The Origin of the Family, Private Property and the State* in 1884, the year after Marx's death, he claimed that the technologically simplest societies were classless and without contradictions. The result – the construction of a supposedly original communism to which humanity would eventually return on a new and higher level of technological development – was, according to Raphael Samuel, "the most striking example of Marxism's indebtedness to bourgeois historical [or anthropological] thought."[9]

Rather than reformulating and recasting the insights of anthropology, then, Marxism at first simply imported them for analyses of technologically simple societies. But this move had ironic consequences: "When Engels postulated a pre-class stage when there were no conflicting principles and everything was sweetness and light, he had no Marxist way by which to explain historical change."[10] Some twentieth-century Marxists such as Lukács went a step further and argued that Marxist theory applied, not to class societies in general, but principally to capitalism. In this view, so-called precapitalist societies were held up as reproachful models of everything that capitalism was not: social life without class, without alienation, and without reification.[11]

---

[9] Raphael Samuel, "British Marxist Historians, 1880–1980: Part I," *New Left Review* 120 (1980): 34.

[10] Bloch, *Marxism and Anthropology*, p. 54.

[11] Georg Lukács, *History and Class Consciousness: Studies in Marxist Dialectics*, trans. Rodney Livingston (Cambridge: MIT Press, [1923] 1971). Lukács was influenced by what he himself later called the romantic anticapitalism of Max Weber and Georg Simmel. See Michael Löwy's "Naphta or Settembrini? Lukács and Romantic Anticapitalism," *New German Critique* 42 (1987): 17–31. For an anthropological defense of "romantic anticapitalism," see Stanley Diamond, *In Search of the Primitive: A Critique of Civilization* (New Brunswick: Transaction Books, 1974).

Such a portrayal fitted hand-in-glove with the largely functionalist and ahistorical theory being developed within academic anthropology from the 1920s to the 1950s. Anthropology was, apparently, Marxist avant la lettre. Even so hard-headed an observer as Perry Anderson, when he surveyed the terrain of British thought in the 1960s, found only social anthropology as an indigenous source for inspiration or encouragement.[12]

This division of labor between anthropology and Marxism was systematically called into question only during the 1960s. In Britain, Talal Asad and others began to investigate the effects of colonialism on the writings of British anthropologists working in Africa and to call for an analysis of the colonial order as a part of the description that anthropologists normally made of local social systems.[13] In a related development in the United States, the work of Eric Wolf and Sidney Mintz emphasized that Latin American societies that had once been analyzed as non-capitalist had in fact been influenced long and intimately by what came to be known as the world capitalist system. Commodity flows, labor migration, and the exertion of imperial power have connected "us" with "them" far longer, according to Wolf and Mintz, than anthropology was previously wont to admit.[14]

While the empirical analysis of African and Latin American societies in the 1970s began to call into question the old boundary between anthropology and Marxism, theoretical discussion did the same. The most consequential conversation in this regard originated in France and centered on the seemingly arcane question of how to analyze kin-based societies from a Marxist perspective.

Maurice Godelier took what I shall call the traditional point of view. He maintained that in technologically simple societies kinship functions as relations of production and that consequently concepts like exploitation are inapplicable.[15] Godelier's move was an example of anthropolo-

---

[12] Perry Anderson, "Components of the National Culture," *New Left Review* 50 (1968): 46–50.

[13] Asad, *Anthropology and the Colonial Encounter.*

[14] The latest and most substantial statements of this strand of North American anthropology are Eric R. Wolf, *Europe and the People Without History* (Berkeley: University of California Press, 1982), and Sidney W. Mintz, *Sweetness and Power: The Place of Sugar in Modern History* (New York: Viking, 1985). Both Wolf and Mintz have been influenced, in some ways, by sociologist Immanuel Wallerstein, *The Modern World-System: Capitalist Agriculture and the Origins of the European World-Economy in the Sixteenth Century* (New York: Academic Press, 1974). Exactly how anthropologists are to capture both the openness of local history and its conditioning by larger-scale structures remains a difficult problem – one to which I will return in the Conclusion.

[15] See Ariane Deluz and Maurice Godelier's review of Claude Meillassoux's work, "A propos de deux textes d'anthropologie économique," *L'Homme* 7 (1967): 78–91. Just at the

gy's usual critical impulse – it sought to undermine naïve universalism by emphasizing social and cultural variety. Such an intervention was, no doubt, salutary in relation to the dogmatic version of Marxist theory that Godelier was addressing, but it had fateful unintended consequences for anthropology, for it effectively protected the orthodox notion of "kinship" from any Marxist reconceptualization. In the terms set forth by Godelier, the task to be undertaken was apparently one of translating anthropological knowledge, as it already existed, into Marxist language.

An alternative to Godelier's juxtaposition of anthropology and Marxism developed out of the tangled interchange among French anthropologists in the 1970s.[16] Below, I attempt to clarify and extend this different approach. At the outset, let me draw attention to what are perhaps my master assumptions. Contrary to traditional anthropological relativism and contrary to Marxist theorists like Engels, I believe (1) that all human societies to the present have been organized by systems of material domination and (2) that these systems everywhere have been, to varying degrees, socially problematic.[17] Relations of production, as Marx called them, are like sand in an oyster. They constitute inevitable points of irritation, however such irritation is dealt with – whether it is expressed, displaced, or finally transformed into something that looks quite different.

moment Godelier was asserting that kinship could function as relations of production, other anthropologists were beginning to question whether in fact "kinship" in the usual anthropological sense exists. See David M. Schneider, "What Is Kinship All About?" in Priscilla Reining, ed., *Kinship Studies in the Morgan Centennial Year* (Washington, D.C.: Washington Anthropological Society, 1972). The functionalist consequences of Godelier's early position become clear in his reanalysis of Mbuti materials in *Perspectives in Marxist Anthropology*, trans. Robert Brain (Cambridge: Cambridge University Press, [1973] 1977), pp. 51–62. Over the years, however, Godelier's stance seems to have changed, at least as it is reflected in empirical analysis. His recent work focuses much more closely on social inequalities and on consent and resistance; see *The Making of Great Men: Male Domination and Power among the New Guinea Baruya*, trans. Rupert Swyer (Cambridge: Cambridge University Press, [1982] 1986).

[16] Joel S. Kahn, "Marxist Anthropology and Segmentary Societies: A Review of the Literature," in Joel S. Kahn and Josep R. Llobera, eds., *The Anthropology of Pre-Capitalist Societies* (London: Macmillan, 1981), gives an admirably clear summary of the debate.

[17] I assume that domination, to be such, must be materially based – whether it is defined in sexual, ethnic, or class terms. If height, for example, were judged a mark of prestige but played no role in linking groups of persons with differential power over a society's total product, then one could not say that tall people dominate shorter ones.

It is not clear that assumption (1), by itself, uniquely characterizes historical materialism. According to many forms of functionalist theory, for example, all past and present societies have exhibited forms of materially-based power differentials. The addition of assumption (2) may be necessary, therefore, to differentiate Marxism. In this respect, the notion that forms of domination in some ways work against requirements of universal human nature (to be explained in Chapter 2) is crucial. For then the continuance of systems of inequality becomes inherently problematic; successful social reproduction becomes an unstable result, open to possible disruption.

If these assumptions – which privilege Marxism over traditional anthropology – can be shown to be realistic grounds for departure, a great deal follows. Anthropology's rhetoric of nostalgia becomes inappropriate as any guide or helpmeet for the future. And, as for the past, so-called primitive societies have to be analyzed differently as well. Kinship becomes not just a symbolic or social system that neutrally orders people's lives, but a central part of the power and culture of many noncapitalist forms of domination.[18]

Marxism, then, has some role to play in recasting anthropological knowledge. But the reverse relation must be examined as well, for historical materialism, at least as it has often been construed, will not escape unscathed by modern social anthropology. Here, the special value of anthropology is its attempt to provide an Archimedean point outside the confines of any one cultural system in order that variation may be observed without prejudice. Whether in fact such a point can finally be reached is debatable, but minimally, the exercise of analyzing another cultural system has the potential to free us from our own categories. We observe capitalism no longer from within but from without. From this standpoint, some of what we have always accepted as natural turns into something strange, and seeing something as strange is a prerequisite of any fuller knowledge.

The process of tacking Marxist analyses back and forth between radically different modes of production has only begun. In the absence of much attention to this problem, there have been persistent tendencies within historical materialism, beginning with the work of Marx himself, to mistake capitalist categories for universal analytical ones.

Let me take an example that will be elaborated on in later discussion. For some time, Marxists and others have held an image of capitalism as organized in a more naked, hard "economic" way than many noncapitalist societies, in which it is difficult to disentangle the economy from

---

[18] The reformation of kinship studies is already well under way. Feminism has been particularly important in this regard. See, for example, Gayle Rubin, "The Traffic in Women: Notes on the 'Political Economy' of Sex," in Rayna R. Reiter, ed., *Toward an Anthropology of Women* (New York: Monthly Review Press, 1975), pp. 157–210; Jane F. Collier and Michelle Z. Rosaldo, "Politics and Gender in Simple Societies," in Sherry B. Ortner and Harriet Whitehead, eds., *Sexual Meanings: The Cultural Construction of Gender and Sexuality* (Cambridge: Cambridge University Press, 1981), pp. 275–329; Jane F. Collier and Sylvia J. Yanagisako, eds., *Gender and Kinship: Essays Toward a Unified Analysis* (Stanford: Stanford University Press, 1987); Jane F. Collier, *Marriage and Inequality in Classless Societies* (Stanford: Stanford University Press, 1988).

the polity or from religion, in which, indeed, all of these sometimes appear to be dominated by "kinship."

This view has, at the same time, vexed Marxists, for if some noncapitalist societies are less "economic" – indeed dominated by something entirely "noneconomic," namely "kinship" – this fact appears to contradict one of the central tenets of historical materialism: that the economy or the base determines the superstructure. If the economy cannot be separated from kinship or religion, how can one say that the economy is determinant?

A number of responses have been given to this question. Some, like Marshall Sahlins, believe that there is no solution and that consequently Marxism cannot be applied to noncapitalist societies.[19] Others, like Emmanuel Terray (and before him, Louis Althusser and Étienne Balibar), have gone to some scholastic length to insist that the concept of determination must be supplemented with another of "dominance."[20] According to this line of thought, in every society the economy is determinant in that it determines which level of society – economic, political, or religious – is dominant. In capitalism, the economy is both determinant and dominant, whereas in noncapitalist societies, it is typically determinant but not dominant. Finally, still other writers, like Perry Anderson, have maintained that in noncapitalist societies superstructures enter into their bases; only in capitalism have the two become entirely separate.[21]

It will be useful to follow Anderson's reasoning in some detail, for he presents more lucidly than most the set of ideas I want to examine:

Capitalism is the first mode of production in history in which the means whereby the surplus is pumped out of the direct producer is "purely" economic in form – the wage contract: the equal exchange between free agents which reproduces, hourly and daily, inequality and oppression. All other previous modes of exploitation operate through *extra-economic* sanctions – kin, customary, religious, legal or political.[22]

[19] Marshall Sahlins, *Culture and Practical Reason* (Chicago: University of Chicago Press, 1976).
[20] Emmanuel Terray, *Marxism and "Primitive" Societies*, trans. Mary Klopper (New York: Monthly Review Press, [1969] 1972), and Étienne Balibar, "On the Basic Concepts of Historical Materialism," in Louis Althusser and Étienne Balibar, *Reading Capital*, trans. Ben Brewster (New York: Pantheon, [1968] 1970).
[21] Perry Anderson, *Lineages of the Absolutist State* (London: New Left Books, 1974). After G. A. Cohen's *Karl Marx's Theory of History: A Defence* (Oxford: Clarendon Press, 1978) was published (see particularly pp. 247–8), Anderson abandoned this position in *Arguments Within English Marxism* (London: New Left Books, 1980), pp. 72–3.
[22] Anderson, *Lineages*, p. 403.

Notice that Anderson's definition of what constitutes the economic is straightforwardly embedded in the particular capitalist category of wage labor. It is not very revealing, then, to be told that other modes of production rest upon extraeconomic sanctions. In so far as they do not rest upon wage labor, inequalities in other societies are of course not "economic," at least on this reading of the term.

Such an objection would constitute only a quibble were it not for the fact that Anderson's definition of the economic has further consequences. It does not, on the one hand, problematize capitalism. When we see the word "economic" we nod our heads and read on – we think we know what it means. And, on the other hand, it makes noncapitalist societies appear exceptional, almost too strange. From the passage quoted above, Anderson continues:

The "superstructures" of kinship, religion, law or the state necessarily enter into the constitutive structure of the mode of production in noncapitalist social formations. They intervene *directly* in the "internal" nexus of surplus-extraction, where in capitalist social formations, the first in history to separate the economy as a formally self-contained order, they provide by contrast its "external" preconditions.[23]

But this argument is misleading. In what sense is law external to the relationship between workers and capitalists? In what sense is religion, at least insofar as it involves fundamental definitions of personhood – so-called free agents – external to surplus extraction in capitalism?

Anderson's characterization of capitalist versus noncapitalist modes of production effectively discourages the analysis of a complex of culturally specific ideas that are crucial in defining and maintaining capitalist inequalities. And, at the same time, it verges on making noncapitalist inequalities almost mystically different, as if persons in such societies stumbled about the world in an ideological haze. Anderson draws the following conclusion in the passage that I have been quoting above:

In consequence, pre-capitalist modes of production cannot be defined *except* via their political, legal and ideological superstructures, since these are what determine the type of extra-economic coercion that specifies them.[24]

But exactly the same conclusion should be drawn for capitalism. It is the superstructure that provides the very terms in which the capitalist mode of production becomes a social reality. Marx's own analysis, in-

[23]Ibid., pp. 403–4.   [24]Ibid., p. 404.

asmuch as it builds on culturally specific notions of persons (persons "free" to sell their labor) and on particular legal definitions of how persons must relate (through "contracts" backed by the coercive power of the state), is embedded in superstructural terms. This embedding is necessary in any analysis of capitalism, in any attempt to understand its "laws of motion." In this respect, *Capital* itself is as much an analysis of a superstructure as of a base.[25]

Although this claim may appear to stand Marxism on its head and to substitute an idealism for a materialism, I argue that it does not. Rather, it highlights what is otherwise concealed: namely, that the realm that we in capitalist societies think of as "economic" is just as peculiar and as culturally constructed as any other way of organizing material life. It is neither "harder," nor more "abstract," nor more of a system "unto itself" than others. Above all, it is not any easier to understand.

Realizing this anthropological point forces, if not an overturning of Marxism, then a revision of how it has often been understood. In particular, it requires an interpretation of the hoary problem of base and superstructure different in emphasis, for example, from G. A. Cohen's exposition.[26] Below, I argue that the base – the system of de facto power in any society – should not be seen as only supporting or lying beneath the superstructure. It is also correct to say that the superstructure typically makes the base what it is. At issue here is the formulation of a distinctively Marxist hermeneutics – one that interprets systems of meaning as these are imbricated with forms of domination.

Marxism, thus anthropologically understood, has at least two advantages. Abroad, it enables an analysis of technologically simpler societies that does not present them as mystically harmonious. And at home, it

[25] G. A. Cohen, *Karl Marx's Theory of History* (p. 224), argues that even though Marx regularly used legal terms (embedded in superstructural ideas) to refer to non-legal entities (in particular, to relations of production), base and superstructure can be rigorously and separately defined. This, I believe, Cohen has established. But it is important to note that this position does not lead to the conclusion that modes of production can be *analyzed* apart from superstructural detail. As Cohen points out (p. 223), his program defines what relations of production are, not how they are maintained. And how relations of production are maintained is a central issue in Marx's *Capital* and, indeed, in historical materialist analysis of any mode of production. My arguments at this point are related to, though ultimately different from, Stephen Lukes's in "Can the Base Be Distinguished From the Superstructure," in David Miller and Larry Siedentop, eds., *The Nature of Political Theory* (Oxford: Clarendon Press, 1983), pp. 103–19. Cohen has responded to Lukes in "Reply to Four Critics," *Analyse und Kritik* 5 (1983): 212–9.

[26] Cohen, *Karl Marx's Theory of History*, pp. 231–4.

furthers the questioning of categories in which we ourselves live our lives – a process that will continue, incomplete, as long as capitalism survives.

———

In the last analysis, it is impossible to understand Marxism except against the background of the theory it has developed against, namely, neoclassical economic theory. Not long after Marx published the first volume of *Capital* in 1867, a number of theorists – W. Stanley Jevons in England, Karl Menger in Austria, and Léon Walras in France – independently published analyses using the principle of diminishing marginal utility, and the outlines of neoclassicism were thus laid down.[27] Both Marxism and neoclassicism were extensions of and reactions to the so-called classical political economy of an earlier era, and over the twentieth century, both developed in tension with and in relation to the other.

An overarching theme of the following chapters is that these two strands of thought – neoclassicism and Marxism – must be examined together. How one understands one half of a conversation depends on the other. Only in the context of an entire discussion do the claims, the rhetorical moves, the political force of any one participant's statements become clear.

In recounting the interchange between neoclassicism and Marxism, the most common analogy used so far has been the quarrel. Each side has been presented as if there were no common ground for the smallest agreement. Although such a description captures much of past polemic, the following chapters contend that such a reading, by missing the overlap, introduces errors into the analyses of both neoclassicism and Marxism.[28]

As I argue below, a Marxist approach that is more than simply a static typology of modes of production requires an understanding of neoclassical theory that is sympathetic, at least in certain respects. People do make decisions, and there are often, as neoclassical theorists assert, patterns in those decisions. Rather than simply rejecting neoclassicism's truths, such as they are, historical materialism must incorporate and go

---

[27] Maurice Dobb, *Theories of Value and Distribution Since Adam Smith: Ideology and Economic Theory* (Cambridge: Cambridge University Press, 1973), chap. 7, and Mark Blaug, *Economic Theory in Retrospect*, 4th ed. (Cambridge: Cambridge University Press, 1985), chap. 8.

[28] Both John Roemer and Jon Elster, among others, have argued similarly. See their contributions to John Roemer, ed., *Analytical Marxism* (Cambridge: Cambridge University Press, 1986).

beyond them. My concern to build toward a Marxist analysis of societies that sees persons as actively constructing their lives is one reason, then, that I begin this book with a chapter on neoclassical theory.

But I have a second reason as well. For I wish to argue against a common anthropological approach that differentiates capitalist from noncapitalist societies by the supposed presence or absence of self-interested and calculating individual action. According to theorists from Bronislaw Malinowski to Karl Polanyi to Marshall Sahlins, neoclassical economics applies to capitalist societies – in which individuals are out to get the most they can – but it does not apply to noncapitalist societies – in which kinship, religion, and politics constrain individual choice.[29] Neoclassical economics for capitalist societies. Anthropology for everything else.

This approach apparently responds to deeply ingrained rhetorical needs in anthropology. It helps to establish the "otherness" of other cultures; it legitimates anthropology within an academic division of labor; and it embodies a certain critical spirit. Indeed it might be said to echo Marx himself. Even though Marx would not have agreed that neoclassical theory provides an adequate understanding of capitalism, he often wrote about technologically simple societies as if individual choice in them were nonexistent. In the *Grundrisse,* he claimed:

Human beings become individuals only through a process of history. He appears originally as a species-being, clan being, herd animal – although in no way whatever as a political being. . . . Exchange itself is a chief means of this individuation . . .[30]

And, again in *Capital:*

Cooperation in the labor process, such as we find it at the beginning of human civilization, among hunting peoples or, say, as a predominant feature of the agriculture of Indian communities, is based on the one hand on the common ownership of the conditions of production, and on the other hand on the fact that in those cases the individual has as little torn himself free from the umbilical cord of his tribe or community as a bee has from his hive.[31]

[29] This line of thought, which came to be known as substantivism in anthropology, extends from Bronislaw Malinowski, "The Primitive Economics of the Trobriand Islanders," *Economic Journal* 31 (1921): 1–16, to Karl Polanyi, Conrad M. Arensberg, and Harry W. Pearson, eds., *Trade and Market in the Early Empires: Economies in History and Theory* (Glencoe: Free Press, 1957), to Marshall Sahlins, *Stone Age Economics* (Chicago: Aldine-Atherton, 1972).

[30] Marx, *Grundrisse: Introduction to the Critique of Political Economy,* trans. Martin Nicolaus (New York: Vintage, [1939] 1973), p. 496.

[31] Marx, *Capital: A Critique of Political Economy,* vol. 1, trans. Ben Fowkes (New York: Vintage, [1867] 1976), p. 452.

I believe that this is wrong. Like all systems of thought that operate by contrasting "us" and "them," when it gets "them" wrong, it also gets "us" wrong. Noncapitalist humans are not herd animals; neither are capitalist ones freed from all social constraint to maximize in a world in which, in Sahlins's words, the sky is the limit.

Below I try to show that whatever insights neoclassical theory affords for capitalism, it provides similar ones for noncapitalist societies. And whatever the limits of neoclassical thought in relation to capitalism, similar ones obtain in relation to noncapitalist societies. These negative conclusions are necessary preliminaries in constructing an understanding of the relationship between anthropology and Marxism.

In the epigraph to this chapter, I quoted Clifford Geertz's ironic opening to a review of the work of Claude Lévi-Strauss: Know what an anthropologist thinks he is and you know in general what he will say about whatever tribe he happens to be studying. All ethnography is part philosophy, and a good deal of the rest is confession.[32] Although insightful, this way of putting the matter limits attention to individual psyches. We might equally say that all ethnography is part philosophy, and a good deal of the rest is politics. Know what an anthropologist thinks his own society is and you know – by negation – what he will say about whatever tribe he happens to be studying.

More perhaps than any other academic discourse, anthropology has defined itself against capitalism. This spirit of anticapitalism has shown itself, not in a reforming zeal that depends ultimately on an acceptance of the present (as in much of sociology, for example), but in a broader alienation from modern society that looks backward to "tradition." Arriving just as the forces of change are about to overwhelm traditional cultural orders, anthropologist after anthropologist has taken as his or her task the reconstruction and validation of lost ways of living – ones presented as sometimes superior to our own. This rhetorical stance, which pervades work of otherwise contending schools of thought, is what James Clifford has called anthropology's "pastoral" mode.[33]

---

[32] Clifford Geertz, *The Interpretation of Cultures* (New York: Basic Books, 1973), p. 345.
[33] James Clifford, "On Ethnographic Allegory," in James Clifford and George E. Marcus, eds., *Writing Culture: The Poetics and Politics of Ethnography* (Berkeley: University of California Press 1986), pp. 98–121. The most influential example of this "pastoral" theme in recent anthropology is Michael T. Taussig, *The Devil and Commodity Fetishism in South America* (Chapel Hill: University of North Carolina Press, 1980). See Terence Turner's criticisms in "Production, Exploitation and Social Consciousness in the 'Peripheral Situation,' " *Social Analysis* 19 (1986): 91–115.

Retrieving – redeeming, Walter Benjamin would say – a past before the fall: Such a vision contains a politics. What is less often realized is that this kind of romantic anticapitalism shares a good deal with its enemy position – rationalistic procapitalism. One is the mirror image of the other. Both are expressed in the same we–they categories. Are we rational? They mired in tradition? Or are our lives only fragmentary? Theirs whole? Is ours the most advanced and efficient economy yet? Or is theirs more meaningfully integrated into the rest of their lives? Is neoclassical economics beautiful and applicable to us and not to them? Or is it ugly and applicable to us and not to them?

Status, contract, Gemeinschaft, Gesellschaft, tradition, modernity – these terms, worried over and debated, criticized and rejected, formulated and reformulated, provide the deep structure of much present-day social theory.[34] I try to escape their net (probably not entirely successfully) by collapsing the couplet: They are us. We are them. This claim is true to the extent that we live interconnected lives and have always done so, particularly in the recent past.[35] More important, we live and suffer in forms of social domination, forms often intermeshed and interdependent.

Having asserted a putative unity (on the basis of Marxist theory), I want immediately to add (an anthropological) qualification. How "they" are "us" is hardly transparent. Local forms of domination are always just that: reproduced in their own particular practices and encoded in their own cultural terms. In such a social and cultural terrain – one in which systems of inequality often crosscut one another – the task of discovering where unity lies requires dialogue and interpretation.

These issues reverberate with particular intensity in historical materialism, for the way that Marxists have analyzed technologically simple societies has always been tied up with their political vision of commu-

---

[34] Reinhard Bendix, "Tradition and Modernity Reconsidered," *Comparative Studies in Society and History* 9 (1967): 292–346. See also Jane Schneider, "European Expansion and Hand-Crafted Cloth: A Critique of Oppositional Use-Value vs. Exchange-Value Models," *Journal of Historical Sociology* 1 (1989): 431–8, and William Roseberry, *Anthropologies and Histories: Essays in Culture, History, and Political Economy* (New Brunswick: Rutgers University Press, 1989).

[35] These connections have, at the least, prevented biological speciation. Arjun Appadurai asks, "But were there ever natives [in the anthropological sense of the term]. . . . ? Most groups that anthropologists have studied have in some way been affected by the knowledge of other worlds, worlds about which they may have learned through migration, trade, conquest, or indigenous narratives." See Appadurai's "Putting Hierarchy in Its Place," *Cultural Anthropology* 3 (1988): 39. In a different key, G. William Skinner has made this point for some time. For his method of dealing with this problem in relation to Chinese data, see "Regional Urbanization in Nineteenth-Century China," in G. William Skinner, ed., *The City in Late Imperial China* (Stanford: Stanford University Press, 1977), pp. 211–49.

nism. Marxism was founded upon a triplet – "they" of the completed past versus "us" of the present versus "them" of the emancipated future. As Stanley Moore has shown, this triplet reduces to social theory's traditional couplet, since the terms in which Marx described advanced communism were the same as those he used for so-called precapitalist societies.[36] In a letter to the *German–French Yearbook* in 1843, Marx wrote:

> That self-reliance, that freedom, which disappeared from earth with the Greeks, and with Christianity vanished into the blue haze of heaven, must again be awakened in the hearts of men. Then only can men move from society [Gesellschaft] to a new community [Gemeinschaft] uniting them for their highest ends – a democratic state.[37]

This highest state according to Marx will be brought into being when not only exploitation, but all exchanges – including wages – are abolished. In such a society, labor will become an end in itself, not a means to anything else, and egoism and self-interest will be overcome. The problem of incentives is abolished, and social harmony reigns in a recovered Gemeinschaft. From herd animal to communist man.

This connection between past and future is the secret of Marxism's attraction to traditional anthropology. Ironically, what began as the West's construction of the noncapitalist "other," a construction that simply negated aspects of its most objectionable self, returned in modified form as a communist utopia. Below, I argue that these simplified contrasts distort the analysis of other modes of production and, at the same time, impede the construction of useful socialist strategy. But this statement is not a confession. It is a political claim.[38]

As I have said, this book examines issues in social theory in relation to data from Maale, Ethiopia. Let me briefly introduce Maale and describe the four chapters that follow.

[36] Stanley Moore, *Marx on the Choice Between Socialism and Communism* (Cambridge: Harvard University Press, 1980). Moore points out that Ferdinand Tönnies, who made Gemeinschaft and Gesellschaft into master words in social theory, was himself influenced by Marx. Concepts moved back and forth, then, in complex ways between Marxism and social theory more broadly construed.

[37] Quoted in Moore, ibid., p. 8. This is, of course, the young Marx. Moore shows that the mature Marx did not give up this vision of communism even though it contradicted aspects of his developing historical materialism. "After the *Manifesto*, and to a greater degree after *Capital*, communism [as distinct from socialism] became for Marx a goal he was unwilling to abandon but unable to defend" (p. 89).

[38] My principal political assumptions are perhaps three: (1) that democratic socialism is a goal worth fighting for, (2) that such a state cannot usefully be viewed as a transparent and conflict-free unity, and (3) that movement toward socialism, at least for any particular case, is not inevitable. I do not defend these statements in themselves, but they are, as the reader will see, embedded in the larger arguments and analyses I develop below.

The Maale, who number about 15,000 persons at present, live in southern Ethiopia. At the end of the nineteenth century, they formed one of the numerous independent chiefdoms and kingdoms (in what is now the south of the country) that were conquered and incorporated into the expanding Ethiopian empire. Partly as a result of this expansion, Ethiopia was able to defeat Italy, its would-be European master, at the Battle of Adwa in 1896. Unlike most other African states, then, Ethiopia remained politically independent during the twentieth century, except for Mussolini's brief occupation in the late 1930s.[39]

In consequence of this and other factors, the Maale were largely unaffected by the economic and political transformations that dominated much of the rest of Africa. There was, for example, comparatively little cash-cropping in twentieth-century Maale. Traditional chiefs and the ritual king were maintained in office until 1975. And slash-and-burn horticulture endured, unendangered by excessively large increases in population.

Located on the periphery of the world capitalist system, the Maale have certainly seen transformations in their lives over the past eighty years. But these changes have grown out of their own local situation and do not correspond to stereotypes of a homogeneous Third World.[40]

Using Maale data, Chapter 1 considers neoclassical models in social anthropology, in particular the works of Alexander Chayanov and Marshall Sahlins. After examining neoclassicism, I conclude that it contains important silences around questions posed by history, power, and ideology. Chapter 2 proceeds to Marxist theory, taking up the notion of mode of production in reference to Claude Meillassoux's work. After an examination of the Maale mode of production in the next essay, Chapter 3, the twinned issue of power/ideology begins to come into focus. But the picture that results is something like a photograph – an epoch frozen, out of historical time. Chapter 4 seeks to animate this still life, to build on the results of the previous mode-of-production analysis in order to understand one place in Maale – Bola – at one moment in time – 1975.

In what I hope is an interpretive spiral of increasing scope, one in which people become more and more real, Chapter 4 returns to the same empirical issues as Chapter 1 and contains something of the same vision

[39] For an overview of twentieth-century Ethiopian history, see Donald L. Donham, "Old Abyssinia and the New Ethiopian Empire: Themes in Social History," in Donald L. Donham and Wendy James, eds., *The Southern Marches of Imperial Ethiopia: Essays in History and Social Anthropology* (Cambridge: Cambridge University Press, 1986), pp. 3–48.
[40] Sidney W. Mintz, "On the Concept of a Third World," *Dialectical Anthropology* 1 (1976): 377–82.

as the theory considered there, neoclassicism. Maale persons are seen as actively making their own lives through social practices and in cultural categories. But, compared to the results of the first essay, the object of Chapter 4 is to show how Maale practices were partially constrained by the structural context in which they were carried out – a repetitive reproduction of power differences during the twentieth century – and by the play of events in one locale – a particular configuration of political blocs in Bola.

This progression of Maale detail is meant to provide the vehicle for perhaps the largest theoretical argument of the book: that the goal of Marxism is not just to construct social theory. Its final aim is to provide the terms for understanding history – history in some specificity.

1. Homo economicus: A Maale mystery

In the 1960s a grand argument arose in anthropology. Formalists, as they became known, maintained that neoclassical economics could be used to analyze any economy. So-called substantivists countered with the charge that such theories are culture- and institution-bound; they can be applied only to capitalist economies. It is difficult now to understand what all the excitement was about, and common opinion appears to have it that the debate was largely misconceived and unproductive. But as far as I am aware, no one has been able to go beyond Frank Cancian's original discussion or Raymond Firth's sensible comments to put her or his finger on the theoretical reasons for the unproductiveness.[1]

More recently, Maurice Godelier has argued that the two sides of the debate actually occupied a common theoretical ground – a possibility that looks increasingly likely as Marxist theory has begun to offer a third vantage point.[2] But the commonality can hardly be, as Godelier maintained, "functionalist empiricism." Functional explanations are a prominent feature of many kinds of Marxist analyses (as I shall argue below), not neoclassical ones, and as for "empiricist," it is difficult to know exactly what Godelier understands by the label (other than that one would not want to be called one). If empiricism means staying strictly on the surface of social reality, confined to directly perceptible qualities, then there are few empiricist analyses, whatever the school of theory.[3] One presumes that no social anthropologist ever saw a lineage principle; certainly no neoclassical economist has ever seen a utility function.

In the absence of any sustained discussion of late, a certain amount of

---

[1] Frank A. Cancian, "Maximization as Norm, Strategy and Theory: A Comment on Programmatic Statements in Economic Anthropology," *American Anthropologist* 68 (1966): 465–70; Raymond Firth, "Themes in Economic Anthropology: A Comment," in Raymond Firth, ed., *Themes in Economic Anthropology* (London: Tavistock, 1967). Pierre Bourdieu, *Outline of a Theory of Practice*, trans. Richard Nice (Cambridge: Cambridge University Press, [1972] 1977) offered general inspiration for this chapter.

[2] Maurice Godelier, *Perspectives in Marxist Anthropology*, trans. Robert Brain (Cambridge: Cambridge University Press, [1973] 1977), p. 21.

[3] See Talal Asad, "The Concept of Rationality in Economic Anthropology," *Economy and Society* 3 (1974): 211–8.

confusion has arisen. Take, for example, the case that I want to examine in this chapter, Marshall Sahlins's model of the "domestic mode of production," itself a reformulation of the work of a Russian economist, Alexander Chayanov.[4] Chayanov's original theory was arguably an attempt to apply neoclassical concepts to the particular features of peasant household production. Sahlins, on the other hand, maintains that the neoclassical elements in Chayanov's work are inconsequential and that, in any case, his own model of the domestic mode of production is substantivist.[5] Finally, to complete the list of all possibilities, Sahlins's work has been listed in a select bibliography of recent Marxist analyses.[6]

Clearly, not all of these claims can be sustained. At least two major issues are entangled here. The first is how to specify alternative bodies of social theory – neoclassicism and Marxism, among others. The second is whether the boundaries of neoclassical theory so specified coincide with the dividing line between capitalist and noncapitalist modes of production. Can, in fact, a label like neoclassical be given a principled description in anthropology? Can such a theoretical approach be used to analyze more than capitalist economies?

I propose to answer these large questions by embedding my discussion in a series of very small facts: the value of children's labor when they guard ripening fields, the definition of "work" in noncapitalist economies, the effects of ostracizing a young man from labor cooperation. I shall present Chayanov's theory, confront it with the Maale data, inquire into whether Sahlins's model of the domestic mode of production fits the data better, and conclude by considering the special character of both approaches as examples of neoclassical theory.

At the outset, I should explain that my goal is to present the strongest possible version of neoclassicism, one that meets as many of the criticisms made by its opponents as possible. This exercise convinces me that neoclassical approaches can be developed into a consistent theoretical program in anthropology, can be useful for certain kinds of problems, and can be applied toward different political ends, both pro- and

---

[4]Marshall Sahlins, *Stone Age Economics* (Chicago: Aldine–Atherton, 1972), chaps. 2–3. Alexander Chayanov's principal work was *Organizatsiya krest'yanskogo khozyaistva* [*Peasant Farm Organization*] (Moscow: Cooperative Publishing House, 1925); it was translated and edited by Daniel Thorner et al. and published as *The Theory of Peasant Economy* (Homewood, Illinois: Irwin, 1966). For more recent work in anthropology inspired by Chayanov, see E. Paul Durrenberger, ed., *Chayanov, Peasants, and Economic Anthropology* (New York: Academic Press, 1984).
[5]Sahlins, *Stone Age Economics*, p. xii.
[6]David Seddon, ed., *Relations of Production: Marxist Approaches to Economic Anthropology* (London: Frank Cass, 1978), p. 413.

anticapitalist.[7] But my purpose is not to missionize, either. Neoclassical theory leaves critical questions unanswered. To be didactic, the moral of the story that I am about to tell is that those who do not appreciate neoclassical theory in the most sympathetic light possible may be condemned to remain within its theoretical boundaries. It is only by seeing exactly what neoclassical theory does (and, therefore, does not do) that it becomes possible to recognize the need for another approach. It is in this sense that the present chapter is preparatory for the next on Marxist theory.

———

Alexander Vasil'evich Chayanov, born in 1888, became a leading agricultural economist in Russia. Influenced by the so-called neopopulist tradition, Chayanov advocated the conservation of peasant small-holding after the Russian revolution and technical progress through cooperatives. For this, he was arrested in 1930 during campaigns to collectivize the countryside, and he died in prison some years later.

Given the political climate in which Chayanov worked, one dominated by an increasingly dogmatic interpretation of Marxism, it is not surprising that it is sometimes difficult to typify the basic theoretical affiliations of his work. Chayanov himself denied that his analysis was an extension of the Austrian neoclassical school, yet he admitted the fundamental importance of neoclassical concepts such as marginal utility. Chayanov concluded, "As regards the Austrian school, the author of the present book stands in approximately the same position as does J. H. von Thünen, for whom the marginal principle has also played no small part."[8]

An examination of von Thünen's work, not to mention a closer reading of Chayanov, leaves little doubt that the theory of peasant production was primarily an attempt to extend neoclassical forms of analysis – of individual decision-making under structural constraints – to peasant

[7] A fuller discussion would explore the degree to which neoclassical analyses may have inherently conservative rhetorical possibilities. Such possibilities would be just that – possible but not necessary outcomes. For example, the class structure of capitalist economies tends to enter many neoclassical analyses as a silent assumption – not something to be focused on, thought about, and explained. Inasmuch as that assumption is forgotten, such analyses can be turned into politically conservative ideology. Consider two claims: Wages are determined by the marginal productivity of labor, or wages are determined by the marginal productivity of labor *given an initial class division between capitalist and workers*. The first, but not the second, can be transformed into a justification of class – that workers get what they deserve, that they receive what they contribute to the final product.

[8] Chayanov, *Theory of Peasant Economy*, p. 46.

farm families.[9] Chayanov began, for example, with postulates typical of neoclassical economics. He argued that for any individual the value of the return of an hour of labor declines as more and more hours of labor are expended. The threat of starvation makes the return from the first hours very valuable indeed, but as more and more is produced from more and more hours of labor, satisfaction declines. Conversely, as the value of the return to each additional unit of labor declines, the "cost" of the labor increases. As a person works longer and longer hours, he or she finds each additional hour more difficult, more tiring. According to Chayanov, the level of production is determined by the balance of these two forces of cost and gain.

What makes Chayanov's theory distinctive is that he went on to show that the balance between cost and gain is related to the institutional arrangements in which production is carried out. According to him, the distinctive feature of peasant as compared to capitalist production is that the former contains no category of wage labor. That fact is critical, since it means that expansion of any household's production must come, as it were, from the sweat of its members' own brows. Capitalist enterprises, by contrast, can expand almost indefinitely by hiring more and more workers as long as capital is available.

If households are the "firms" of peasant economies, household composition determines the relative strength or weakness of the enterprise. The ratio of household consumers to workers (C/W), the dependency ratio, is a crucial variable, according to Chayanov. A high dependency ratio reflects a high relative proportion of consumers (typically many children). That means, in turn, a relatively weak household enterprise in which each adult worker has to produce more just to provision her or his household. In other words, for households with high dependency ratios, the balance that Chayanov postulates between the cost and gain of an extra hour of labor shifts in favor of working longer hours.

Following this line of reasoning, Chayanov noted that in time households generally went through a number of phases with respect to the dependency ratio. Consider what happens as a household moves through a hypothetical developmental cycle. A new unit is established at the time of marriage. As children are born and added to the family, food requirements increase. But children, initially at least, do not add to the

[9]See James R. Millar, "A Reformulation of A. V. Chayanov's Theory of the Peasant Economy," *Economic Development and Cultural Change* 18 (1970): 219–29.

household work force, and that is where the pinch comes. As subsistence requirements increase, the number of workers remains constant and the dependency ratio rises. According to Chayanov, there is only one possible outcome: Each household worker has to work longer hours. As more and more children are born, the burden on the household increases until the eldest child begins to work. At that point, the dependency ratio begins to decrease so that each household worker can begin to work fewer hours.

The exact pattern of Chayanov's phases varies from society to society and depends on the particular type of household developmental cycle; still, decades before anthropologists devised the concept of developmental cycle, Chayanov had hit on its essentials for the Russian peasant case. Stated formally, "Chayanov's rule" says that the amount of time a household member works is proportional to his or her household's dependency ratio – the number of household consumers divided by the number of workers. As the relative proportion of consumers increases, each worker has to work longer hours. As the relative proportion of consumers decreases, each worker can work shorter hours.

In view of the confusions in the literature (and, admittedly, the ambiguities in Chayanov's work itself), it must be emphasized that he is not proposing a subsistence theory of peasant production, that is, that peasants are interested in producing only for their own use and that they do not respond to opportunities to produce a surplus above subsistence.[10] Such an interpretation would rest upon an argument about peasant motives contrary to Chayanov's initial assumption that peasants seek their own gain. This reading is, however, the one presented by Marshall Sahlins.[11] Sahlins interprets Chayanov's system as one of "production for use," "an economic system of determinate and finite objectives," an economy in which "needs are limited." Compare what Chayanov has to say:

Of course, our critics are free to understand the labor–consumer balance theory as a sweet little picture of the Russian peasantry in the likeness of the moral French peasants, satisfied with everything and living like birds of the air. We, ourselves, do not have such a conception and are inclined to believe that no peasant would refuse either good roast beef, or a gramophone, or even a block of Shell Oil Company shares, if the chance occurred. Unfortunately, such chances do not present themselves in large numbers, and the peasant family wins every

[10] Mark Harrison, "Chayanov and the Economics of the Russian Peasantry," *Journal of Peasant Studies* 2 (1975): 389–417.
[11] Sahlins, *Stone Age Economics*, pp. 82–92.

kopek by hard, intensive toil. And in these circumstances, they are obliged not only to do without shares and a gramophone, but sometimes without the beef as well.[12]

Any economic unit, including the peasant farm, is acquisitive – an undertaking aiming at maximum income. In an economic unit based on hired labor, this tendency to boundless expansion is limited by capital availability and, if this increases, is practically boundless. But in the family farm, apart from capital available expressed in means of production, this tendency is limited by the family labor force and the increasing drudgery of work if its intensity is forced up.[13]

Both substantivists such as Sahlins and Marxists such as Meillassoux have repeatedly criticized these assertions for inappropriately generalizing capitalist forms of rationality, for not respecting cultural differences, and – most important – for not recognizing the institutionally specific patterns of noncapitalist economies. Meillassoux, for example, writes that the application of neoclassical concepts in anthropology ". . . is more than mere error or sheer ethnocentrism; it betrays the imperialism of the science of Imperialism which wants to submit 'development' to the universal laws of capitalist exploitation. . . ."[14]

Such criticisms may, of course, be applicable to certain neoclassical analyses. That particular forms of neoclassical theory have been uncritically extended at times to new and inappropriate institutional contexts perhaps few neoclassicists themselves would deny. But the stronger version of this argument – that neoclassical forms of analysis are necessarily in error – is harder to defend. Indeed, I believe it is possible to show that Chayanov's work clearly contradicts such a claim.

In order to begin that demonstration, let me note that Chayanov did not postulate that peasant families maximize profits. Quite the opposite, he tried to show that the category "profit," in its strict sense, has meaning only in wage–labor economies. Instead, Chayanov started with the general proposition that peasants make decisions so as to maximize "gains" and to minimize "costs." But since gains and costs are not defined at the outset, this initial postulate cannot be tested.[15] Indeed, at this stage, it is not an empirical proposition at all but simply a method of analysis. This method, I shall argue, is the defining feature of neoclassicism: Its goal is to understand the rationale, the pattern in a set of individual decisions.

[12]Chayanov, *Theory of Peasant Economy*, pp. 47–8.　　[13]Ibid., p. 119.
[14]Claude Meillassoux, " 'The Economy' in Agricultural Self-Sustaining Societies: A Preliminary Analysis," in David Seddon, *Relations of Production*, p. 128.
[15]See Cancian, "Maximization as Norm, Strategy, and Theory."

On this reading, it is strictly nonsensical to ask whether peasants (or anyone else) "maximize." Everyone does – by definition. With no prior specification of what is being maximized, the notion of maximization itself becomes only the postulation of *some* relatively enduring pattern in sets of individual decisions. As Amartya Sen points out, ". . . if you are consistent, then no matter whether you are a single-minded egoist or a raving altruist or a class conscious militant, you will appear to be maximizing your own utility in this enchanted world of definitions."[16] Once a maximand has been specified – profits or prestige or whatever – then a substantive proposition results, one that can be empirically tested against particular social realities. But terms such as "profit" and "prestige" take their meaning from and can only be defined relative to particular institutional arrangements; such seemingly transparent phrases are cover terms for complex institutional orders.

This is clear in Chayanov's case. The empirically empty categories of cost and gain have to be understood relative to the particular context in which peasant householders make decisions. Costs to a capitalist are, for example, moneys spent on wages, raw materials, and machines; for a peasant householder, in contrast, costs are defined primarily by the drudgery of his or her labor. Consider the consequences that follow from this difference during adverse economic times.[17] In an economic slump, capitalist firms are likely to decrease production and to cut costs by laying off workers. For peasant households, the response is often just the opposite. Because production is institutionalized differently, workers cannot be laid off, and assuming that the drudgery of labor is not thereby pushed up too far, peasant households are likely to increase – not to decrease – labor time so as to maintain their former standard of living.

In other words, an application of neoclassical method in Chayanov's case has led to a result that some substantivist and Marxist critics have asserted is impossible, namely, an appreciation of the critical structural differences between types of economy and a demonstration that each institutional arrangement has its own "rationality." In the same environment in which a capitalist firm rationally decreases production, a

---

[16] Amartya K. Sen, "Rational Fools: A Critique of the Behavioral Foundations of Economic Theory," *Philosophy and Public Affairs* 6 (1977): 323. Sen's analysis is an attempt to develop an alternative to a definitional view of maximization. The result is a much more complex (and interesting) view of human action than I am considering here or than has predominated in economics. Ironically, however, I would argue that it is precisely the simpler, definitional view of maximization that has allowed neoclassicism to be applied to *any* economic structure.

[17] See Millar, "A Reformulation of A. V. Chayanov's Theory."

peasant household rationally increases its output. The difference in response stems not from any supposed contrast in emphasis on material versus nonmaterial values, but from the fundamentally different ways in which capitalist and peasant household economies are institutionalized.

Chayanov's theory is, then, a simple one. Given his assumptions, there would appear to be no other possible result: As the household dependency ratio increases, each household worker has to work longer hours. For Russian peasant communities, Chayanov marshalled an array of evidence to support his model. Except for one case, however, he did not have direct data on labor time. Chayanov (and later Sahlins) assumed instead that the field area farmed by a household could be taken as an indirect measure of household labor time. If the equation of field size with amount of labor time is accepted, then Chayanov's theory of the Russian peasant economy is supported by clear statistical tendencies. As others have pointed out, Chayanov erred on minor theoretical points, and because his analysis did not consider the effects of class differentiation, it did not capture the whole reality of the Russian peasant economy.[18] Lenin, for example, argued that households on either side of middle-strata peasants were caught up in a different dynamic from the one Chayanov described, rich peasants turning themselves into capitalists, poor peasants being forced into the ranks of the proletariat.[19] But for middle peasants in areas where land was available, Chayanov's theory apparently held rather well.

In general terms, especially in the broad contrast between capitalist and peasant production that it adduces, Chayanov's theory appears to offer a promising starting point for an analysis of noncapitalist economics. But can Chayanov's model be extended to more than just the Russian case? Are there institutional differences among noncapitalist forms of production just as important as those between capitalist and noncapitalist? Let me turn to the Maale economy of southern Ethiopia in 1975, specifically to an area called Bola. (As will become clear in Chapter 4, Bola was inhabited by non-Maale as well as by Maale. The Maale households with which I am concerned here were concentrated in the hamlet

[18] Harrison, "Chayanov and the Economics of the Russian Peasantry."
[19] Vladimir I. Lenin, *The Development of Capitalism in Russia: The Process of the Formation of a Home Market for Large-Scale Industry* (Moscow: Progress Publishers, [1899] 1956).

of Dofo, one of several in the Bola vicinity.) How does Chayanov's theory fare among the Maale of Bola?

The shape of the household developmental cycle is a first desideratum. The Maale, at least those in the central highlands around Bola, have a stem family household system. All daughters move out of their parents' households at marriage, and younger sons stay only until their first child is born. Eldest sons, in contrast, continue to live and to cultivate with their parents after marriage.

There is, then, a typical trajectory through which most households pass, and at any one time, Maale communities are composed of households in a number of phases: young men's households with dependency ratios in the medium range, households of middle-aged men typically with high dependency ratios, and elders' households usually with low ratios.[20]

According to Chayanov's theory, the higher the dependency ratio, the longer members of a household should work. Households of the highest ratios, middle-aged men's households caught in a demographic squeeze of many young children and few workers, should work the longest hours.

Although my fieldwork procedures in 1975 were not designed to test Chayanov's theory, a time survey carried out for general ethnographic purposes nevertheless offers some relevant data.[21] I selected nine sample households for intensive study, and for one-week intervals spaced at three points in the horticultural cycle, I interviewed household members at the end of each day and made a record of their activities along with an estimate of the time spent on each task.

In order to study households of widely different composition, I selected three households from each of three successive phases in the developmental cycle: first, households headed by young men (younger brothers) with two children or fewer, all under working age; second, households headed by middle-aged men with three to seven children, all under working age; and third, households headed by elders living with at least two adult working children. By selecting households from different areas of the community and from different lineages, I attempted to minimize selection biases.

---

[20] For a detailed description of household organization and composition in Bola see Donald L. Donham, *Work and Power in Maale, Ethiopia* (Ann Arbor: UMI Research Press, 1985), pp. 73–115.

[21] See Allen Johnson, "Time Allocation in a Machiguenga Community," *Ethnology* 14 (1975): 301–10, for a more sophisticated methodology than the one used here.

Translating Chayanov's theory into the empirical terms given by a time survey raises at least three complex questions: What is to count as (1) work? And how exactly should (2) consumer and (3) worker units be calculated? I shall take up each of these problems in turn.

(1) It is clear that the definition of work in Chayanov's theory does not refer to indigenous conceptual categories. Different cultures classify activity systems differently, and the concept roughly glossed as "work" takes on different meanings in different cultures.[22] For instance, in North American society, one is likely to say that a person "is not working" if he or she is not engaged in paid employment. The analysis of conceptual systems and how they relate to the wider political economy is an essential part of a larger study (see Chapter 4), but such an analysis does not define work in Chayanov's more limited inquiry.

Rather, work for Chayanov is the time directly spent on producing and preparing the means of material sustenance. This definition should not be taken to imply that other activities necessary to the household's continuance, "labor" perhaps in a wider sense, do not exist. Child care is an obvious example. As a household's dependency ratio rises, increasing amounts of household time will have to be devoted to child care. But this does not modify the operation of Chayanov's theory: Along with increased time spent on child care, the household will also have to allocate more time to food production and preparation. These latter are the starting points and hence a strategic variable in Chayanov's analysis.

In Maale, the principal lines of production in 1975 were horticulture, livestock-raising, and beekeeping. Since an hour spent on horticulture may have a very different productivity from an hour spent on livestock-raising, the existence of different systems of production immediately raises another problem. Unless households of all dependency ratios spend the same proportion of their time on each line of production, Chayanov's proposed relationship may not hold. For example, if households of high dependency ratio were somehow able to exploit more productive lines of labor employment than others, they would not have to work longer hours. Instead, each hour of their work time would simply produce a greater final output.

For the particular Maale community on which I am reporting, this potential difficulty does not appear important. Unlike the pattern in lower and drier parts of Maale, livestock-raising and beekeeping in Bola were

[22] See David Parkin, "The Categorisation of Work: Cases from Coastal Kenya," in Sandra Wallman, ed., *Social Anthropology of Work* (London: Academic Press, 1979). I shall return to this issue in relation to capitalism in the Conclusion.

uniformly secondary. Horticulture was by far the dominant activity, and there is no indication that crop mixes (another source of possible productivity differences) varied across households. For the purposes of simplification, then, I assume below that labor time spent in horticulture can be taken as approximately equal to production time. I shall inquire later whether this assumption – let us call it assumption A – could skew the results.

There are still other problems in establishing labor time, in distinguishing work from nonwork, from a time survey. This is particularly true of women's activities, in which it is almost impossible to disentangle time spent on grinding and food preparation from that spent on child care from that spent on talking with neighbors. Indeed, this difficulty tends to be a general feature of all Maale production. Unlike capitalist economies in which the distinction between work and nonwork is timed to the minute (at least for many laborers), work in Maale is not a strictly segregated activity.

Despite this, most of the time that men and women actually spent in the fields was given over to labor. There were, in fact, few reasons for being in the fields except to work. Therefore, in order to minimize the difficulties introduced by the overlap between work and nonwork, I have counted only time in field production by both men and women in my calculations. Production time is not only easier to measure than food preparation time, but one could also argue that it should be a more sensitive indicator of lengthening the work day. After all, food has to be produced before it can be prepared. Whether this assumption – assumption B – could introduce error into the results is a question taken up below.

(2) Once a method for estimating the relative length of work days for households is established, the next problem is to define units for measuring dependency ratios, the relative number of household consumers and workers, C and W. How much, for example, does a seven-year-old child consume relative to an adult male? Or how much work in the fields does a young wife (with other duties such as child care and food preparation) carry out relative to her husband? I have already pointed out that Chayanov assumed that all workers do the same kind of work, work of the same productivity, for different lengths of time. The same uniformity conditions apply to consumption: The assumption is that householders consume the same products in different quantities. In the absence of an empirical survey of consumption in Maale, I have defined C in the following calculations by adapting figures from published nutri-

tion studies.[23] Adults, both male and female, fourteen years of age and older are assumed to require 1.0 consumption units, children aged seven to thirteen, 0.75, and children two to six, 0.5.

(3) Finally, a method for calculating worker units, W, must be devised. One solution would be to derive relative labor units from the empirical data on work time. Data from the nine sample households showed that males aged fourteen to fifty worked an average of 4.5 hours a day in the fields, and those over fifty worked an average of 2.6. Unmarried girls fourteen and older worked an average of 2.2 hours, but married women worked only 1.5 hours in the fields. These figures could be used to calculate relative worker units for men (1.0), elders (0.6), married women (0.3), and unmarried girls (0.5).

As long as household dependency ratio is being compared to variables other than work time (as, for example, on p. 44), this method of calculation is obviously the most realistic one. But for Chayanov's hypothesis (to be tested in figure 1), it will not be satisfactory, for both W in the ratio C/W and total household work time would be calculated from the same data. In other words, our two principal variables, dependency ratio and household work time, would not be specified independently. In the face of this impasse, for figure 1 we are forced back to the cruder alternative that Chayanov himself used: assuming all adults as 1.0 worker units. The only problem becomes one of drawing the line between (adult) workers and (child) consumers for the Maale case.

Deciding how to distinguish workers from non-workers should depend, of course, on the specific features of Maale production. It appears that Maale boys and girls generally begin "full-time" horticultural work at about age fourteen. Younger children certainly carry out activities that one might term work in a wider sense, but it is crucial to notice that these activities are rarely directed toward production (and hence would not count according to the assumptions above). Young girls, for example, spend considerable time in grinding grain, fetching water, and caring for still younger children. Even when children's activities such as boys' herding *are* directly productive, they are typically neither horticultural nor organized household by household.[24] Goat herding is done by

[23] T. Scarlet Epstein, "The Data of Economics in Anthropological Analysis," in A. L. Epstein, ed., *The Craft of Social Anthropology* (London: Tavistock, 1967), pp. 153–80.

[24] The importance of the social organization of children's work has not always been appreciated. For example, Moni Nag, Benjamin White, and Robert Peet, in "An Anthropological Approach to the Study of the Economic Value of Children in Java and Nepal," *Current Anthropology* 19 (1978)': 293–306, try to relate peasants' fertility decisions to the value of children's work, but unless children's work is organized strictly house-

boys about six to ten years old for the community as whole; if a household does not have a boy of the requisite age, its goats are still cared for.
Cattle herding is the responsibility of boys of about ten and older, but
once again, households are not the relevant organizational unit. Minimal lineage segments cooperate in herding cattle, and sometimes one
boy herds the cattle of up to four or five households.

There is only one important role for children below fourteen that is
both devoted to horticultural production and organized household by
household, hence that could possibly count as work in the scheme developed here. That is guarding ripening fields against birds and other
predators. When fields ripen in Maale, platforms are built in strategic
locations from which children scare away birds and other pests. Older
children do a limited amount of second weeding, rustling through the
sorghum stalks, while younger children typically play flutes and sling
stones at birds. Unless fields adjoin, children usually guard alone.

Should hours spent on guarding be counted as household work time
just as hours spent on weeding or hoeing are? Again, we are faced with
activities with widely different levels of productivity, and I have assumed below that hours spent on guarding were sufficiently unproductive that they can be ignored in calculating work time. Given this assumption, assumption C, it is appropriate to fix the age of adult workers
at fourteen or above.

Finally, I can come to the point: *the present data show exactly the opposite
relationship to the one proposed by Chayanov.* Figure 1 (overleaf) presents data
on length of the work day versus household dependency ratio. According to Chayanov's theory, as dependency ratios increase, the length of
the work day should also increase; that is, the slope of the line shown in
figure 1 should be positive. In fact, figure 1 shows the reverse – a negative
slope. As dependency ratios increase, length of the work day in horticultural production decreases, at least in the small sample of households
on which we have data. How can this apparent paradox be explained?

Before we can conclude that the Maale data contradict Chayanov's
theory, we have to reexamine the assumptions made above. Assumption A – that horticultural production can be taken as approximately
equal to total production – would introduce error only if households of
high dependency ratios were somehow devoting relatively more time to
productive activities that were not counted. As I have already pointed

hold by household (a matter that the authors do not consider), this kind of argument
is not sound.

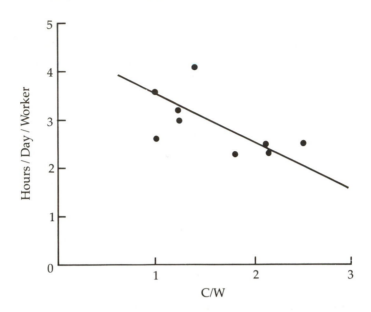

Figure 1: Hours of field labor per day per worker versus the dependency ratio of selected Maale households in Bola during 1975

out, livestock-raising and beekeeping were the other principal lines of production. But it was precisely households with relatively low dependency ratios, elders' households, that owned the vast majority of cattle, and high ratio households, therefore, had little to do with cattle-keeping. There was also no indication from census information that men in high dependency households tended significantly more beehives than others. Assumption A, therefore, does not appear to introduce any significant distortion into our analysis.

Assumption B posited that only food production and not preparation time was to be counted in figure 1. In other words, I assumed that preparation time added only a constant proportion to production time, and that in measuring the relative length of the work day, neglecting the former would introduce no error. This would not be the case, however, if households of low dependency ratio exchanged a part of their (unprepared) produce, a surplus above subsistence requirements, either through the market or through traditional forms of circulation. That would mean that other households of higher ratios would be doing relatively more preparation and that this uncounted time might account for the fact that high ratio households appear to work less than Chayanov hypothesizes.

It is generally true, in all of Maale, that elders' households with low dependency ratios often produced extra grain to trade for cattle. (When

I wanted to buy grain, for example, I was told to seek out a worshado, "father of a multitude," an elder with many working children.) But this was not true of Bola during 1975. No grain found its way into the local market, and only one household, an elder's household (not included in the time survey above), produced enough extra grain to trade for a calf from a bond friend. Assumption B, then, would not appear to offer a sufficient explanation for the negative slope of figure 1.

Assumption C, finally, postulated that children's time in guarding fields was unproductive enough that it could be neglected in calculating the household work day. If this were not true, if children's time in guarding fields saved enough grain that their parents could afford to spend less time in production than other adults, then the negative slope of figure 1 would be explained. In other words, children from about six to fourteen would save enough grain by guarding fields to meet not only their own and younger siblings' subsistence requirements but also part of their parents' needs.

There are a number of indications that guarding fields did not increase the final harvested product nearly so much. First, fields in Maale were generally grouped into contiguous blocks. Whether by chance or by planning, at least one of the fields of a block was ordinarily cultivated by a household with children who could guard. Even though the other fields of the block were not as well-guarded, they benefited to some extent, particularly against the predations of monkeys and baboons. Second, if children's time spent in guarding were the explanation for figure 1, we would expect that children in high dependency ratio households would guard longer hours than those in low ratio households. They did not. Children in both kinds of households devoted the same amount of time to guarding (approximately two hours a day). Assumption C, therefore, does not appear to hold our answer.

Now, apart from the possible problems of method that we have been able to dismiss, it goes without saying that figure 1 might be the result of a small and unrepresentative sample of Bola households. Certainly I have not proven the point statistically. The possibility that figure 1 may be accurate, however, is strengthened by fuller data on another Maale community called Bio in 1983 that show exactly the same lack of relationship between work time and dependency ratio (see figure 9, p. 218 of the Appendix).

Let us therefore proceed with the information that we have: High dependency ratio households in Bola seem not to have worked longer hours. What other kinds of data might confirm such a conclusion? And, if confirmed, how can this paradox be explained? Households that needed the most appear to have worked the least.

If Chayanov's theory does not appear to describe the Maale case, the next possibility to be investigated is Sahlins's model of the domestic mode of production. Sahlins extended as well as modified Chayanov's work, and it may be that the modified theory will offer an explanation of our Maale mystery. Before deciding, however, we are forced to return to abstract theoretical issues. For Sahlins, in his model of the domestic mode of production, claims to offer an alternative to and a critique of neoclassical theory in anthropology.

Sahlins's revisions of Chayanov's work were basically two: first, that households are not closed economic units but linked to one another through various forms of circulation and, second, that many of these forms involve social, political, and religious values that modify Chayanov's purely economic analysis. For example, politically ambitious households may produce a surplus above their own subsistence needs and use it to attract political followers. Since some households "overproduce," others thereby enjoy the possibility of "underproducing." The net effect is that the positive slope of Chayanov's graph of work time versus dependency ratio may be inflected in particular ways by various social and political environments. The pattern of deviation, according to Sahlins, should correlate with the specific kind of social and political environment; with this, he concludes, "it becomes possible to conceive a truly anthropological economics."[25]

As the saying goes, man does not live by bread alone. "Economics" cannot easily be separated from "kinship" and "politics," particularly in technologically less developed societies. In this sense, Sahlins's modifications place Chayanov's bare theory in a more realistic framework. But do Sahlins's revisions so affect the theory that, as he argues, we should no longer place it in the category of neoclassical analyses? Has he given us a fundamentally different ("substantivist," as he calls it) kind of theory? The answer depends, of course, on what we mean by "neoclassical," and that issue requires further discussion.

The defining feature of neoclassical analysis is, I believe, its departure from the point of view of individuals. Perhaps present-day cultural anthropologists will be surprised by the assertion, though Max Weber would

---

[25] Sahlins, *Stone Age Economics*, p. 30.

not have been: Neoclassical analyses depend on "interpretation."[26] They require understanding the meanings and motives that activate individual decisions. The particular ends of individual actions, material or not, are unspecified. "We do not assume," says Ronald Rogowski, a political scientist applying neoclassical theory, ". . . that an individual will seek to maximize income, power, votes, or any other 'good.' Hence no goals that are pursued with tolerable consistency can be called 'irrational.' "[27] Rather, what *is* assumed is that individual goals or preferences can be arranged into a more-or-less consistent hierarchy: If A is preferred to B, and B to C, then A should also be preferred to C. In other words, neoclassical analyses posit individuals (households in the present case) consistently pursuing a hierarchy of particular values subject to local institutional constraints – allocating scarce resources to determinate ends.

On this reading of neoclassicism, Sahlins's theory, despite his protestations, shares all the fundamental points. His theory is still based on individual preferences. According to him, hierarchies of values peculiar to each culture, ranging from material needs to kinship morality to status claims, motivate households of varying dependency ratios to spend varying amounts of time in production. All of these concepts – individuals' motives conditioned by particular cultural values, stable hierarchies of preferences leading to different actions by different kinds of households – are entirely orthodox.

Sahlins's arguments to the contrary stem, it seems, from a belief that neoclassical theory rests on maximization as an empirical proposition. According to Sahlins, people in capitalist societies maximize. Others do not. Capitalism is determined by "production for exchange," an insatiable quest for material profit, for "as much as possible." "The sky is the limit." The domestic mode of production, on the other hand, is determined by "production for use": ". . . wants are finite and few, and technical means unchanging but on the whole adequate."[28] Thus Sahlins calls hunters and gatherers the "original affluent society," but for him, affluence means not level of wealth but psychological satisfaction. Hunters and gatherers are poor but satisfied. They, like all producers of use values, resemble bees who "neither seek nor covet more."[29]

[26] Max Weber, *Roscher and Knies: The Logical Problems of Historical Economics*, trans. G. Oakes (New York: Free Press, [1903–1906] 1975).
[27] Ronald Rogowski, "Rationalist Theories of Politics: A Midterm Report," *World Politics* 30 (1978): 301.
[28] Sahlins, *Stone Age Economics*, p. 2.
[29] Marshall Sahlins, "The Intensity of Domestic Production in Primitive Societies: Social

What Sahlins's formulation does not comprehend is that *even* satisfied hunters and gatherers, if any exist, can be analyzed as maximizing. Nor is this kind of example peculiar to noncapitalist economies. For the moment, let us consider capitalism from the point of view of workers, not capitalists. For workers, a neoclassical analyst would point out that leisure has a value just as do material goods. In any society there must come a point when workers prefer leisure to additional labor. Maximization, as the phrase has been used in anthropology, is perhaps an unfortunate label, since it implies "wanting the most." But the key idea is not so much wanting the most as wanting consistently.[30] Given the institutional contexts in which they act, workers have ordered hierarchies of needs: certain goods, leisure, and so forth. The opposite of maximization is not, as Sahlins would have it, domestic production; it is unintelligible disorder.[31]

Is, then, Sahlins's model of the domestic mode only neoclassical analysis masquerading in different language? Not quite. It is true, I think, that every aspect of the domestic mode can be translated into the clearer terms of ordinary neoclassical theory. In that sense, Sahlins's model would appear to offer no alternative to, nor critique of, neoclassicism.[32] In one crucial respect, however, Sahlins departs from the ordinary procedures of economists like Chayanov, and a careful consideration of that departure will allow a sharper specification of how neoclassical analyses depend on the particular institutional and cultural contexts in which they are applied.

To explain, let me return to the question of how hierarchies of individual values are determined in actual empirical analyses. How do we know individual preferences? Basically, the answer goes, only by observing what people do in particular instances and by inferring the hierarchy of tastes that must have motivated such actions. Immediately, however, we are faced with a circularity, if we have closed off, by definition, any

Inflections of the Chayanov Slope," in George Dalton, ed., *Studies in Economic Anthropology* (Washington: American Anthropological Association, 1971), p. 31.

[30] Firth, "Themes in Economic Anthropology," p. 8.

[31] Nor, strictly speaking, is Herbert Simon's concept of "satisficing" an alternative to maximization in the sense I am using the term; see his *Models of Man: Social and Rational* (New York: John Wiley, 1957). Rather, satisficing replaces older analyses of profit maximization in capitalist economies that assume that decision-makers have complete knowledge of the future. See Jerome Rothenberg, "Values and Value Theory in Economics," in S. R. Krupp, ed., *The Structure of Economic Science: Essays on Methodology* (Englewood Cliffs, N. J.: Prentice-Hall, 1966), p. 232.

[32] Elsewhere, I have argued that substantivism more generally – including Karl Polanyi's concepts of reciprocity and redistribution – does not offer a theoretical alternative to neoclassicism. See Donham, *Work and Power*, chap. 1.

other way of determining preferences. How can we infer preferences from actions and then explain the same actions as a result of the postulated preferences? The only escape from this tautology is to determine tastes at some time t_1, to assume further that tastes remain constant while some other variable changes from t_1 to t_2, and then to predict the outcome at t_2. According to Gary Becker, "The assumption of stable preferences provides a stable foundation for generating predictions about responses to various changes, and prevents the analyst from succumbing to the temptation of simply postulating the required shift in preferences to 'explain' all apparent contradictions to his predictions."[33]

This method of defining individual ends is not the one used by Sahlins, and in this sense his model – given its other features – is not neoclassical enough. Instead of adopting an agnostic attitude toward values or tastes and allowing them to be defined indirectly by particular institutional and cultural contexts, Sahlins argues a priori that all kinds of domestic production are determined by values qualitatively different from those in capitalist production. According to Sahlins, the domestic mode of production is determined by "production for use," the capitalist mode by "production for exchange."

These are, of course, Marx's phrases, but for Marx the difference between the two lies not so much in individual intentions or in cultural values (though these are not denied) but in the contrast between wage and non-wage economies, hence in the difference between class systems.[34] For Sahlins, however, the definition of these two economic systems never goes beyond individual intentions and the cultural values that condition them. Production for use takes place when wants are finite and when people neither seek nor covet more. Production for exchange is based on unlimited individual needs, an insatiable quest for as much as possible.

It is clear that Sahlins's insistence on the contrast between value systems was meant to emphasize, to come to terms with, the real diversity in how economic systems are institutionalized. In some very crucial sense, economic systems *are* different. But Sahlins's attempt at this point had an effect that was the reverse of what he intended, namely, to preclude

---

[33] Gary S. Becker, *The Economic Approach to Human Behavior* (Chicago: University of Chicago Press, 1976), p. 5.

[34] See Robert Brenner's important article, "The Origins of Capitalist Development: A Critique of Neo-Smithian Marxism," *New Left Review* 104 (1977): 25–92. Brenner argues that "the correct counterposition cannot be production for the market versus production for use but the class system of production based on free wage labour (capitalism) versus pre-capitalist class systems" (p. 50).

the possibility of ever reaching the level of institutional analysis. Consider first his description of capitalism – "the sky is the limit." The simple fact that few factories in capitalist countries operate on Saturday and Sunday would appear an initial embarrassment for such a description. Following this line of thought, we are led to ask further whether the insatiable quest for material gain is a value uniformly held across capitalist society. By workers as well as capitalists? If so, we would expect to find workers even in good times fighting to lengthen the working day; presumably they would have to be forced out of the factories at the end of the day. To ask these questions is, of course, to highlight the difference between workers and capitalists and to suggest that values and rationalities are conditioned by class. By typifying capitalism as a whole by one uniform value, Sahlins was prevented from ever posing these questions or inquiring into them.

The emphasis on prior abstracted values – what one might call cultural reductionism – also affected how Sahlins analyzed domestic production. Consider the difference in Sahlins's and Chayanov's analyses of why domestic producers do not increase production. Sahlins's answer proceeds straight to cultural values inculcated in individuals. Simply put, they do not want more things. Like bees, they neither seek nor covet more. The institutional fact that work is performed as wage labor, household labor, or whatever is irrelevant; domestic producers simply do not want any more. In the language of neoclassical economics, they have reached their "bliss point."[35]

Chayanov, in contrast, by adopting no prior position on values came to a more circumstantial and revealing appreciation of institutional differences. Peasant producers may well have fewer material needs than most persons in capitalist economies, but it is crucial to note that whatever their needs, householders have to rely on their own labor. They may well, in some sense, "want" more but be unwilling to "pay the cost." And cost, as Chayanov observed, has to be understood in the institutional context of household production; if cost could somehow be reduced, production might well be increased.

This brings me to a provisional conclusion: By allowing individual preferences to act as proxy variables indirectly determined by institutional contexts, neoclassical analyses can offer valuable insights into how, in Karl Polanyi's phrase, "the economy is instituted."[36] Besides Cha-

---

[35] W. R. Stent and L. Roy Webb, "Subsistence Affluence and Market Economy in Papua New Guinea," *Economic Record* 51 (1975): 522–38.

[36] The analysis of institutions was, of course, precisely what substantivism claimed to pro-

yanov's study of households, one could cite Frank Cancian's analysis of how risk-taking is affected by economic stratification or Martin Orans's study of how "maximizing" in India is constrained by forms of economic and political inequality.[37] But I should state my case carefully. Even though such studies offer insights into how institutions operate from the point of view of individual strategies, no neoclassical analysis can explain why one institutional complex is present and not another. Indeed, this is logically impossible, for we have seen that such analyses commonly assume institutional information as given, as exogenously determined. What is assumed in an analysis cannot at the same time be explained by it.[38] With this (major) qualification, it is now possible, I hope, to appreciate the connections between neoclassical analyses and the various kinds of economic structures to which they are applied.

Seen in this light, a number of stock criticisms of neoclassical analyses fall by the wayside. Neoclassical analyses involve no necessary assumption about how egotistical, hedonist, or individualistic persons are. "The postulate that an agent is characterized by preference rules out neither the saint nor Genghis Khan."[39] Hierarchies of values can vary all the way from those of complete altruism to narrow self-gain so that there is no cogent reason for confining neoclassical method to certain types of societies – capitalist, individualistic Gesellschaften. Second, neoclassical analyses do not necessarily oppose individuals to society, nor do they assume that individuals exist outside society. One could, and I shall, claim just the opposite – that hierarchies of tastes are socially conditioned. Third, neoclassical theory does not make individuals into universal, ahistorical, natural beings independent of their historical contexts or peculiar cultures.[40] Specifically, postulating stable preferences

vide. See Karl Polanyi, Conrad M. Arensberg, and Harry W. Pearson, eds., *Trade and Market in the Early Empires: Economies in History and Theory* (Glencoe, Ill.: Free Press, 1957).

[37] Frank A. Cancian, *The Innovator's Situation: Upper-Middle Class Conservatism in Agricultural Communities* (Stanford: Stanford University Press, 1979); Martin Orans, "Maximizing in Jajmani Land: A Model of Caste Relations," *American Anthropologist* 70 (1968): 875–97.

[38] Oskar Lange, "Marxian Economics and Modern Economic Theory," *Review of Economic Studies* 2 (1934–35): 189–201.

[39] Frank Hahn and Martin Holis, "Introduction," *Philosophy and Economics* (Oxford: Oxford University Press, 1979), p. 4.

[40] In work done after that on the domestic mode of production, *Culture and Practical Reason* (Chicago: University of Chicago Press, 1976), Sahlins continues to maintain that his concept of culture offers a critique of utilitarianism or neoclassical method – what he calls "practical reason." But most neoclassical economists are not very concerned with how individual preferences originate; all they require is that preferences remain relatively stable over time. If anthropologists tell economists that preferences are conditioned by "cultures," sets of enduring values and predispositions, economists may well be grateful. Far from constituting an alternative, such an idea is exactly what neoclassicism needs.

over relatively short periods of time in particular social contexts does not involve the assumption that human nature is everywhere unvarying and eternal.[41] Whatever the intrinsic limitations of neoclassical analyses, they are not these. Recognizing this fact will, I think, make the formulation of any alternative theory easier.

Despite its theoretical shortcomings, does Sahlins's theory of domestic production nevertheless suggest a correct explanation of the Maale data? Recall that Sahlins argued that households are not closed economic units, that various patterns of circulation of goods among households can cause particular kinds of deviation from Chayanov's slope. For the Maale case, this argument suggests the possibility that high dependency households may have received a net flow of goods from other, better-endowed households rather than working longer hours. Such a pattern, if it existed, would explain the paradox of figure 1.

Investigating this possibility, we note that the Maale do indeed have traditional ways by which needy persons obtain crops from kinsmen and neighbors. To give crops in this context is described by a particular verb, zimane. Great cultural store is set upon generosity and, in fact, the Maale concept of iginni or "relative" is defined as much in reference to generous mutual aid as to biological kinship. Persons therefore can "become relatives," igintane, through various forms of exchange and mutual help. Wives apparently often asked their fathers or brothers for such help, and occasionally men begged kinsmen and neighbors for help, sometimes maternal kinsmen who lived in a community other than their own.

My census of Bola asked people to recall the number of sacks of grain that they received and gave away in these forms of circulation, and the resulting information shows, as Sahlins's theory would predict, that elders' households gave away more than they received. Five elders' households (all with low dependency ratios of 2.0 or less) gave away an average of 3.8 sacks of grain and received only 0.6 sacks.

At the other extreme of the dependency ratio continuum, however, middle-aged households did not receive, according to their reports, more than they gave away. Five middle-aged households (all with high dependency ratios of 3.3 or greater) gave away an average of 2.0 sacks and

[41] Frank Hahn, "Notes on Vulgar Economy," ms., Marshall Library of Economics, Cambridge University.

received only 0.4 sacks in return. In several cases, I determined that givers reported their gifts while takers did not, and it seems clear that there was a tendency (consistent with a certain amount of embarrassment about having received help) to underreport the amount of grain received. But even assuming a fair degree of underreporting, it is unlikely that middle-aged households received significantly more grain than they gave away. Sahlins's redistributive hypothesis appears to fare little better than Chayanov's theory.

One can imagine still other solutions. Middle-aged households could have cut their consumption levels relative to others. As I have already noted, I do not have data on consumption levels, but one would expect that such cuts could have gone only so far before the reproduction of the next generation was endangered. Alternatively, consumption patterns could have operated so that members of needy households ate in others' households more often than the reverse. Again, I do not have quantifiable information on this point. Given the cultural value placed on generous hospitality, such a pattern may have operated to some extent. At the same time, other cultural norms – specifically, that a person should not visit another household during mealtime too often lest he be said to have come simply "because he was hungry" – limited transfers of cooked food between households. None of these possible explanations, Sahlins's included, appear to account convincingly for figure 1.

If patterns of circulation of (1) cooked food and (2) raw grain do not appear to offer an explanation for the Bola data, there remains, I believe, one last possibility, namely, the circulation of (3) labor. To examine that possibility is to jettison an explicit institutional assumption of Chayanov's, that households are self-contained and bounded labor units. And it is also to call into question Sahlins's characterization of the domestic mode of production as a Hobbesian anarchy of independent household existences. Even though he recognized the web of connections among households created by circulation, Sahlins maintained that in the organization of production, each household is an independent monad:

The domestic mode anticipates no social or material relations between households except that they are alike. The social economy is fragmented into a thousand petty existences, each organized to proceed independently of the others and each dedicated to the homebred principle of looking out for itself. . . . the domestic mode has all the organization of the so many potatoes in a certain famous sack of potatoes.[42]

---

[42] Sahlins, *Stone Age Economics*, p. 95.

But was the Maale labor process so uncoordinated? So anarchic? Or were households possibly organized among themselves to facilitate the flow of labor? True, wage labor was absent. But were there other institutional arrangements in which labor could be transferred from household to household?

To answer these questions requires a closer examination of the labor process in Maale. That only about half of all field work was carried out by household members working by themselves alerts us to how inadequate an analysis would be that focused solely on Maale domestic groups. Domestic groups or households were just one among several structures that participated in production; the other half of work was accomplished in various kinds of larger social units organized to work cooperatively. In Bola there were three types of cooperative work arrangements, mol'o, helma, and dabo, and these three fall into two structural types.

The first kind of work group, represented by mol'o and helma, is what has been called a reciprocal work group.[43] It is composed of a bounded group of households that work in rotation on each other's fields. Since a schedule of rotation is followed, each household receives as much labor from others as it gives to them. The mol'o and helma cannot, therefore, create any net circulation of labor among households.

The second kind of work group, the dabo, is an example of what has been called a "festive" work group (although festivity is clearly not its most salient structural feature). Here, the sponsoring household brews beer or prepares food and, as the Maale say, "begs" neighbors to come and help them on the appointed day. After the work is done, the sponsoring household retains an obligation, a loose and unenforced obligation, to send a worker at some future date to the festive work parties of the households who have worked for it. Unlike the neatly bounded work groups discussed above, exact reciprocity in dabo labor is not built into the system of cooperation. To what degree giving and receiving dabo labor was in fact balanced remains an open question.

Investigating this problem requires a relatively self-contained universe of households. That is, most households' dabo partners should come from within the group studied, not outside. The Maale in Bola vicinity were such a group: In 1975, 91 percent of the workers in their dabo parties came from within their boundaries. Another requirement

[43] Charles J. Erasmus, "Culture, Structure and Process: The Occurrence and Disappearance of Reciprocal Farm Labor,"*Southwestern Journal of Anthropology* 12 (1956): 444–69. See also M. P. Moore, "Co-operative Labour in Peasant Agriculture," *Journal of Peasant Studies* 2 (1975): 270–91.

is that the self-contained universe of households be studied for a long enough time that balances within the system can become manifest. On that score, I kept a record of the dabo work parties sponsored during the entire span of planting and weeding fields in 1975, a period of four months. This period was a strategic choice, since it was the season of peak labor demand in Maale, the bottleneck during which about half of all dabo were sponsored.[44]

To go straight to the point, the solution to our Maale mystery, or at least a large part of the solution, appears to lie in the pattern of dabo labor imbalances. With two notable exceptions, households of low dependency ratios, predomiantly elders' households, consistently gave away more dabo labor than they received. Conversely, households with high dependency ratios, predominantly middle-aged couples' households, received more dabo labor than they gave away. Finally, young couples' households and most widows' households in the middle range of dependency ratios experienced neither a large deficit nor a large surplus. In sum, there was a net transfer of labor, mostly from elders' households to middle-aged couples' households.

In order to demonstrate numerically that such transfers took place, a number of preliminaries are required: (1) A few households worked in and sponsored dabo so infrequently during my study period that their imbalances might have been the result only of sampling. Consequently, five households only weakly integrated into the dabo system, whose total of dabo days given added to those received was less than twelve, are eliminated from the analysis below (that is, from figure 2).

(2) Three households were obviously deviant cases and have to be explained on principles other than those I shall deduce below. One middle-aged man, for example, had a very high dependency household but managed to draw no surplus labor from his neighbors. For various reasons, he had alienated neighbors who had begun to refuse to work cooperatively with him; in 1975 during my survey, he cultivated a very small field and, after being effectively ostracized, afterwards moved away. The other two exceptions were elders' households with relatively large supplies of domestic labor who yet supplemented them with net surpluses of labor from neighbors. One was relatively rich in cattle – the only exception to a remarkably even distribution of wealth among the

---

[44] Even in the (unlikely) event that imbalances during my study period were numerically balanced by reverse flows of labor at other times of the year, the total effect on yields would not have balanced, since the level of labor input during planting and weeding probably affected final yields more than labor inputs at any other time.

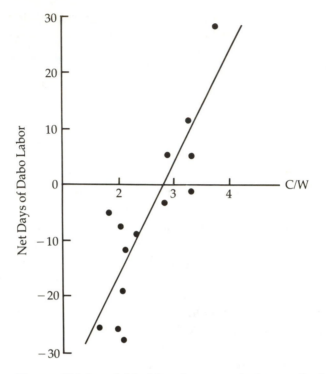

Figure 2: Net days of dabo labor given or received versus the dependency ratio of Maale households in Bola during 1975 (after Donham, *Work and Power*, p. 159)

Maale of Bola – and the other household was headed by a half-Maale trader of moderate wealth who had married a Maale woman. Evidence from the market village just next to the Maale community reported on here (this information is detailed in Chapter 4) shows that both high relative wealth and trading activities modify the pattern discussed here and are correlated with net surpluses of dabo labor.

Given these exceptions and qualifications, the correlation of dabo imbalances with household dependency ratios is striking. Figure 2 shows the least squares linear relationship between the two variables.[45] Households with as many as three children between two and six years old (dependency ratio of about 2.8) typically had reached a critical balance point. They gave out about as much dabo labor as they received and apparently still managed to meet their consumption requirements. With

[45]The correlation coefficient, r, is 0.89; that is, 78 percent (r^2) of the variability in dabo imbalance can be explained by variation in dependency ratio. The correlation shown in figure 2 is significant at the 0.001 level.

less favorable ratios of domestic labor (more children), most households depended on a surplus of dabo labor drawn from their neighbors. And with more favorable labor supplies, households, typically elders' households, consistently gave away much more dabo labor than they received. This makes the conclusion suggested by figure 1 more plausible: High dependency ratio households apparently did not work longer hours. Instead, they relied, at least partially, on net surpluses of dabo labor.[46]

So far I have analyzed elders' households as unitary wholes and have shown that they contributed a net surplus of labor to other households. I should make clear that it generally was not elders themselves who worked for others, but younger members of elders' households. Recall the composition of a typical elder's household: the elder, his wife, his eldest son and the latter's wife, and any unmarried sons and daughters. It was usually the eldest son or unmarried sons or daughters who worked in other households' dabo. Yet the household head, the elder, had authority over the disposition of his dependents' labor, just as he had final authority over the disposition of the product of their labor. Household heads oversaw, supervised, and organized the labor process of the community.

In short, the direction of Sahlins's modification of Chayanov's theory – that social, political, and religious factors significantly affect material life – is borne out in the present analysis. But it is borne out in a different, an institutionally more complex, and a more orderly way than in Sahlins's formulation of the domestic mode of production. In production, Maale households were in no sense so many potatoes in a sack. The production process was no more (probably less) anarchic than a General Motors assembly line.[47]

---

[46] A final possibility should be explored – namely, that the labor embodied in dabo beer balanced the amount of labor done by the work party. Unfortunately, this conjecture is difficult to test empirically, and the only attempt to deal with the question that I am aware of is Fredrik Barth's study "Economic Spheres in Darfur," in Raymond Firth, ed., *Themes in Economic Anthropology* (London: Tavistock, 1967), p. 166. Barth estimated that the labor embodied in Darfur beer was about one-third that accomplished by work parties. For the Maale case, I have calculated that the labor embodied in Maale dabo beer was about half that carried out by the work party (see Donham, *Work and Power*, pp. 179–80). Although the *net* labor flows were approximately half of the simple imbalances shown in figure 2, they were still sizable. Also, it should be remembered that these labor flows occurred at the principal bottleneck in the productive cycle, when the magnitude of labor input had it greatest effect on final yields.

[47] With the present results in mind, it is of some interest to return to Chayanov's work. He (and Sahlins) assumed that field size was an indirect measure of a household's labor time. In Bola, we have seen that this assumption would be false and dangerously misleading. The labor time that went into a Bola plot was not necessarily only that of the household owning the field. But if an analyst assumed that households were bounded

It will have become clear by now that the story I have told, like all mysteries, was composed according to a certain artificial order. Was the circuitous way of telling the story worth the time? Would not a simple description of the labor process have been, as they say, more economical?

I think not. The value of neoclassical theory in general and of Sahlins's work in particular is that they force us into a more rigorous and fine-grained analysis than we might have made otherwise. To an unsuspecting observer, the Maale labor process would have appeared egalitarian and uncomplicated. Any Maale person would have explained, "Yes, if I work for so-and-so, then he will help me later." It was Sahlins's (I argue neoclassical) theory that prompted a deeper analysis of the Maale case. By following such an approach to its logical conclusion, we were forced to specify the particular institutional context of Maale production – the unexpected way in which differences in dependency ratio signaled different roles in giving and receiving labor. Otherwise, when the assumptions appropriate to other institutional orders were generalized to the Maale case, individual actions appeared merely bizarre.

This inextricable connection between particular neoclassical analyses and particular institutional settings means that, in one sense, substantivists like Karl Polanyi were correct: There is no universal economic theory. Neoclassical theory as such does not exist. There are only neoclassical theories, particular neoclassical analyses. This has been pointed out by orthodox neoclassical economists themselves: "The statement that the fundamental principles of economics are universally valid . . . may be true only as their *form* is concerned. Their *content*, however, is determined by the institutional setting. And without this institutional content, the principles are nothing but 'empty boxes' from which we can obtain only empty generalities."[48] By filling in the empty boxes to specify particular institutional orders, we are forced to consider relationships and interconnections systematically. This, it seems to me, is the source of most neoclassical insights.

labor units and that field size reflected household labor time, we can now safely predict that the Bola results would confirm Chayanov's rule. Households of higher dependency ratio would appear to work longer hours. It is unlikely, of course, that exactly the same factors as operated in this Maale community were present in the Russian peasant cases studied by Chayanov. But since he did not specify the wider institutional context in which households were embedded, we cannot a priori exclude that possibility.

[48] Nicholas Georgescu-Roegen, *Analytical Economics: Issues and Problems* (Cambridge: Harvard University Press, 1966), pp. 109–10.

But neoclassical analyses also have their limits – limits that turn out to be importantly restrictive. In relation to the present case, a number of larger questions remain unposed and unanswered. First, there is no evidence to suggest that the patterns of Bola in 1975 were the same at other times. In fact, the opposite is the case. Subsequent research in the same area during 1983 showed that the slope of the relationship between labor time and dependency ratio had become strongly positive, just as Chayanov predicted (see figure 10, p. 219 of the Appendix). Evidently, historical context conditions the connection between Chayanov's variables in a way we have not yet explored. Second, the existence of the pattern of labor transfers analyzed above depended upon the fundamental inequality between household heads and others. What gave male household heads the power to dispose of the labor of their grown, co-resident children? What were the beliefs and practices that supported, renewed, or perhaps challenged that structure of inequality? These questions introduce a discussion of the limits of neoclassical analyses. Let me begin by reference to three issues: history, power, and ideology.

In the face of problems posed by historical transformations, political domination, and ideological beliefs, neoclassical theory is, I believe, essentially helpless.[49] What "essentially" means is not clear, so let me turn to the first problem, historical change. As I have noted above, neoclassical studies typically postulate stability of individual preferences over the time period being considered. Since preferences obviously do change during historical time, the coverage of neoclassical analyses is necessarily restricted to relatively short periods. Over these short periods, neoclassical studies assume as givens particular institutional orders and hierarchies of individual values. What is assumed cannot at the same time be explained. Why is there a stem family household system in Maale? No neoclassical analysis can provide an answer.

Rather, assuming that a stem family household system *does* exist in Maale and assuming that individual Maale actors pursue a certain hierarchy of ends in regard to production, we have been able to set up a closed system of interrelated variables. If – somehow – one variable changes, then we can see the resulting reverberation through the sys-

---

[49] Jon Elster has argued for the relevance of neoclassical approaches to Marxism in "Marxism, Functionalism, and Game Theory," *Theory and Society* 11 (1982): 453–82. Here, I am concerned to sketch the limits of such approaches, limits also discussed by G. A. Cohen in *History, Labour and Freedom: Themes From Marx* (Oxford: Clarendon Press, 1988), pp. 14–6.

tem. In that sense, neoclassical analyses can offer certain insights into historical transformations, but why the "independent" variable changed in the first place is a question for which we have no answer. Ralf Dahrendorf's comments are relevant at this point: "What happens in the market is a constantly repeated game that is sufficient unto itself. Only a *deus ex machina* . . . can initiate change in the market, and even then one cannot predict what direction change will take."[50]

Neoclassical theory's helplessness before history is related to the second topic, its lack of analysis of domination. The quickest way to illustrate this point is by recalling that so far we have treated households of all sizes and compositions as *single* decision-making units. But are they? To pose the question is to answer it. Maale is perhaps no more conflict-ridden than other societies of its kind, but the cases of wife-beating, women leaving their husbands for relatives' houses, and arguments between fathers and sons are enough (even over the short space of three years of fieldwork) to convince one that households are composed of a number of persons, not one.

Household heads, as I have said, have the formal authority to make decisions about production and about how the final product is to be used. They occupy a dominant position vis-à-vis their wives and coresident children, who do not fully control the fruits of their own labor. But of course wives and children are not totally without recourse, and the actual power that a household head is able to wield is always the complex outcome of superior political resources interacting with various kinds of resistance. The pattern of who is positioned against whom varies over the developmental cycle: in the beginning, young husbands versus young wives, when divorce was most frequent; toward the end, elders versus their coresident eldest sons, and expressed much more openly, mothers versus their daughters-in-law. It was particularly women, the Maale said, who broke up households.

To relate power to history, I would point out that it is the evolution of political domination that conditions many, perhaps most, patterns of historical transformation. For the case at hand, one can imagine the balance of power shifting in favor of household heads (as against their dependents) sufficiently to transform a stem into an extended family system. Or the reverse might occur, the balance shifting toward children so that a stem family might change into a conjugal family system. These

---

[50] Ralf Dahrendorf, *Essays in the Theory of Society* (Stanford: Stanford University Press, 1968), p. 227.

are no more than hypotheses, but Dahrendorf, again, makes the more general point:

The structures of power in which the political process takes place offer an explanation of not only how change originates and what direction it takes, but also of why it is necessary. Power always implies non-power and therefore resistance. The dialectic of power and resistance is the motive force of history. . . . Here is the nexus where norms are laid down, called into question, modified and called into question again. Here is the source of initiative, and thus of the historicity – and that means the vitality, the openness, the freedom – of human societies.[51]

How norms are laid down and authority allocated brings me to the third topic, ideology. By ideology I mean systems of belief that uphold sectional interests while appearing to express general ones. In designating certain ideas as ideological, I want to avoid any simple distinction between ideas that reveal the world and those that hide the world. Unless we make a fairly low estimate of human intelligence and equate ideology simply with trickery and false consciousness, we have to admit that ideologies are, in some sense, true, at least partially so. As E. P. Thompson has argued, it is precisely because ideological systems contain partial truths that they can serve as ideologies.[52] For an illustration, recall the Maale belief that it was women who broke up households: Women *did* break up domestic units, they often *were* quarrelsome – in the structural context in which they acted. What is specifically ideological was the Maale generalization from particular context to eternal verity – that women are by nature irresponsible and hence not fit for political authority.

The extent to which the dominated themselves accept such ideological formulations appears always to be problematic. The range of positions extends from virtual acceptance to open rebellion. With regard to the neoclassical analysis above, it is important to note that the extreme case of acceptance is required in order that households can be approximated as unitary decision-makers, that wives and children acquiesce to the authority of household heads. But acquiesence is not complete (else social change, as Dahrendorf pointed out, would never occur). There seems always to be a sense in which the dominated both believe and reject. This patient contradiction and the possible transformation of mostly believing to mostly rejecting is an aspect of social life that neoclassical anal-

[51] Ibid.
[52] E. P. Thompson, *Whigs and Hunters: The Origin of the Black Act* (Harmondsworth: Penguin, 1975), pp. 258–69.

yses – with their stable hierarchies of personal values – necessarily cannot capture.

History, power, and ideology furnish, then, grand questions for macroanthropology. Neoclassicism can provide full answers to none of them. Its scope and ambitions are narrower. One could say that neoclassical theory trains a bright light on a very small area. It is possible both to appreciate the brightness and to regret the smallness. In the next two chapters, I shall argue that the Marxist theory of modes of production illuminates a larger area of social and cultural life.

2. Epochal structures I: Reconstructing historical materialism

> *My mother was a political radical. On one occasion, many years ago, when she was already quite elderly, I received her in San Juan, Puerto Rico, where she had come for a brief vacation. As we drove from the airport to the city, we passed through an enormous slum, called "El Fanguito," which stretched along a brackish estuary. My mother gazed silently out of the window until I asked her what she was thinking. "I am thinking," she said, "that there must be a lot of rich people in this country." Astonished, I exclaimed, "How can you gaze upon that, and declare that there are rich people here?" "Ah," she countered, "if there are this many poor people here, there have to be a lot of rich people."*
>
> Sidney Mintz

How, after all, is one to understand Marxism? Given the volume and complexity of Marx's own works (from the *Manuscripts* to *Capital*), not to mention the variety of positions taken by his followers (from Louis Althusser to E. P. Thompson), answering this question is more than usually difficult.[1]

At the outset it should be emphasized that *any* answer has to be constructed not only from Marx's works but from those of his critics. A consistent and fully articulated vision of historical materialism cannot simply be "found" in the works of the founder. Marx was wrong in certain places and inconsistent in others, as he himself realized in his persistent rethinking and rephrasing of ideas. To remain uncritical about Marx is to take up a fundamentally un-Marxist stance. The problem, then, is not so much to present Marx's own views (although I believe that the following discussion represents the central tendencies of his thought) as to construct a defensible historical materialism in view of modern social thought.

Some observers, of course, have argued that no coherence remains in the Marxist tradition. Leszek Kołakowski entitled a recent major work

[1] The subtitle to this chapter repeats a phrase of Jürgen Habermas. See "Toward a Reconstruction of Historical Materialism," *Communication and the Evolution of Society*, trans. Thomas McCarthy (Boston: Beacon Press, [1976] 1979), pp. 130–77.

Main Currents of Marxism: Its Rise, Growth, and Dissolution.[2] And Alvin Gouldner, in a different vein, argued that Marxism was founded on an original contradiction and has oscillated ever since between two contrary positions – what he called "scientific" and "critical" Marxism.[3] Scientific Marxism, according to Gouldner's ideal type, treats societies as entities subject to laws of development, laws independent of and presumably determinative of individual human wills. On this reading, revolutions do not occur before conditions are ripe, so that an important part of revolutionary politics becomes biding one's time. Critical Marxism, on the other hand, focuses on interpreting systems of meaning, systems in which both oppressors and oppressed live their lives. By interpreting and accounting for the apparent persuasiveness of ideologies, a critical analysis uncovers the hidden potency of humankind. Revolution, therefore, is always on the agenda; radical change depends only on consciousness and the courage to act.

As the reader may have guessed, I am going to argue that historical materialism requires both a notion of stuctural determination and one of human agency:

> Men make their own history, but they do not make it just as they please; they do not make it under circumstances chosen by themselves, but under circumstances directly encountered, given and transmitted from the past.[4]

The problem will be to move beyond an easy eclecticism (a little of this, a little of that) to show exactly how analyses of structural determination are incomplete and in what senses a comprehensive understanding of history actually requires a theory of human agency.[5] As in the preceding chapter, I shall tack back and forth between abstract social theory and

---

[2] Leszek Kołakowski, *Main Currents of Marxism: Its Rise, Growth, and Dissolution,* 3 vols., trans. P. S. Falla (Oxford, Clarendon Press, 1978).

[3] Alvin Gouldner, *The Two Marxisms: Contradictions and Anomalies in the Development of Theory* (New York: Seabury Press, 1980, and New York: Oxford University Press, 1982).

[4] Marx, "The Eighteenth Brumaire of Louis Bonaparte," in Marx and Engels, *Collected Works,* vol. 11 (London: Lawrence & Wishart, [1852] 1979), p. 103.

[5] The notion of agency is not well defined in recent discussions in social theory. I use it in two senses, the first of which predominates in this chapter and the next and might be called epochal agency: that is, patterns of individual action, motivated by particular meanings and practices, the result of which is the reproduction of certain broad structures of inequality. This sense of agency is hardly opposed to the idea of structure; exactly the opposite, it is required in order to understand how structures are reproduced. The second kind of agency, what might be called historical agency, is different; it involves struggles between groups of various kinds, set in specific space-time, that put into question the continuance of inequalities. This "questioning" may or may not result in fundamental transformations. See E. P. Thompson, *The Poverty of Theory and Other Essays* (New York: Monthly Review Press, 1978); Perry Anderson, *Arguments Within English Marxism* (London: Verso, 1980); Anthony Giddens, *Central Problems in Social Theory: Action, Structure and Contradiction in Social Analysis* (Berkeley: University of California Press, 1979).

embedded empirical analysis. This chapter on historical materialism prepares the way for the next on Maale political economy.

Building on G. A. Cohen's work, I shall construct what I believe to be proper interpretations of the key terms of historical materialism, Marx's concepts of "forces of production," "relations of production," and "determination" (eventually, different translations of Marx's original terms will be introduced).[6] The stage will then be set for a presentation of the work of Claude Meillassoux.[7] Despite the criticisms that I shall develop of it, Meillassoux's work is arguably the source of the most far-reaching questions raised by Marxist anthropology to date.

But the specification of bare structures will not be enough, for I shall not have explained how social inequalities are reproduced through time. Such a task will require, in addition, a discussion of typical patterns of meaning, experience, and practice. It is precisely at this point that Cohen's and Meillassoux's expositions are silent, and it is here that the works of Pierre Bourdieu and Anthony Giddens begin to offer guidance.[8] Ultimately what is required is the construction of a Marxist hermeneutics – one that will interpret the world of meanings that inform relations of production, whatever the mode of production.

This leads to the conclusion that the very notion of mode of production is a double-faced one of both structure and practice. It is impossible to understand how structures are reproduced except through meaningful human action (after all, structures do not act). And, similarly, it is impossible to understand practices, except as they are conditioned by structures, themselves the product of past practices. This constant duality is, as it happens, reflected in the semantics of the English word "mode" (and before it, the German "Weise"), the double meaning of which is both form or structure and way or style of doing something.

Marx's concept of essential human nature is, as a number of recent commentators have argued, a touchstone for his entire system of

[6] For an introduction to Cohen's framework, see his "Forces and Relations of Production," in John Roemer, ed., *Analytical Marxism* (Cambridge: Cambridge University Press, 1986), pp. 11–22. The most developed statement of his analysis remains *Karl Marx's Theory of History: A Defence* (Oxford: Clarendon Press, 1978). See also his *History, Labour and Freedom: Themes from Marx* (Oxford: Clarendon Press, 1988).

[7] Claude Meillassoux, *Maidens, Meal and Money: Capitalism and the Domestic Community* (Cambridge: Cambridge University Press, [1975] 1981).

[8] Pierre Bourdieu, *Outline of a Theory of Practice*, trans. Richard Nice (Cambridge: Cambridge University Press, [1972] 1977); Giddens, *Central Problems*. See also Philip Abram's notion of "structuring" in *Historical Sociology* (Ithaca: Cornell University Press, 1982), and Sherry B. Ortner, *High Religion: A Cultural and Political History of Sherpa Buddhism* (Princeton: Princeton University Press, 1989).

thought.[9] In order to define Marx's ideas by contrast, one can imagine a range of possible positions from one extreme (human needs are everywhere the same – the same, that is, as in capitalist society) to its opposite (humans are so formed by their milieux that their needs and aspirations are fundamentally different). Not surprisingly, the first extreme often gets associated with notions of biology and natural givens, whereas the second is usually expressed in terms of cultural relativity.

Marx rejected both of these positions. The first idea, that humans are everywhere the same, would not be defended by many social scientists these days (with perhaps the exception of extreme sociobiologists or vulgar neoclassical economists). Still, it is a powerful popular notion and one that Marx attacked again and again in his own day. Its political commitments are clear. Humanity is capitalist man writ large; it is foolhardy to dream of other ways of organizing society, for capitalist inequalities are the result of natural qualities of human beings.

The opposite extreme, that human nature offers no constraints on social arrangements, is a considerably stronger position within current social science. As I tried to show in the previous chapter, neoclassical economic theory in its most attractive form – the kind of social theory that underpins much of Max Weber's work, for example – depends on such a view. Humans make choices, particular choices with a view toward attaining certain ends. But those ends vary from place to place, and all that an analysis can posit is a more-or-less stable hierarchy of *some* ends. What unites mankind is, at best, a capacity, a generic potential for "culture." But particular cultures vary, as Clifford Geertz would have it, from that of "transformed Aztecs lifting pulsing hearts torn live from the chest of human sacrifices" to that of "stolid Zuni dancing their great mass supplications to the benevolent gods of rain."[10]

This second view has important consequences that also contrast with Marxist theory, for it sees humanity as essentially plastic and therefore in need of culture – *any* culture, apparently. According to Geertz, cultural patterns provide the terms in which "we give form, order, point, and direction to our lives" and without which we would be "unworkable monstrosities," "mental basket cases." To summarize briefly, to

[9] John Plamenatz, *Karl Marx's Philosophy of Man* (Oxford: Clarendon Press, 1975), chaps. 2–3; Bertell Ollman, *Alienation: Marx's Conception of Man in Capitalist Society*, 2d ed. (Cambridge: Cambridge University Press, 1976), chaps. 7–17; John McMurtry, *The Structure of Marx's World-View* (Princeton: Princeton University Press, 1978), chap. 1; Norman Geras, *Marx and Human Nature: Refutation of a Legend* (London: New Left Books, 1983); Jon Elster, *Making Sense of Marx* (Cambridge: Cambridge University Press, 1985), chap. 2.
[10] Clifford Geertz, *The Interpretation of Cultures* (New York: Basic Books, 1973), p. 40.

provide a foil against which Marx will stand out, this image of human-kind promotes a view of cultural analysis as a (bookish) sort of "trans-lation" of one symbolic system to another, encourages a primarily aes-thetic attitude toward other cultures, and perhaps most important in relation to Marxism, limits the analyst's political commitments to a re-spect for diversity. "The essential vocation of interpretive anthropology is not to answer our deepest questions, but to make available to us an-swers that others, guarding other sheep in other valleys, have given, and thus to include them in the consultable record of what man has said."[11] Capitalism in this view is not universal; instead, it is only one of a thousand cultural systems, among which it is impossible rationally to choose.

Marx's social theory is different. Whether one is convinced or not, it is impossible to deny that Marxism *is* aimed at answering our deepest questions. At the base of historical materialism is a notion of human nature and of essential human needs as both socially conditioned (and therefore different from epoch to epoch) and, in some respects, univer-sally the same. The aspect of socially conditioned (and therefore vary-ing) human needs will perhaps be clear enough. By contrast, Marx's concept of universal human nature requires further explanation, for this idea is intimately connected both with Marx's commitment to socialism and with how he locates tensions and impulses for change in other eco-nomic formations.

For Marx, free and creative labor is *the* fundamental and universal human need. To forestall confusion, it is necessary to point out that Marx's concept of labor is not confined to the narrow one that has come to dominate our thought in capitalist societies. Rather, "labor," social activity in the material world, potentially comprises notions of self-expression, rational development, and aesthetic enjoyment. As Allen Wood points out, ". . . science and art seem to serve as his [Marx's] chief models for the forms which production will take in the post-capitalist 'realm of freedom.' "[12] Nor does Marx's notion of labor depend on a simplified opposition between "material" and "cultural" (and hence an exclusion of the latter from consideration). For Marx, just as for modern cultural anthropology, man is a symbolic animal:

A spider conducts operations which resemble those of the weaver, and a bee would put many a human architect to shame by the construction of its honey-

---

[11] Ibid., p. 30.
[12] Allen W. Wood, *Karl Marx* (London: Routledge & Kegan Paul, 1981), p. 28.

comb cells. But what distinguishes the worst architect from the best of bees is that the architect builds the cell in his mind before he constructs it in wax. At the end of every labour process, a result emerges which had already been conceived by the worker in the beginning, hence already existed ideally.[13]

What is distinctive about humans, according to Marx, is not simply that we depend on symbols but that we, in a sense, create ourselves through symbolically formed action in the world – "labor." At the beginning of every labor process, a person begins with a certain symbolic project and a certain set of needs. In association with others and through action in the world, such a person not only satisfies those needs; he or she also produces new needs. This self-creation is what distinguishes human beings from animals. It is our "species-being."[14] And it is this aspect of our being human that creates an objective need for a kind of society in which individuals in association with others can maximally reach their powers of creativity and expression.[15]

. . . free conscious activity constitutes the species–character of man. . . . conscious life activity directly distinguishes man from animal life activity. . . . It is true that animals also produce. They build nests and dwellings, like the bee, the beaver, the ant, etc. But they produce only their own immediate needs or those of their young; they produce one-sidedly, while man produces universally; they produce only when immediate physical need compels them to do so, while man produces even when he is free from physical need and truly produces only in freedom from such need. . . . It is therefore in his fashioning of the objective that man really proves himself to be a *species being*. Such production is his active species-life. . . . man reproduces himself not only intellectually, in his con-

---

[13] Marx, *Capital*, vol. 1, trans. Ben Fowkes (New York: Vintage, [1867] 1976), p. 284.

[14] Marx's arguments about the "species-being" of humanity play the role of an assumption in his theories about society. They can be defended philosophically and politically, but considered as part of a scientific attempt to understand human societies, these arguments are assumptions that cannot be tested in themselves. They allow "testable" propositions to be formed.

[15] Whether this need is subjectively felt in any particular society is another question. Jon Elster defines objective alienation as the situation that occurs when satisfiable needs are large compared to actual and to satisfied needs. This definition contrasts with subjective alienation, in which actual needs are large but satisfied ones small. See *Making Sense of Marx*, pp. 74–8. In general, epochal analyses (such as Chapter 3) correlate with the notion of objective alienation, but historical analyses (Chapter 4) depend upon the degree of subjective alienation.

I believe that Elster is wrong when he writes, "In precapitalist society men were not objectively alienated, since even with a reorganization of the production it would not have been possible to satisfy needs much wider than those actually satisfied" (p. 77). Nonetheless, it is true that the distance between what is and what could be has been enormously expanded by technological progress, particularly by capitalist production. As a correlate, revolution – a process in which men and women more or less consciously attempt to reshape society – is a relatively recent phenomenon in world history.

sciousness, but actively and actually, and he can therefore contemplate himself in a world he himself has created.[16]

Quite literally, we produce, transform, and create ourselves through labor. Thought and action continually interact to produce new thought and new action. Marx's vision is one of what might be called humankind in the active voice.

To revert to either of the positions on human nature discussed above – humanity as everywhere the same or everywhere different – is to translate Marx's vision into the passive voice. Either biology creates men and women or culture creates them, and we are left with no internally-generated dynamism or tension. Notice the subtle switch from active to passive voice, as it were, in a passage by Clifford Geertz that echoes Marx:

Beavers build dams, birds build nests, bees locate food, baboons organize social groups, and mice mate on the basis of forms of learning that rest predominantly on the instructions encoded in their genes and evoked by appropriate patterns of external stimuli: physical keys inserted into organic locks. But men build dams and shelters, locate food, organize their social groups, or find sexual partners under the guidance of instructions encoded in flow charts and blueprints, hunting lore, moral systems and aesthetic judgments: conceptual structures molding formless talents.[17]

Culture, here, replaces biology. Culture molds and creates a formless humanity, culture in the active voice and mankind in the passive. It is not that such a view is simply wrong. Indeed, Geertz's insistence on the centrality of interpretation in the human sciences has much to offer, particularly to Marxism. But compared to historical materialism, modern cultural anthropology lacks the key notions of radical human needs and of humanity's self-creation through labor in response to those needs. No doubt, culture as intersubjectively produced meaning creates socially-formed persons, but surely people create and produce culture. It is only by neglecting the second half of this dialectic that anthropologists have turned cultural systems into reified texts, waiting to be interpreted and translated.[18]

It is no accident that almost all of Marx's concepts to be explicated next – "forces of production," "relations of production," and "mode of

[16] Marx, "Economic and Philosophical Manuscripts," *Early Writings*, trans. Rodney Livingstone and Gregor Benton (New York: Vintage, [1934] 1975), pp. 328–9.
[17] Geertz, *Interpretation of Cultures*, p. 50.
[18] See William Roseberry, "Balinese Cockfights and the Seduction of Anthropology," *Anthropologies and Histories: Essays in Culture, History, and Political Economy* (New Brunswick: Rutgers University Press, 1929), pp. 17–29.

production" – build on the root "to produce." Production is the privileged point of entry for understanding social totalities, for understanding how people make their own history but not exactly as they choose.

———

The notion of structure is an indispensable aspect of Marx's social theory. Recently, G. A. Cohen has done much to clarify and systematize this area of Marx's thought.[19] My exposition below is indebted to Cohen's work, though I depart from it at certain critical junctures.

In regard to the concept of structure, at basic issue is the simple notion that societies have some degree of internal consistency, that certain types of economy "go with" certain types of polity, "go with" certain types of religion. Social totalities, in other words, have "structures," more-or-less consistent arrangements of parts that stamp a character on the whole – despite variation. These structures can take only a limited number of forms, since not everything goes with everything else. As a consequence, world history unfolds as a discontinuous succession of epochs. The broad patterns that hold across epochs, the basic ways of producing human social life, are what makes it possible to talk of capitalist or feudal societies, indeed, what makes it possible to talk more generally of modes or ways of producing.

The idea of some degree of consistency and structured arrangements to society's parts is, of course, hardly unique. What distinguishes Marx's theory is, first, how the parts are defined and, second, how they are seen as interrelated. Marx's partition of social systems is inscribed in his key terms – Produktivkräfte and Produktionsverhältnisse. Unfortunately, Marx himself never offered clear definitions of these terms. Pareto once complained that Marx's words were like bats – one could see in them both birds and mice. This ambiguity has been compounded by problems of translating German into other languages.

The usual English translations of Produktivkräfte and Produktionsverhältnisse – forces of production and relations of production – are misleading in certain respects. Produktivkräfte are not just tools and technology, nor are Produktionsverhältnisse simply relationships among people in production. According to Gören Therborn, Marx's concept of Produktivkräfte was taken directly from Adam Smith's notion of "pro-

———

[19] Besides Cohen's *Karl Marx's Theory of History*, see John McMurtry, *The Structure of Marx's World-View* (Princeton: Princeton University Press, 1978), and William H. Shaw, *Marx's Theory of History* (Stanford: Stanford University Press, 1978).

ductive powers."[20] "Power" was translated by Marx into German as "Kraft," and then Marx's English translators rendered "Kraft" back into English as "force." The choice between force and power is significant to the degree that force normally refers to things outside human beings, whereas power is more easily seen as a human capacity. For example, it is odd to refer to knowledge and know-how as a force, but it can be called a power. Since Marx's Produktivkräfte certainly included human capacities among its central referents, I shall use "productive powers" to refer to what today most writers in English call "forces of production."[21]

To begin with Cohen's definition, productive powers are anything that can be *used* in productive interaction with nature. To qualify as a productive power, "a facility must be capable of use by a producing agent in such a way that production occurs (partly) as a result of its use, and it is someone's purpose that the facility so contribute to production."[22] Notice what this definition presupposes: First, an objective knowledge of what contributes to production in any place at any time; second, a hermeneutic understanding of culturally relative systems of meaning, so that a person's intention to produce can be adequately interpreted. It is the intersection of these two considerations that defines productive powers according to Cohen's definition.

On this reading, productive powers are not simply raw materials or tools; more inclusively, they are human skills, productive knowledge, and even technical aspects of cooperation in the labor process, all of these being intentionally used to produce.[23] These factors Marx considered equally "material" in that they can be used to produce materially. But most modern readers and even some "materialists" would

---

[20] Gören Therborn, *Science, Class and Society: On the Formation of Sociology and Historical Materialism* (London: New Left Books, 1976), pp. 362–5.

[21] As Cohen points out, the phrase "productive powers" also has its problems. Strictly speaking, we cannot say that a tool *is* a productive power; rather it *has* such power when put in motion by a human being (*Karl Marx's Theory of History*, p. 37).

[22] Ibid., p. 32. See Jon Elster's extended commentary on Cohen's definition in *Making Sense of Marx* (Cambridge: Cambridge University Press, 1985), pp. 243–53, particularly his discussion of the difference between extensive and intensive notions of development of powers.

[23] Cohen argues that work relations themselves are not productive powers, but that knowledge of ways of organizing labor is (*Karl Marx's Theory of History*, pp. 113–4). For a critique of Cohen, see Richard W. Miller, *Analyzing Marx: Morality, Power and History* (Princeton: Princeton University Press, 1984), p. 194. Finally, William Shaw has argued that work relations should be counted as a subtype of "relations of production" (*Marx's Theory of History*, pp. 32–6).

probably classify objects, knowledge, and the technical aspects of cooperation as variously material, ideal, and social.

This unusual way of defining the category of the material is related to Marx's central notion of human nature, of human beings creating themselves through productive action in the world. Productive powers are the resources that people use in that process. Marx's focus is on persons acting, using ideas and objects to change nature. Notice the difference it would make if the category of the material were confined to objects outside human beings, outside human consciousness. Then, if one were a materialist, one would see human society only as it is conditioned by its environment, the "objective" material world. This point of view, it must be emphasized, is different from Marx's materialism; it translates an active vision of humankind into the passive voice.[24]

It might be objected that the preceding definition of productive powers is altogether too broad, that it includes almost everything social. After all, do not all social arrangements, in some sense, contribute to production? Marx himself wrote, ". . . *all* human relations and functions, however and in whatever form they appear, influence material production and have a more or less decisive influence upon it."[25] Consider an example discussed by Cohen (and Marx before him) of a group of farmers who, in order to work their fields, must be protected by soldiers.[26] Is protection, then, a productive power? Not according to the definition above. Soldiers' protection is not directly used in productive interaction with nature; it is not required by the production process itself. This is not to say, of course, that in some wider social sense, soldiers' services do not make production possible, and, as I shall point out directly, Marx was centrally concerned with just such sorts of contingent connections between productive powers and their social integuments.

Having outlined a definition of productive powers, I should note their outstanding characteristic for Marx's theoretical scheme as a whole: that productive powers tend to expand in world history. At least two aspects of this assertion should be clarified. First, no evolutionary teleology is

---

[24] Marxism's definition of the material gives it a different theoretical cast from, for example, strands of North American anthropology such as evolutionism and cultural ecology. Anthropologists in the latter traditions tend to view the "hard" realities of environment, technology, and population as basic. Human beings have to adapt their culture to them. But notice the peculiar one-sidedness in this point of view: Technology, population, and even environment are to some extent created and shaped by men and women. The concept of adaptation, by itself, cannot capture the active side of human history.

[25] Marx, *Theories of Surplus Value*, Part I, trans. Emile Burns, S. Ryazanskaya, ed. (Moscow: Progress Publishers, [1905–10] 1963), p. 288.

[26] Cohen, *Karl Marx's Theory of History*, pp. 33–4.

implied. Instead, in the most general sense, the anterior cause of this tendency is located in human nature itself. Humans everywhere have felt a need to actualize themselves through labor. And through labor, people have developed their powers and skills in a continuous dialectic with nature. Increase in productive knowledge is, then, a critical part of what makes human beings human.

But more specifically, the expansion of productive powers has to be seen relative to different kinds of societies. (This will be clearer in a moment, when I point out that relations of production affect the expansion of productive powers.) Different relations of production give variously placed social groups different (and sometimes opposed) interests in technological improvement. But no revolutionary group in any society, it seems, has ever had direct interests in reducing labor productivity. This means that, given *any* socially conditioned impulse toward technological improvement, the development of productive powers is, in Eric Olin Wright's phrase, "sticky downwards."[27] That is, societal transformations tend to preserve the level of productive powers already achieved.

This image of technical progress as a variously paced, fitful climb upward must be understood in relation to the second point I wish to emphasize: The tendency for powers to expand can be seen only at a world level. Particular societies may and indeed have stagnated; some have even experienced local declines in the level of productive powers. As I shall point out below, relations of production can prevent technical development beyond a certain point. For any particular society in stasis, there is no reason to believe that new social relations compatible with the further expansion of powers *must* develop. In fact, what has happened most often in world history is that technical knowledge diffuses from place to place, and typically the most "advanced" societies are not the ones that give rise to the next evolutionary development. Rather, peripheral groups that are the recipient of the productive knowledge of their more "advanced" neighbors often leap-frog ahead.[28]

I have referred to the level of development of productive powers. Just what this notion entails should be considered. A society's mass of productive powers is determined by two factors: first, average labor productivity, and second, population. The product of these two factors yields

---

[27] Eric Olin Wright, "Giddens's Critique of Marxism," *New Left Review* 138 (1983): 27–9.
[28] Yuri I. Semenov, "The Theory of Socio-Economic Formations and World History," and Ernest Gellner, "A Russian Marxist Philosophy of History," in Ernest Gellner, ed., *Soviet and Western Anthropology* (London: Duckworth, 1980), pp. 29–82.

the level of productive powers. In this formulation, population itself is not a productive power, yet it enters into the determination of the level of productive powers.[29]

To return to Marx's argument, the next step is famous but not well understood: The level of productive powers "determines" the Produktionsverhältnisse, so-called relations of production.

> The general conclusion at which I arrived and which, once reached, became the guiding principle of my studies can be summarized as follows. In the social production of their existence, men inevitably enter into definite relations, which are independent of their will, namely relations of production [Produktionsverhältnisse] appropriate to a given stage in the development of their material forces of production [Produktivkräfte]. The totality of these relations of production constitutes the economic structure of society, the real foundation, on which arises a legal and political superstructure [Überbau] and to which correspond definite forms of social consciousness.[30]

What are Produktionsverhältnisse? Once again, Marx's language confounds our expectations, for Produktionsverhältnisse are not just social relationships formed in production but, more centrally, the basic structure of power that determines differential control over the division of the fruits of society's labor. Otherwise put, Produktionsverhältnisse are "productive inequalities," and it is this phrase I shall use in translating Marx's term rather than the more literal "relations of production."[31]

Productive inequalities are, then, relationships among groups that place some in materially superordinate positions in relation to others. Moreover, superordination depends precisely on subordination. As the epigraph to this chapter suggests, if there are "poor" people, there must be "rich" people.[32] The labor of the first supports the existence of the second. *How* this difference is instituted, it must be emphasized, is not specified. To qualify, productive inequalities must delineate differences in power over society's total product. But productive inequalities do not

---

[29]This is a different formulation from Cohen's and is inspired by Elster's discussion in *Making Sense of Marx*, pp. 249–53.

[30]Marx, *A Contribution to the Critique of Political Economy*, trans. S. W. Ryazanskaya (Moscow: Progress Publishers, [1859] 1970), p. 20.

[31]One difficulty with the phrase "productive inequality" is that it may suggest that inequality is a required aspect of production in any form. Although there is good reason to believe that all societies to date have been organized around material inequalities, I do not assume that this outcome is inevitable. Productive inequalities can theoretically take a number of values – including zero.

[32]Sidney W. Mintz, "American Anthropology in the Marxist Tradition," in Sidney W. Mintz et al., eds., *On Marxian Perspectives in Anthropology: Essays in Honor of Harry Hoijer, 1981* (Malibu: Undena Publications, 1984), pp. 18–9.

have to be constituted in relation to immediate control over productive powers themselves.

Here I depart from G. A. Cohen's analysis – and, indeed, from most conceptions of historical materialism formed in the context of capitalism. According to Cohen, the proximate form of production relations is ownership by persons of productive forces or persons. "Ownership," however, is a legally defined, superstructural right, and it is clear that relations of production (or productive inequalities, as I have called them) must be defined independently of the superstructure, since Marx also claimed that inequalities determine the superstructure. Consequently, Cohen argued that every superstructural right can be matched with a corresponding de facto power. It is these latter relationships, expressed in terms of de facto power over productive forces, that properly define relations of production, according to Cohen.[33]

This conceptual strategy works for capitalism because the relevant superstructural notions that define inequalities do in fact center on ownership and control of resources: A capitalist, who owns means of production, buys labor power and as a result of control established over persons in production reaps a profit. Before the labor process begins, it is the particular distribution of powers over productive forces – the capitalist with his means of production, the proletarian with only his labor power – that conditions the resulting distribution of the product.[34] In technologically simpler societies, however, particularly in those without state structures, immediate control over productive powers does not determine the division of the fruits of a society's labor. For example, I shall argue below (pp. 94–8) that when Maale gave cattle as tribute to the ritual king, they did not do so because the king "controlled" resources like land. It is true that the king was said to "own" the land, but in this case ownership referred to the right to collect tribute, not to control land as a productive factor.[35]

It might be said that the very fact of labor tribute meant that, in a wider sense, the king controlled the labor of commoners. But if so, it is crucial to note that "control" in this formulation means something dif-

---

[33] Cohen, *Karl Marx's Theory of History*, pp. 34–5.
[34] That direct control over productive powers defines productive inequalities in capitalism – but not in other modes of production – is the grain of truth in Perry Anderson's exposition otherwise criticized in the Introduction (pp. 9–11).
[35] I believe that William Shaw is wrong, then, when he writes that ownership relations of production – what I am calling productive inequalities – are "relations within which . . . [people] regulate their mutual access to the productive forces and, *as a consequence,* to the products of production" (my emphasis), *Marx's Theory of History*, p. 28. Such a consequence occurs for capitalism but not for all modes of production.

ferent from the concept in the capitalist example above. Indeed, "control" has become synonymous with *any* systematically reproduced material inequality – however that inequality is instituted, whether for so-called economic, political, or ideological reasons. If this is so, the primary, universal feature of productive inequalities becomes precisely differential power over the production of society's total product – not "control," in the narrow sense, of productive powers themselves.

In this reformulation, Cohen's distinction between rights and powers remains fundamental for historical materialism.[36] A person may have a right to material resources but not the power to exercise it; he may have power over resources but not a right. Productive inequalities are de facto powers – not rights – over labor and its products. They locate fundamental asymmetries in production: One group lives, to some extent, on the labor of others.[37]

Why do productive inqualities occupy such a central place in Marx's thought? The answer is that they locate the basic divisions within any society, the lines of potential opposition – of contradiction. Marx saw these as the potential fault lines along which tensions tend to build up, are routinely dissipated by small readjustments, and are sometimes violently resolved by radical realignments. These fault lines are structural; they do not necessarily lead to actual struggle and conflict (indeed, the function of the superstructure is precisely to prevent such occurrences). Nevertheless, contradictions always exist as potentialities; they lie just below the surface.[38]

The concept of productive inequality has to be related, finally, to Marx's view of human nature. Every person needs to realize himself or herself in free, creative activity in the world. Productive inequalities set up social obstacles to that process; they alienate groups from the social product that is required for human self-realization at any particular techno-

[36] Cohen, *Karl Marx's Theory of History*, chap. 8. Steven Lukes has contested the possibility of matching norm-governed relationships with de facto powers: "Can the Base be Distinguished from the Superstructure," in David Miller and Larry Siedentop, eds., *The Nature of Political Theory* (Oxford: Clarendon Press, 1983), pp. 103–19. Cohen has responded in "Reply to Four Critics," *Analyse und Kritik* 5 (1983): 195–222.

[37] Referring to Cohen's distinction between powers and rights in defining productive inequalities (relations of production), Elster writes: "The question is whether the programme can be carried out in all cases. I doubt that it can, since in many cases there is no independently existing control that is stabilized by the legal relations" (*Making Sense of Marx*, p. 403). But no such independently existing control is required. Productive inequalities are abstract descriptions of power relations. What actually "exists" is a superstructural set of meanings and practices. I return to this issue in the Conclusion.

[38] For a review of the notion of contradiction and an exposition of its central place in social – not merely logical – analysis, see Giddens, *Central Problems*, chap. 4.

logical level. Different sets of productive inequalities institute different degrees of alienation, different depths of inequality, that vary from relatively shallow and easily contained ones to those that can be resolved only by revolutionary transformations.[39] In this sense, contradictions in technologically simple societies are less dynamic, less tense, than those in capitalist ones.

It is precisely Marx's concept of essential human nature that makes his theory different from orthodox functionalist theories of social integration. In functionalism, there is no notion that particular social and cultural orders can come into conflict with human nature. Instead, societies must be organized somehow, and complex societies can only be organized hierarchically. Social hierarchies, in turn, must be legitimated, and the systems of values and beliefs that seem to be best at this task are evolutionarily selected. One expects a certain amount of conflict at all levels of the system inasmuch as common values are not perfectly inculcated into each new generation. But conflicts do not sum into a pattern, nor do they propel social change; they are merely the friction that must be overcome in all forms of social integration.

Contrast Marx's point of view expressed in this well-known passage from *Capital*:

The specific economic form in which unpaid surplus labor is pumped out of direct producers determines the relationship of domination and servitude, as this grows directly out of production itself and reacts back on it in turn as a determinant. On this is based the entire configuration of the economic community arising from the actual relations of production, and hence also its specific political form. It is in each case the direct relationship of the owners of the conditions of production to the immediate producers – a relationship whose particular form naturally corresponds always to a certain level of development of the type and manner of labor, and hence to its social productive power – in which we find the innermost secret, the hidden basis of the entire social edifice. . . .[40]

If productive inequalities are the "hidden basis of the entire social edifice," how are they regularly reproduced? How is a system of power that limits the actualization of what Marx took to be universal human

---

[39] As Allen Wood, *Karl Marx*, p. 36, argues, "The degree to which people are alienated is a function of the extent to which their lives fall short of actualizing the human essence, of exercising their essential human powers. These powers, however, are not fixed but historically varying and on the whole expanding. Oppressed people will therefore become more and more alienated the greater the gap becomes between the essential powers belonging to the human species and the degree to which their own lives participate in the development and exercise of these powers."

[40] Marx, *Capital*, vol. 3, trans. David Fernbach (New York: Vintage, [1894] 1981), p. 927.

needs able to persist? Nothing we have said so far provides a satisfactory answer.

Let me outline a response to this question for capitalist society, one made famous by Marx's analysis in *Capital*. At the start of any production process, capitalist society is divided by productive inequalities into two opposed classes: capitalists who control the great mass of productive powers versus workers who control no such powers, except their own capacities for labor. Capitalists, therefore, have the means to set up enterprises; they have the money to buy machines and to hire workers. Workers, by contrast, own nothing but their own labor power. Without access to other powers, workers cannot initiate production on their own. They have only two options: to sell their labor power to capitalists or to starve. Because workers control their own labor power, they can choose *which* capitalist to work for. But the structure of the economy requires them to work for *some* capitalist.

So capitalists buy labor power and workers sell it. At this point, production proper commences, and we begin to see, for the first time, how control over productive powers is translated into power over workers in the production process – what William Shaw aptly calls "work" relations of production.[41] It is, by and large, the capitalist who organizes and directs production; it is he who appoints managers who oversee and maintain the pace of work. And the constant imperative is always the production of more in less time. Workers, of course, are not helpless; they can resist in various ways, organize into unions, and so forth. But the capitalist retains the upper hand. And retaining the upper hand, he appropriates the product at the end of the production process. By virtue of the fundamental power asymmetry established in production, the capitalist is typically left with a surplus after selling the product and paying his costs – a surplus created by the labor of workers. This surplus labor can then be turned into yet more capital, and the circle is completed. The contradiction between workers and capitalists has not only been reproduced; it has been deepened and augmented, for the capitalist is relatively richer and workers relatively poorer (relative, that is, to each other).

This circular movement – from an original pattern of control over productive powers to control over people in production to a restoration (and

[41] Shaw, *Marx's Theory of History*, pp. 32–6.

perhaps augmentation) of the original pattern of control over productive powers – is what Marx called a reproduction schema. Notice particularly that the story told above is directly dependent on a whole array of particular legal institutions – contracts defined and backed by the power of the state – and cultural concepts – not the least of which is that labor is a commodity to be bought and sold just like any other thing. In other words, in constructing this story of reproduction, we have left the realm of de facto powers specified in the notion of productive inequalities and have entered a socially and culturally specific world of particular practices with particular meanings: the superstructure.

We are forced to the conclusion that (1) Marx's own reproduction schemata for capitalism include what he called the Überbau or superstructure, and more generally (2) it is precisely the superstructure that allows for and that explains the reproduction of productive inequalities.

For a last time, we are misled by Marx's language. Ordinarily, if something is described as having a base and a superstructure, we think of the base as a foundation. It supports the superstructure; without the foundation, the superstructure would fall to the ground. Yet, if the argument presented here is correct, the truth of historical materialism is closer to the opposite. Superstructures provide one of the keys to historical materialism; they explain how productive inequalities are reproduced.

What, then, can be said about superstructures, about reproduction schemata? Perhaps the first point to make is a negative one. Not all legal and political arrangements nor all systems of ideas can be counted as part of what Marx called the superstructure. Such a course would lead to innumerable difficulties. Science, for example, would have to be placed in the superstructure (when we have already placed aspects of it in the productive powers). And if *all* forms of law, politics, and ideas were seen as maintaining productive inequalities, then we would have disposed of Marx's key concept of contradiction – that is, we would have deprived the dominated groups of society of any impulse to resist. In a phrase, we would have functionalized Marx's social theory.

E. P. Thompson, in a study of law in eighteenth-century England, sums up the role of contradiction in the legal order this way:

We reach, then, not a simple conclusion (law = class power) but a complex and contradictory one. On the one hand, it is true that the law did mediate existent class relations to the advantage of the rulers. . . . On the other hand, the law mediated these class relations through legal forms, which imposed, again and again, inhibitions upon the actions of the rulers. . . . There were even occasions (one recalls John Wilkes and several of the trials of the 1790s) when the Government itself retired from the courts defeated. Such occasions served, paradoxically, to consolidate power, to enhance its legitimacy, and to inhibit revolutionary movements. But, to turn the paradox around, these same occasions served to bring power even further within constitutional control.[42]

Without compromising the existence of contradiction, the notion of reproduction schemata requires only three things: (1) The existence of systems of ideas in public discourse that culturally construct the power of superior groups by predominantly (but not totally) naturalizing productive relations. (2) The organization of institutions that will adjudicate social conflicts (including those arising out of economic contradictions) so as, by and large, to allow contradictions to be reproduced anew. (3) The institutionalization of coercive force that can be used to protect the superior positions of dominant groups whenever (1) or (2) fails. These three aspects of reproduction schemata, which combine variously the functions of "mask" and "weapon," relate respectively to (1) ideology, (2) law, and (3) political organization.[43] I shall take up each in turn.

(1) In the formulation above, I spoke of ideology as constructing and naturalizing power. In doing so, I deliberately avoided any formulation that might suggest that power may stably exist apart from ideology. In this sense, it would be misleading to say that ideology "legitimates" power, as if power could exist on its own. The second part of my definition, naturalization, means first of all that the great majority of the group in power will see their positions as so clothed in an aura of factuality, so meaningfully given that they naturally act to preserve their power. (This does not prevent individuals from, as Marx said, "going to the other side.") And, second, naturalization requires that a large enough section of the exploited group live within dominant values and beliefs a large enough portion of the time so that opposition is at least divided.

As I pointed out in the last chapter, the extent to which exploited groups accept dominant values is a complex problem. In any case, it would be a mistake to see ideology as simple trickery or false consciousness. As E. P. Thompson argued in relation to law, "people are not as stupid as some structuralist philosophers suppose them to be. They will not be mystified by the first man who puts on a wig."[44] Most ideologies contain partial truths, and their "falseness" is due not to blanket error

[42] E. P. Thompson, *Whigs and Hunters: The Origin of the Black Act* (Harmondsworth: Penguin, 1977), pp. 264–5.
[43] McMurtry, *The Structure of Marx's World-View*, p. 120.
[44] Thompson, *Whigs and Hunters*, p. 262.

but to unwarranted generalization across contexts. Part of the exercise of constructing reproduction schemata is, then, to understand the particular productive contexts in which ideologies "make sense." Within those contexts, ideologies contain their truths. But what makes ideologies ideologies is precisely a lack of recognition of the context that renders their claims persuasive.[45]

(2) Even if ideology played its role perfectly (it never does), there would still be a need for socially recognized ways of resolving conflict. Not every society has specifically legal institutions such as courts and professional judges, yet all have regularized ways of settling, or at least dampening, social conflicts. Conflicts can perhaps be grouped into two kinds: those that coincide with economic contradictions as defined by productive inequalities, and those that crosscut such contradictions.

Conflicts that coincide with contradictions are, obviously, the most dangerous for social reproduction. For those cases, *if* societies are to persist in the same mode of production, methods of resolution must exist that will uphold the power of dominant groups. Exactly how this is accomplished is often a complex matter and varies from outright denial of rights to certain categories of persons (slaves in slave-based societies), to the formal exclusion of categories of persons from participation in legal procedures (women, even those directly involved, are not allowed to participate in divorce cases in some technologically simple societies), and finally to the de facto exclusion of still other groups from recourse to the law (workers in capitalist societies are generally too poor to fight certain legal matters).

Conflicts that crosscut contradictions are a good deal less threatening and may even contribute to social stability. For example, lords (allied with peasants) fighting other lords (allied with other peasants) can do much to prevent the contradiction between all lords and peasants from becoming too visible, from erupting into overt conflict. Accordingly, such kinds of conflicts may resist methods for settling them longer than those discussed above.

(3) Finally, neither ideology nor law is enough. Both are usually backed by coercive force. The "amount" of institutionalized coercive force varies with the depth of material contradictions. For example, the power differences between husbands and wives in relatively egalitarian hunting and gathering societies are slight. Still, the power of men over women in such societies is sometimes reinforced by gang rape. Whatever the

[45] See Bourdieu, *Outline of a Theory of Practice*, pp. 159–71.

amount, organized coercion typically reinforces and depends on both ideology and forms of conflict resolution. All are parts of the reproduction of productive inequalities.

To recapitulate the concepts discussed so far, productive powers are anything that can be used in the material process of production – tools, raw materials, scientific ideas, the technical aspects of organizing labor. Productive inequalities, the next category Marx introduced, are patterns of effective power over the production process and over the total social product. Reproduction schemata, finally, are the set of superstructural discourses and practices within which productive inequalities are constructed and reproduced.

Through conscious action, people (unconsciously) reproduce the whole mode of production in which they live – their way of life. Social reproduction does not occur entirely behind the backs of actors. It is probable that people in all societies have some understanding of the inequalities that order their lives, some insight into the oppression that limits their being. This knowledge remains, however, typically partial and unclarified, hard to dredge up to the light of day, difficult to systematize in public discourse. It remains repressed – a part of what Fredric Jameson has called the political unconscious.[46]

———

According to Marx, productive powers "determine" productive inequalities, and productive inequalities "determine" the superstructure. How are we to understand determination in these assertions?

This is perhaps the core question in historical materialism, one around which countless debates have raged. Whatever else Marx's own writings do, they do not deal with determination clearly and unambiguously. Let me begin with our ordinary notions. If we say that X determines Y, we usually mean that X causes Y so that given X, Y is uniquely specified; X somehow effects the presence of Y but not vice versa.

Transferred to Marx's concepts set out above, this description ends in what has been called vulgar Marxism. Such an interpretation can be supported by some of Marx's more incautious statements: "The hand mill gives you society with the feudal lord; the steam mill society with the industrial capitalist."[47] As Leszek Kołakowski impatiently points out,

[46] Fredric Jameson, *The Political Unconscious: Narrative as a Socially Symbolic Act* (Ithaca: Cornell University Press, 1981).
[47] Marx, "The Poverty of Philosophy," in Marx and Engels, *Collected Works*, vol. 6 (London: Lawrence & Wishart, [1847] 1976), p. 166.

what the hand mill and steam mill both give us is flour. It is obvious that the same technology – steam mills – can exist in different modes of production, for example, in capitalism and socialism.

Besides evident empirical difficulties, this notion of determination introduces other problems as well. As we have already seen, superstructures are not just linearly caused by productive inequalities; rather, the very existence of inequalities depends on superstructures. How can we say that X determines Y when the continued existence of X depends on Y?

A common response at this point is to retreat toward one of two concepts, toward "the last instance" or toward "dialectics." At first glance, both appear to offer a way of loosening up historical materialism, of retaining some notion of economic conditioning of society, but not at the cost of empirical irrelevance. The first phrase is, of course, Engels's, and it has been elaborated on by Louis Althusser and his students.

According to the materialist conception of history the *ultimately* [in letzter Instanz] determining element in history is the production and reproduction of real life. More than this neither Marx nor I have ever asserted. Hence if somebody twists this into saying that the economic is the *only* determining one, he transforms that proposition into a meaningless, abstract, senseless phrase.[48]

The second notion, that of dialectics and of a dialectical interaction between productive powers and inequalities, reaches back to Hegel and Spinoza for inspiration. Perhaps the most interesting argument for this position within current Marxism is Bertell Ollman's. Ollman emphasizes the dialectical interaction of *all* of society's parts in one organic totality. Determination in this view is quite different from simple causation:

It is in this context that we must place Marx's otherwise confusing and confused use of "cause" and "determine." There are not some elements which are related to the factor or event in question as "causes" . . . and others as "conditions." . . . Instead, we find as internally related parts of whatever is said to be the cause or determining agent *everything* that is said to be a condition, and vice versa [my emphasis].[49]

The problem with these reactions to vulgar Marxism is that both are imprecise enough that it is difficult to isolate just what substantive claims are being made. Marx's concepts become, then, only a vocabulary for talking about empirical cases, a set of terms that directs attention to cer-

---

[48] Engels, "Friedrich Engels to Joseph Bloch," in Robert C. Tucker, ed., *The Marx–Engels Reader*, 2d ed. (New York: Norton, [1890] 1978), p. 760.
[49] Ollman, *Alienation*, p. 17.

tain areas of social life. So if the revolution did not occur, it was because "the last instance" did not arrive, but we can rest assured that the economy is still "determinative." Similarly, with the notion of productive powers and inequalities as a dialectical union, it is hard to imagine *any* occurrence that could not be described in such terms.

Compared to either of the alternatives above, the great merit of G. A. Cohen's discussion is that it gives a historical materialist description of determination that is both precise enough to be theoretically useful and, with some modification, flexible enough, to comprehend the evident facts. In brief, Cohen argues that Marx's (conceptually unclarified) notion of determination rests on what sociologists and anthropologists have long called functional explanation.[50]

To avoid confusion, perhaps we should, as Cohen does, distinguish functional explanations from functionalism. Functional explanations have a distinct logical form in which the effects of a trait enter into the explanation of the presence of that trait: for example, when Y's presence is partly explained by the positive consequences Y has for X. (As we shall see, functional forms of analysis have interesting parallels with dialectical ones.) Functionalism, on the other hand, is a congeries of various schools of social theorists, most of whom use functional explanations in one way or another, but all of whom are additionally committed to a view of human nature as essentially plastic, of society as essentially free from contradiction.

To repeat, a functional explanation is one in which the positive consequences of Y for X are part of the explanation for the presence of Y. In other words, X "selects" Y because of Y's effect on X.

When Marx maintains, therefore, that productive inequalities determine the superstructure, he means that for any set of productive inequalities, there are only a certain number of reproductive schemata possible – namely, those that have the consequence of stabilizing that particular degree of difference in social power. The system of productive inequalities, therefore, selects some such schema. In this sense, productive inequalities determine the superstructure, even though the superstructure is necessary for the existence of inequalities.

Similarly, one step down in Marx's social architecture, when we say

---

[50] Cohen was not the first to notice the role of functional explanations in historical materialism. Arthur L. Stinchcombe, *Constructing Social Theories* (New York: Harcourt, Brace & World, 1968), pp. 93–8 and 141–3, called attention to this connection, and before him, Robert K. Merton in his classic article on manifest and latent functions in *Social Theory and Social Structure* (New York: Free Press, 1949). No one, however, has made Cohen's points in such a sustained and thoughtful manner.

that the level of productive powers determines productive inequalities, we mean that for any given level of powers, there is only a limited set of productive inequalities possible – namely, those that are compatible with and in fact promote the further development of the powers.[51] The level of productive power therefore selects some such set of inequalities. In this sense, productive powers determine productive inequalities, even though inequalities actively promote the development of productive powers.

The general form of determination of inequalities by productive powers and of the superstructure by inequalities is the same. In one respect, however, the kind of functional argument in these two cases is different, for the first results in movement, the second in stability. Productive powers select inequalities that are consistent with and that encourage the further expansion of powers. Thus there is a continual process of interaction and a continual tendency (variously paced in different modes of production) for powers to expand.

This spiraling interaction continues until the (dynamic) powers are no longer compatible with the (static) productive inequalities. Then, according to Marx, social transformation is on the agenda. Because of the nature of universal human needs, the expansion of powers tends eventually to take precedence over productive inequalities, and one set of inequalities is transformed into another, and therewith, the entire scheme for social reproduction is reordered:

At a certain stage of their development, the material productive forces of society come in conflict with the existing relations of production, or – what is but a legal expression for the same thing – with the property relations within which they have been at work hitherto. From forms of development of the productive forces these relations turn into their fetters. Thus begins an epoch of social revolution. With the change of the economic foundation the entire immense superstructure is more or less rapidly transformed.[52]

[51] My phrasing at this point is deliberately different from Cohen's. According to him, the set of productive inequalities selected is the one that promotes the *optimum* development of the productive powers. "The class which rules through a period, or emerges triumphant after epochal conflict, is the class best suited, most able and disposed, to preside over the development of the productive forces at the given time," *Karl Marx's Theory of History*, p. 149. It seems to me that whether the optimum set of inequalities is selected or not depends on the intensity of competition among societies. With the rise of the world capitalist system, such competition was greatly increased. States that did not develop were fair game to be dominated or even to be incorporated within the boundaries of others. But during earlier periods of world history, this kind of interaction was much less intense, and because it was less intense, there was no systematic mechanism to weed out less than optimal forms of productive inequalities – which nonetheless promoted some development of the productive powers.
[52] Marx, *A Contribution to the Critique of Political Economy*, p. 21.

The form of functional interaction between powers and inequalities tends, therefore, toward positive feedback and growth. This is not the case for the relationship, one step higher, between inequalities and the superstructure. There, reproductive schemata stabilize and maintain a constant set of inequalities, a more or less constant distribution of social power between groups. Given small and large attempts to disrupt and to transform productive inequalities, the superstructure functions to restore the system to the status quo ante. The relationship between inequalities and superstructure is an example of what has been called homeostatic interaction.[53]

A functional description of determination accomplishes many of the goals that previous reactions to vulgar Marxism set out to achieve; in particular, it captures much of the intuitive appeal of the dialectical model but states the problem of interaction between social factors in a more rigorous way. Imagine, as G. A. Cohen has asked us to do, a society that is perfectly law-abiding. In such a society, men and women would enjoy powers *because* of their (superstructural) rights. This seems to refute the idea that rights are determined by productive inequalities. But that is not the case, as Cohen has argued, because the set of rights that exists does so partly by virtue of the fact that it upholds a particular system of domination, one appropriate for the level of the productive powers. "The content of the legal system is dictated by its function, which is to help sustain an economy of a particular kind. Men do get their power from their rights, but in a sense which is not only allowed but demanded by the way historical materialism explains rights by reference to powers."[54]

If a functional reading of determination solves many problems, it is nevertheless true that functional forms of argument contain a myriad of pitfalls. The full range of difficulties cannot be reviewed here.[55] One particular problem needs discussion, however, for Cohen's otherwise illuminating presentation does not draw out its full implications. That is the problem of what Carl Hempel called functional alternatives.[56] There

---

[53] Martin Orans, "Domesticating the Functional Dragon: An Analysis of Piddocke's Potlatch," *American Anthropologist* 77 (1975): 320.

[54] Cohen, *Karl Marx's Theory of History*, p. 232.

[55] For an introduction to these problems, see Stinchcombe, *Constructing Social Theories*. For a critique of Cohen's attempt to defend functional explanations, even in the absence of specification of *how* the functional fact contributes to what is being explained, see Jon Elster's review of *Karl Marx's Theory of History* in *Political Studies* 28 (1980): 121–8, with Cohen's following reply.

[56] Carl G. Hempel, "The Logic of Functional Analysis," *Aspects of Scientific Explanation* (New York: Free Press, 1965).

is often more than one Y (Y_1, Y_2, Y_3 . . .) that can fulfill any given function. That being so, we cannot explain the particular presence of Y_1, say, by referring to its function, for Y_2 or Y_3 could have served the same need. Y_1's function, then, is a necessary but not a sufficient explanation for the presence of Y_1.

The critical question becomes: What is the size of the set of functional alternatives? Philosophers Hempel and Cohen disagree. Hempel believes that sets of functional alternatives are typically composed of almost infinite numbers of traits that fulfill the same function. On such an assumption, it is easy to see why he rejects functional explanation as banal. Cohen (and, implicitly, Marx before him), however, appears to believe that functional alternatives, though they may exist, are quite limited, sometimes limited to just one trait. On this view, functional explanations are anything but trivial; if the set of functional alternatives is one, then specifying Y's function affords a sufficient explanation for the presence of Y.

For analyses of both the past and the future, a great deal depends on which of these views is closer to the truth. Consider the limiting cases when the set of functional alternatives tends toward one versus that when it tends toward infinity. The first, diagrammed below, gives us old-fashioned, evolutionary Marxism, the position that Marx himself, despite occasional doubts and emendations, seems to have favored:

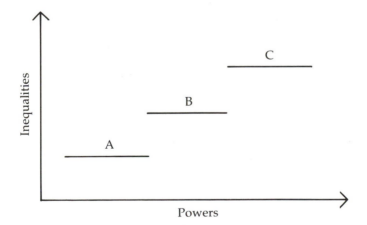

Figure 3: The relationship between productive powers and inequalities that results in unilineal Marxism

In this view, for each level of development of the productive powers, there is only one set of productive inequalities possible; history therefore

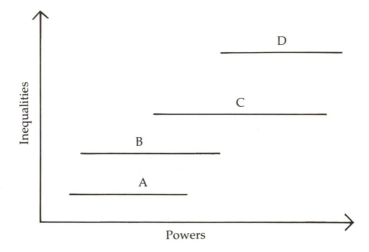

Figure 4: A relationship between productive powers and inequalities that results in multilinear Marxism

proceeds in a series of discrete steps from A to B to C. Both the past and the future are specified – socialism is inevitable because it is the only economic system consistent with highly developed powers.

A different story emerges if the number of functional alternatives is even moderately few. If several sets of productive inequalities are compatible with any given level of powers, then the grand design of world history becomes considerably more complex. One possible trajectory, for example, would be A to C to B to D. The future, too, looks less certain, for there may be functional alternatives to socialism.[57]

Perhaps the obvious should be stressed: Which of these positions is closer to the truth is not a philosophical question; it is an empirical one. Even a cursory survey of the patterns and complexities of world history suggests that the answer is, not surprisingly, somewhere between the two extremes presented above. The set of functional alternatives in most cases is probably greater than one but much less than infinity. Typically, functional explanations are, therefore, neither sufficient and full nor banal and useless.

The difficulties of carrying out functional explanations should not be minimized. How does one decide, for example, if a certain aspect of the superstructure is actually incompatible with productive inequalities?

[57] Philippe Van Parijs has pointed out the importance of functional alternatives to a view of history in "From Contradiction to Catastrophe," *New Left Review* 115 (1979): 87–96.

Consider a case that occurs in John McMurtry's study.[58] A radical book is published in Canada attacking its racist and capitalist social system (whether we should consider book publishing a part of the superstructure is not clear, but let us assume that it is). How could this have happened, if the function of the superstructure is to uphold productive inequalities? McMurtry's answer is that, effectively, the book did not challenge Canada's class system. But surely this kind of argument ends in tautology – we conclude that the book did not challenge the system *because* it was published. For the argument to stand, we need some way of deciding whether the book challenged inequalities that is independent of whether it was published.

From Chapter 1 it will be recalled that neoclassical analysis escaped a similar impasse by introducing a time dimension into its arguments. For historical materialism, the escape comes from cross-cultural comparison. Let us assume that a change in productive inequalities occurred in a certain society after productive powers expanded beyond a certain level, X. If we discovered that the old type of productive inequality never occurred in a large sample of other societies above a level of productive powers X, then we could conclude that the change occurred partly *because* the old inequalities were incompatible with the new level of productive powers. Without comparison across societies (and, it should be noted, a typology of productive inequalities, along with a way of measuring the level of productive powers), historical materialist arguments all too often collapse into helpless tautologies.

Marx's framework set out above was developed mainly in regard to Western European history. What happens when these notions are applied to a radically different kind of political economy? Is the analysis illuminating? Or is historical materialism shown to be only a partial explanation?

In order to answer these questions, Claude Meillassoux began to apply historical materialist concepts to precolonial African societies in 1960, and his ensuing work has provided the point of origin for much of Marxist thought in anthropology.[59] Later writers have modified and criticized

[58] McMurtry, *The Structure of Marx's World-View*, pp. 164–5.
[59] Claude Meillassoux, " 'The Economy' in Agricultural Self-Sustaining Societies: A Preliminary Analysis," in David Seddon, ed., *Modes of Production: Marxist Approaches to Economic Anthropology* (London: Frank Cass, [1960] 1978); *Anthropologie économique des Gouro de Côte d'Ivoire* (Paris: Mouton, 1964); "On the Mode of Production of the Hunting Band," in Pierre Alexandre, ed., *French Perspectives in African Studies* (London: Oxford University

Meillassoux's work in various ways, but the questions Meillassoux asked and the way he posed them have formed the basis for later discussion. Meillassoux's work is, therefore, a strategic place from which to begin an analysis of Marxist theory for noncapitalist societies.

In the most recent statement of his views, Meillassoux has developed what he calls, like Marshall Sahlins before him, a domestic mode of production. But Meillassoux criticizes Sahlins: "Sahlins' weakness remains that he nowhere specifies the historical period to which this 'mode of production' applies. Although several of the characteristics he proposes are related to productive forces, he never specifies what level of knowledge has been acquired, what techniques of producing energy, or what mode of exploitation of the land exists."[60]

To specify the relevant level of development of productive powers in the domestic mode, Meillassoux proposed four criteria: (1) the development of cereal horticulture as the dominant form of production, (2) the use of land itself, therefore, as a productive power, (3) a dependence on human strength, rather than on animal or machine power, as the principal source of energy, and (4) the use of means of production that require only an individual investment of labor for their construction.

The next step in Meillassoux's formulation is, as we would expect from the logic of historical materialism, a description of how productive inequalities are determined by the level of development of productive powers. According to Meillassoux, only particular productive inequalities – ones based on domestic relationships – are compatible with the level of development of productive powers just described.

In order to argue this point, Meillassoux compared the technical requirements of hunting and gathering to those of cereal horticulture. With hunting and gathering, there is an immediate return to labor; various forms of cooperation may be involved, but after a hunting or gathering expedition, the total product is divided, and there is no reason for continued cooperation by the same group. Bands, therefore, frequently change in composition, and ties of descent, long-term bonds of social obligation, are weakly developed.

Cereal horticulture has different requirements, according to Meillassoux. Productive powers are more highly developed, and in particular,

Press, [1967] 1973), pp. 187–203; "From Reproduction to Production: A Marxist Approach to Economic Anthropology," *Economy and Society* 1 (1972): 93–105; *Maidens, Meal and Money*. See also critiques of Meillassoux by Emmanuel Terray, *Marxism and "Primitive" Societies* (New York: Monthly Review Press, [1969] 1972), and by Pierre-Philippe Rey, "The Lineage Mode of Production," *Critique of Anthropology* 3 (1975): 27–79.
[60] Meillassoux, *Maidens, Meal and Money*, p. 7.

land itself is used in production. Compared to hunting, where products of the land, whatever they might be, are simply harvested, horticulture requires the direct investment of labor in land in expectation of future return. This sets up particular requirements for social relations. Somehow, there must be a relatively stable form of cooperation that preserves seeds from one cycle to the next and that allows workers to eat while new crops are ripening.

> Time and continuity become essential features of the economic and social organization. . . . At all times the workers of one cycle are indebted for seeds and food to the workers of the previous one and this cyclical renewal of the productive inequalities theoretically never ends. . . . at any moment, one man, the oldest one of the group, owes his subsistence to none of the living members of his community but only to the dead ancestors, while all the other members of his community are indebted to him. Hence, the eldest is logically appointed to receive and manage the product of his junior partners to whom, in turn, he will *advance* seeds and food until the next crop. One can easily find here the material and temporal bases of the emergence of the "family" as a productive and cohesive unit and of "kinship" as an ideology: priority of the relations between people over the relations to things . . . concern for reproduction; notions of seniority and of anteriority; respect for age; cult of the ancestors; fecundity cult, etc.[61]

In horticulturally based societies, therefore, productive inequalities oppose elders to others in their productive units. Elders possess a degree of power to dispose of household resources not enjoyed by other members of their households. The specificity of this case can be appreciated when it is compared to a hypothetical example in which no asymmetries exist: Men, women, and adult children of a household all work in democratically determined ways, and all participate in deciding what to do with the household product. In such an economy, no one would wield a greater degree of power over the production process than anyone else. But Meillassoux's example of elder-headed households is different: Women and children enjoy the right to subsistence, a historically determined level of consumption, but the head of the household has the power to control what might be called the domestic surplus – the amount beyond what is consumed.[62]

[61] Meillassoux, "From Reproduction to Production," pp. 99–100.
[62] My use of the notion of surplus should not be confused with others that attempt to draw a causal arrow from surplus to inequality. As Harry Pearson argued some time ago, the immediate causality is surely the other way around; power creates surplus. See Pearson, "The Economy Has No Surplus: A Critique of a Theory of Development," in Karl Polanyi, Conrad Arensberg, and Harry W. Pearson, eds., *Trade and Market in the Early Empires* (Glencoe: Free Press, 1957), pp. 320–41. Pearson's article inspired a controversy in the anthropological literature that culminated in Martin Orans's sensible "Surplus," *Human Organization* 25 (1966): 24–32.

It must be emphasized that it is not necessary that the elder use this power for his own benefit (though that possibility, however benefit is defined, is present). He may well use his power to augment his children's future inheritance. In other words, a productive inequality does not depend on how power is used but on the fact of power itself. Compared to elders, women and children do not control the fruits of their labor. Therefore productive inequalities set up contradictions between elders and others in their households, contradictions that are compatible with and that allow for further expansion of the powers of production.

So far, Meillassoux's argument has progressed from the nature of productive powers to that of productive inequalities: Cereal horticulture requires a certain stability in the social units carrying out production, a certain management and storage of grain. These requirements are met by the constitution of households presided over by elders. Meillassoux then introduces another set of functional requirements. These are what he called the requirements for reproduction – the demographic reproduction of production units.

The social organization of the domestic agricultural community is built . . . both upon *the relations of production* in so far as these emerge from the economic constraints imposed by agricultural activity – undertaken under conditions defined by the level of productive powers – and upon the *relations of reproduction* necessary to perpetuate the productive cell [emphasis in original].[63]

According to Meillassoux, if production were the only factor conditioning production units, we would not be able to explain two important aspects of household organization. The first is the typically large size of domestic groups. Technically, production could be carried out by smaller groups of people, but then it would be more likely that households could not reproduce themselves. The occasional incidence of infertility or early death, for example, would affect the reproduction rate of small households more than large ones. Reproduction requires households of relatively large numbers.

The second aspect that productive requirements could not explain is exogamy. Why do brothers and sisters not marry? The answer, according to Meillassoux, is found in reproductive requirements. By exchanging women, households even out the local effects of unbalanced sex ratios. "This mobility [of women] makes it possible, whatever the number of pubescent men and women born into each community [i.e., pro-

---

[63] Meillassoux, *Maidens, Meal and Money*, p. 38.

duction unit], to ensure an optimal reproduction rate, by means of a better distribution of the genetic capacity of the women."[64]

The grand conclusion to this line of argument is that these considerations require someone to manage household reproduction. This requirement is met by a set of power relationships in which elders not only control and supervise production but also manage the marriage of their daughters. Exogamy opens households outward, and it is the elder who supervises extra-household relationships. In a phrase, elders control reproduction. Reproduction and production interrelate, for the women whose marriages are controlled are, in Meillassoux's words, "the producers of the producers." There is even a sense in which control over women is a more fundamental source of power than control over production:

. . . political authority gained through the control of women can be extended to a larger community than can an authority gained through the material management of subsistence. As the group grows, food management becomes burdensome while matrimonial politics is demonstrably more efficient. The community can expand and integrate several productive cells by decentralizing control over subsistence goods (i.e. over hearths and granaries). Segmentation can now take place at the economic level of production and distribution by the formation of autonomous productive cells, while cohesion is maintained and reinforced at the matrimonial level which defines a larger exogamous political cell (the extended family, the lineage, the clan). When this happens the elder's authority depends less on material than matrimonial management and on his ability to deal with similarly constituted communities.[65]

At this point, Meillassoux stepped from a Marxist to a functionalist social theory. Explaining the difference between these kinds of theory involves two tasks. First, as feminist writers have argued, is a critique of Meillassoux's theory of reproduction.[66] The second task is positive: namely, an extension and clarification of Meillassoux's analysis of production. Not the least ambiguity to be faced is just who "elders" are. This difficulty has been compounded by the translation of Meillassoux's French term, "aîné," into English as "elder." Aîné means not elder but

---

[64] Ibid., p. 43.   [65] Ibid., p. 45.
[66] Bridget O'Laughlin, "Production and Reproduction: Meillassoux's 'Femmes, greniers et capitaux,' " *Critique of Anthropology* 8 (1977): 3–32; Olivia Harris and Kate Young, "Engendered Structures: Some Problems in the Analysis of Reproduction." in Joel S. Kahn and Josep R. Llobera, eds., *The Anthropology of Pre-Capitalist Societies* (London: Macmillan, 1981), pp. 109–47; Olivia Harris, "Households as Natural Units," in Kate Young, Carol Wolkowitz, and Roslyn McCullagh, eds., *Of Marriage and the Market: Women's Subordination Internationally and Its Lessons*, 2d ed. (London: Routledge & Kegan Paul, 1984), pp. 136–55.

eldest; the English term, of course, contains no implication of sibling order. As we shall see, this semantic difference must be sorted out in the exact specification of productive inequalities.

———————

Let me begin with Meillassoux's notion of reproduction. At the climax of his argument, Meillassoux writes, ". . . in contrast to capitalism, *power in this mode of production rests on control over the means of reproduction – subsistence goods and wives* – and not over the means of material production" [emphasis in original].[67]

As I have already argued, control over the means of production yields power in capitalism. We had no right to expect that such control would play a similar role in noncapitalist societies. Second, not only has Meillassoux specified where productive inequalities lie in horticulturally-based societies, he has attempted, in the quote above, to explain the *source* of power asymmetries. Rather than constructing the complex reproduction schemata that are required to generate and regenerate power differences, however, Meillassoux's argument operates by sleight-of-hand. What insight does it afford to say that power in this mode of production rests on control over women? Presumably, Meillassoux is referring to power differences among men. But if so, how are power differences between men and women to be explained? Meillassoux gives no answer, unless one is prepared to think of women as inanimate (but fertile) objects. An analogous and equally tautologous analysis of feudalism would claim that power rests on control over serfs. It is, of course, precisely power over serfs, or over wives, as the case may be, that we want to explain.

This is what Marx attempted to do when he constructed reproduction schemata for capitalism: to show how various patterns of power over people result from kinds of control over productive powers – ideas, forms of cooperation, tools, and raw materials. The concept of *re*production allowed Marx to show how an original pattern of control over productive powers leads to a system of power over people in the concrete work process, which, in turn, results in a replication (and sometimes enlargement) of the original pattern of control over productive powers. What is being reproduced in Marx's analysis is a set of contradictions, a set of power relations.[68]

[67] Meillassoux, *Maidens, Meal and Money*, p. 49.
[68] Emmanuel Terray, "On Exploitation: Elements of an Autocritique," *Critique of Anthropology* 13 & 14 (1979): 35.

Meillassoux's notion of reproduction is different. Like functionalists generally, he assumes that the fundamental prerequisite in domestic-based societies is not the reproduction of power differences, but the demographic reproduction of whole social units – households and lineages. This prerequisite is satisfied by elders' control over the exchange of women. Let me illustrate the incompatibility of this type of argument with historical materialism by transferring the same logic to capitalism. We would postulate a functional requirement that firms have to be reproduced. In order for firms to be reproduced, one would argue, capitalists must control workers to the extent that the level of wages always allows a profit.

The form of this argument outwardly resembles that of Marx's. Both are functional explanations that attempt to explain X by X's effects. But the social unit that is assumed to be reproduced is different in the two arguments: in our Meillassoux-like example, the firm; in Marx's analysis, the capitalist class. If we were to assume that the primary functional requirement of capitalist economies is the reproduction of firms, we would have no way of understanding competition between firms or the fact that some firms do not in fact survive. Indeed, we would not be able to understand the entire dynamic of the capitalist mode of production, cycles of booms and busts, the impetus for technological innovation, and so forth. All of these, Marx related to the reproduction of classes – not firms.

A related consequence attends Meillassoux's analysis of the domestic mode. We have no way of understanding the competition between households for people. Certainly, the contest is different from the one in capitalist economies, and it has very different consequences. But ethnography after ethnography shows that the powerful in technologically simple societies become powerful by accumulating dependents whose labor they control in one arrangement or another. Some marry more wives than others; some adopt more children than their neighbors; some accumulate more clients. To the extent that powerful persons win the competition in wealth in people, others must lose. Some households are, therefore, *not* reproduced; the dynamic of these modes of production requires that they not be reproduced.

I argue that we should reject Meillassoux's analysis of the primacy of reproduction – that aspect of his theory works at cross purposes with the rest – and that we turn to the second task mentioned above – clarifying his discussion of production.

This second goal requires attention to the problem of functional alternatives. Recall Meillassoux's argument in outline. Cereal horticulture has certain functional requirements that are met by domestic organization. We cannot assume, however, that there is only one way of fulfilling those requirements. Even a cursory review of the ethnographic literature reveals that there are multiple ways. A full analysis of this problem would require an entire reformulation – from the point of view of historical materialism – of the field of kinship, marriage, and the family, including a review of the variations known in the literature and a determination of which variants are compatible with which level of productive powers.

To pose only some of the questions that would have to be answered: Why do households in societies with uxorilocal residence retain daughters and give out sons, whereas households in ones with virilocal residence retain sons and give out daughters? Are these two types genuine functional alternatives or do they occur in association with different levels of development of the productive powers? What accounts for male dominance? Why is it that only husbands – not wives – appear to carry out the function of controlling household surpluses? And what accounts for the incest taboo? Why is it that the vast majority of brothers do not keep sisters in their own production units by marrying them? Many of these questions have been posed, and some have been partially answered in non-Marxist scholarship, but it is fair to say, I think, that no comprehensive historical materialist analysis of the field of kinship yet exists.

It is crucial to note the extent of the project required at this point, even if one cannot, as I cannot in this chapter, carry out a full analysis. Meillassoux, in contrast, jumps directly from the level of productive powers to control of the household surplus by *males*, males with a *patrilineal* ancestor cult, males who are able to retain *all* married sons under their own control. Let me illustrate the logic of the kind of investigation that is needed at this point by concentrating on only two sources of variation: those involving different ways of instituting household "headship" and those related to different ranges of control "heads" can enjoy.

With respect to the first topic, it is perhaps well to emphasize the specificity of the notion of household in the present discussion. Households, in the sense of domestic and residential groups, exist in all societies, in all types of economy. When Meillassoux refers to domestic groups (and their heads), however, he has in mind a much more restrictive and particular notion than simply residence. Briefly put, households are economic units in which heads, typically husband–fathers, (1) oversee the labor of their wives and children and (2) enjoy effective control of their own and part of their wives' and children's labor and product. Within this kind of economic structure, how is headship instituted? A number of ways recur in the ethnographic record. Let me describe three.

The first is perhaps the simplest case, in which household heads oversee all production and control the entire domestic surplus. Individual members of a domestic group may have special responsibility for work on particular fields, but the head oversees the disposition of the final product and of any surplus left over after consumption. Consumption levels are, therefore, not just simple biological givens; they are, to some extent, politically determined matters in which heads often find themselves in opposition to their wives and children.

The situation described above is the most secure kind of headship, for it prevents any access of other members of the household to resources except by consumption. Somewhat different are the cases in which control is defined relative to types of crops or livestock. Wives, for example, may control the production of certain goods, male household heads, others. The secret of headship in these cases is that the head invariably controls the production of strategic goods, what anthropologists have called prestige goods. Take the example of the Siane of New Guinea.[69] Women control the production of root crops; husbands cannot enter their wives' gardens without permission, and they have no say over how crops from those fields are used. It turns out, however, that the only way of converting root crops into wealth in Siane is by using them to raise pigs – and husbands have rights over pig production. Even though Siane women formally have greater control over the fruits of their labor than women in the first case, they do not effectively control domestic surpluses. Rather, male heads – husbands – enjoy this prerogative by controlling pig production.

Yet a third alternative obtains in those societies in which every member of a domestic group controls her or his own production. At first glance, such an arrangement would seem perfectly egalitarian. Understanding the particular way that domestic obligations are organized, however, is crucial. Among the Fur of the Sudan, for example, hus-

[69] Richard F. Salisbury, *From Stone to Steel: Economic Consequences of a Technological Change in New Guinea* (London: Cambridge University Press for Melbourne University Press, 1962), p. 63.

bands, wives, and grown children have their separate fields and granaries.[70] Each helps the others with certain tasks. Each controls his or her own granaries and provides his or her own food. But – this is the crucial fact – wives are obligated to provide the food for nonworking children. Only when a wife's stores are exhausted will a husband dip into his stocks. As a consequence, wives may occasionally accumulate resources in an especially good year, but only men have regular access to domestic surpluses. It is still husband-fathers who have effective control of most of the resources available for various kinds of investment and politicking.

These three alternatives (no doubt others exist as well) produce slightly different domestic political economies. Each sets up a different economic and political relationship between heads and others in domestic units. Consequently, each produces slightly different patterns in situations of social change.

Besides the contrasting ways household headship can be constituted, there are also a number of different ways that children can be recruited into production units. To simplify the discussion, let me (as Meillassoux does) restrict attention to societies with patrilineal descent and virilocal residence. Even within such limits, there are significant variations related to the timing of children's exits from parents' households. It is possible that all male siblings will stay in their parents' household after marrying, or that only one will stay, or that none will stay. These possibilities result in different developmental cycles – in grand family, stem family, and conjugal family household systems, respectively.

I list these variations not only to emphasize the problem of functional alternatives but also to point out what has not, I think, been appreciated about Meillassoux's formulation of the domestic mode. Assuming that male heads of all of these kinds of domestic groups control domestic surpluses in exactly the same way, it does *not* follow that the resulting productive inequalities can be described as those of elders versus juniors. The type of inequality in each case depends on the exact type of household developmental cycle. The particular shape of the developmental cycle, by indicating the range of persons through time over whom male household heads have power, indicates exactly who is poised against whom in productive relationships. In the progression of types of developmental cycles, from conjugal to stem to grand family systems, the power of household heads expands to cover more and more people.

---

[70] Fredrik Barth, "Economic Spheres in Darfur," in Raymond Firth, ed., *Themes in Economic Anthropology* (London: Tavistock, 1967), pp. 149–89.

Consider first a conjugal household system in which all sons (and daughters) move out of their fathers' households at marriage. There would be no productive inequality, no power relationship established in production, between elders on the one hand and juniors on the other – unless juniors are defined as unmarried young men. After marriage, all young men move out of their fathers' households to establish their own production units with new power over their young wives. The basic and unchanging opposition is that between husbands and wives.

Households in systems of stem-family development are more complex, and productive inequalities are different. One son, usually the eldest, continues to produce under the authority of his father, even after marriage. In such cases, older household heads typically come into position of relative power, since they control the labor of the married eldest son and his wife. Even so, productive inequalities cannot be summarized as those of elders versus juniors. Younger married sons are independent. The relevant contradictions are those between husbands and wives and between elderly fathers and married eldest sons.

Grand family systems, finally, are the most complex. All sons remain in their fathers' productive units after marriage. The point at which grand families segment varies, but let us assume that brothers remain together under the authority of the eldest after their father dies. Only in this case of extended development does Meillassoux's formulation of productive inequalities in the domestic mode hold: Eldest brothers (aînés) are opposed to all younger brothers (cadets), and husbands to wives. Meillassoux's particular formulation is, then, only one of a family of possibilities. It can by no means be deduced from the level of development of the productive powers.

Until this point, I have suggested that the type of power enjoyed by heads depends on the type of household developmental cycle. This is the usual anthropological shorthand: Societies are said to "have" developmental cycles. It is important to examine this shorthand, for it involves referring to productive inequalities in terms of rights – husbands and wives have the right to expect their eldest son to remain in their household and so forth. As I have explained above, socially defined rights are properly a part of the superstructure; productive inequalities are the de facto powers that match those rights.

On inspection, our anthropological shorthand involves an upside-down view of the world, just as do other superstructural ways of putting matters. Rather than elders' power depending on the type of developmental cycle, the developmental cycle arguably depends on the type and degree of power that elders can muster. It is the pattern of contradictions – the set of productive inequalities – that conditions the developmental cycle. Societies, then, do not simply "have" developmental cycles. Rather, men and women with varying types and degrees of power (specified in superstructural discourses and practices) tend to produce and reproduce various sorts of household systems. The level of development of the productive powers limits the range of possible inequalities, but it does not, as Meillassoux assumes, uniquely specify them. A variety of productive relationships exists, and a more complex and flexible formulation than Meillassoux's is required in order to comprehend that variation.

My goal in this chapter has been twofold: on the one hand, to bring the results of recent discussions in Marxist theory into anthropological discourse, and on the other, to use the peculiarity of a type of political economy unknown to most social theorists – specifically, so-called tribal ones – to clarify wider issues in historical materialism. This has required a reformulation of G. A. Cohen's exposition of the fundamentals of historical materialism. I have argued that a new definition of productive inequalities is required, if societies radically different from capitalism are to be included within the purview of historical materialism. I have also claimed that a greater attention to the problem of functional alternatives is needed, if the notion of determination is to be made compatible with the actual complexity of social evolution. These general issues in Marxist theory led finally to anthropology and to a critique of Claude Meillassoux's work. Refracted through the lens of historical materialism, the subject of kinship, anthropology's traditional stronghold, begins to look different. In the next chapter, I shall attempt to illustrate that difference in an analysis of the Maale way of producing.

3. Epochal structures II: The anatomy of Maale production

The framework constructed in the preceding chapter has no claim on our attention except as it guides and illuminates the examination of actual cases. Marx and Engels themselves insisted that historical materialism is not a self-contained philosophy that can be used to trim the edges of history:

When reality is described, a self-sufficient philosophy loses its medium of existence. At best its place can be taken only by a summing-up of the most general results, abstractions which are derived from the observation of the historical development of men. These abstractions in themselves, divorced from real history, have no value whatsoever. They can only serve to facilitate the arrangement of historical material, to indicate the sequence of its separate strata. But they by no means afford a recipe or schema, as does philosophy, for neatly trimming the epochs of history. On the contrary, the difficulties begin only when one sets about the examination and arrangement of the material. . . .[1]

So, as Marx and Engels said, the difficulties now begin. The analysis of Chapter 1 treated households as givens. The problem in this chapter will be to use Marxist theory to explain household structures themselves. Our problem, in other words, will be to understand the Maale way of producing.

Let me begin with the level of development of productive powers. The Maale case fits Meillassoux's specification of productive powers for the domestic mode. From the late nineteenth century until 1975, productive powers were relatively stable in Maale. Slash-and-burn horticulture was always the main line of production, and human energy always the main source of power in the production process. The only exception involved a small development by 1975 of ox-drawn scratch plowing; such plowing was employed by less than a third of highland households

[1] Marx and Engels, "The German Ideology," in Marx and Engels, *Collected Works*, vol. 5 (London: Lawrence & Wishart, [1932] 1976), p. 37.

and only then for selected fields that had already been cultivated by hand.

For clearing new fields, each adult man possessed a simple tool kit: for chopping down trees, a hand axe; for clearing secondary growth, a curved billhook with a wooden handle; and for cultivating and weeding, iron-tipped hoes in various shapes. Crops were stored in granaries, small thatched-roofed replicas of Maale houses set on platforms off the ground. And, finally, food was processed with an equally simple technology: Every adult woman possessed a large gourd and harness for carrying water on her back, a pair of stones for grinding grain, a clay griddle for baking unleavened bread, and various sized clay pots for cooking and storage. Only relatively wealthy Maale – and not all of them – possessed a few manufactured metal utensils in 1975.

The iron working necessary to produce axes and hoes was done by males of an endogamous outcaste group called gito. The gito, alone with another caste to be described below, lived interspersed over Maaleland, even though they were not thought of as "Maale." Gito blacksmiths worked iron individually with a simple technology of charcoal fires, bellows, and an anvil. The other outcaste group, the mani, were potters and tanners; women of the caste potted without a wheel, and men tanned the large cowhides that Maale used for sleeping mats.

Besides horticulture, other lines of production such as cattle-keeping, beekeeping, and hunting had their technologies in Maale. Raising cattle required few tools, save ropes and crude corrals that every adult Maale man could make. Increasingly during the twentieth century, however, Maale bought firearms from northern traders in order to protect their cattle from Banna raiders from the south – a threat that continued in cycles of varying intensity through 1975. Beekeeping involved the construction of beehives – long cylinders of straw-covered bark closed at both ends by wooden disks. And in hunting (game was scarce by 1975), traditional bows and poisoned arrows were widely used, even though firearms were also present. Metal tips for the arrows were constructed by gito, and poison was prepared by men of the mani caste.

In addition to tools, land was also a productive power in Maale. Since horticulture was practiced in the form of slash-and-burn cultivation, it was not land in any form that counted but land with the right kind of forest cover. The swidden cycle in the Maale highlands differed from that in the lowlands. In the highlands, there were two plantings a year and two kinds of cycles, correlated with the big and small rains. Big-rain fields were planted with sorghum, corn, and finger millet on relatively heavier soils originally covered with forest growth. These fields were cultivated from three to five years and then left to regenerate for fifteen to twenty. Small-rain fields, in contrast, were placed on lighter soils, often on hillsides with relatively little cover; they were planted only twice, the first time during the small rains with sorghum and tef (an Ethiopian grain), and then again during the following big rains with finger millet.

In the Maale lowlands that surrounded the highland core on all sides, horticulture was less productive, and cattle-raising was correspondingly more important. Often, Maale in the lowlands compensated for their grain deficit by trading cattle for highland sorghum and corn. In any case, since rainfall in the lowlands was less abundant than in the highlands, there was correspondingly only one type of field and only one cultivation per year. These fields were planted during the big rains with fast-maturing sorghums. They were cultivated for two or three years and then left to regenerate for approximately twenty.

Finally, besides land and tools and the knowledge of their use, labor was the last major productive power in Maale. Labor was, in fact, the limiting factor of production for Maale producers, since land was relatively abundant and tools were easily obtained. Labor organization was, correspondingly, complex, and there were, as Chapter 1 has already shown, four kinds of social units that carried out horticultural work: households, helma, mol'o, and dabo.

Households typically passed through a number of distinctive phases, moving toward stem-family composition. In Chapter 1, comparisons of relative labor supply over those phases were derived by restricting the notion of labor to horticultural work. Since all working members of Maale households participated in most horticultural tasks (and so could substitute for one another), domestic units were treated as more-or-less homogeneous pools of labor. Now we must reconsider the division of labor in Maale – the whole differentiated array of people's productive interactions with nature.

From this broader point of view, it is immediately clear that Maale households were not built of completely similar units of labor. Many tasks were divided into two great spheres – male and female. Such tasks were, in a phrase, engendered and engendering. That is, a person became male or female and reaffirmed his or her gender by continually performing such work; a male, for example, could not regularly do female work without becoming "female." Most biological males took up male-engendered tasks, but a small minority crossed over to feminine roles. Called ashtime, these (biological) males dressed like women, performed female tasks, cared for their own houses, and apparently had sexual relations with men.[2] The opposite case, of biological females taking up male-engendered roles, appears to have occurred less frequently and to have had fewer social consequences. Such behavior did not set up a new gender category nor prevent females from living with husbands.

Not only were some tasks engendered, but it was precisely these that children were taught first. Female work included fetching water and firewood, grinding grain, cooking meals, preparing beer, feeding and caring for children. By the age of six or so, young girls began to carry water in miniature gourds strapped on their backs and to grind grain, building up the heavy calluses on their palms that all Maale women have. By ten, young girls took over more of their mothers' work, caring for younger children, cooking, and so forth. Girls learned to carry out these tasks in a particular style. In movement and work, measured and deliberate, girls were taught to kept their sexual selves covered: While boys went naked, girls wore short, string skirts. In cooking or at other tasks, women bent over at the waists with their knees together; when they sat, it was always with both legs straight in front, knees together.

In contrast, male tasks included hunting, the care of goats and cattle, beekeeping, cattle raiding, and the heavy horticultural work of clearing new fields. Young boys by the age of six or so began herding goats and were away from their homes most of the day; at that point, they began to learn archery. By ten, they often graduated to herding cattle (except in the most dangerous areas), and they sometimes accompanied cattle to distant pastures where they lived in cattle camps. Beekeeping, raiding with guns, and heavy horticultural work were tasks that followed. In all of these, boys became men through tasks performed, again, in a particular style: Traditionally, men, even old men, wore no clothes.[3] Men always sat or squatted with their knees wide apart. Given to quicker

[2] In 1975, I was aware of only one ashtime in Maaleland, though informants asserted that more had existed in the nineteenth century. Indeed, part of the Maale king's traditional installation had consisted in a ritual ordination of an ashtime. The king installed in the 1930s, however, had refused to carry out this part of the rite, and in general, it appears that imperial Ethiopian culture – centered on Orthodox Christianity – put increasing pressure on Maale roles such as that of ashtime during the twentieth century.

[3] During the twentieth century, Maale men rapidly took up northern styles of clothing, particularly when they travelled. To Orthodox Christian northerners, rulers of the empire, nakedness indicated sin and heathenism.

A girl in a string skirt, a boy with a toy bow and arrow in 1951. By the 1970s, some girls wore ready-made cotton skirts, some boys ready-made shorts. Even then, few had seen foreigners with cameras.

and more expansive movements, men were the free and uncovered sex.

Households, then, were built out of two fundamentally different and complementary sorts of labor, and any household that did not have both was not a fully functioning economic unit.[4] But households, even fully-

---

[4] The bulk of horticultural work – the mainstay of the economy – was not gendered. Both

formed ones, were not sufficient unto themselves, and cooperative work groups knit households together into a number of larger structures. These groups – helma, mol'o, and dabo – could accomplish horticultural tasks much more quickly than households (sometimes the horticultural cycle required large inputs of labor during a relatively short period of time). And work groups probably also increased labor productivity through conviviality and coordinated effort.[5]

These, then, were the powers that Maale used to produce their material life: technology, land, and labor. According to Marx and to Meillassoux, the level of development of these powers determines productive inequalities. Were domestic inequalities, as Meillassoux has characterized them, the result in Maale?

––––––––

Meillassoux's formulation does not prepare us for what we find. In addition to domestic inequalities within households, we find tributary relations between commoners, on the one hand, and chiefs and a ritual king, on the other. These tributary relations were of a peculiar kind. The Maale polity was not a state in which the extraction of tribute was backed by a monopoly of coercive power. Coercive power was in fact only weakly developed.[6] Rather, the giving of tribute was bound up with ritual and cosmology, with notions that tribute to the chiefs and king was necessary in order to insure biological fertility.

Control over fertility – the bringing of rain, the sprouting of crops, the births of children, calves, and goats, the creation of all wealth in Maale and the corresponding destruction of all enemy generative power – was the master symbol of Maale political economy. All good fortune was thought to be the result of the special powers of a hierarchy of living persons, and behind them, lines of deceased ancestors. Tribute at once established and acknowledged this hierarchy. At the apex of the system was the ritual king.

In the nineteenth century, Maaleland was divided into thirteen chief-

men and women dug and cultivated, weeded, harvested, and transported produce to granaries, as I pointed out in Chapter 1.
[5] Work groups were certainly "used" in Maale production, and as will become clear later, it took a certain amount of social savvy to be able to carry out this use. If cooperative work groups themselves do not qualify as productive powers, then the social knowledge of how to use them does, as well as the purely technical aspects of cooperation.
[6] The ritual king, with the agreement of another official, the gojo, had the right to order mani outcastes to execute Maale who continually offended public order. In general, the king appears to have used the mani as a kind of rudimentary police force, but this use was strictly circumscribed by the power of other officials and by public opinion.

doms, each presided over by a hereditary chief known as goda or master. No master worked, but instead drew labor tribute from the inhabitants of his chiefdom. Subchiefs called gatta organized work on masters' fields. Each subchief, blowing an antelope horn, periodically summoned commoners from districts of the chiefdom to work on the master's field.

Above the thirteen masters was the kati or ritual king. The king had no particular area of his own but presided over all of Maaleland, drawing labor tribute from all the chiefdoms. First, the king sent a messenger to a master, then the master instructed one of his subchiefs to take workers to the king's fields. These fields were located in the center of Maaleland and could not be cultivated by anyone except the king. One plot was named warshabashe, "too much for a multitude." Besides labor tribute, the ritual king could also demand tribute in kind. For all the sacrifices made when he prayed to his ancestors for rain, the king sent orders to the masters, who informed their subchiefs, who in turn decided whose cattle or goats should be sent to the king.

If coercion was only weakly developed in the Maale polity, how was this system of tribute maintained? There was, of course, a certain amount of reinforcement of the notion of the special powers of the chiefs and kings during good years. After receiving tribute, the king propitiated his ancestors, and indeed the rains came. But a string of good years probably also encouraged a certain amount of laxness; if current patterns of observance of social obligations are any guide, some Maale inevitably did not give tribute. What happened in those cases? Unlike officials in states, the king and chiefs had relatively few resources with which to compel the obedience of subjects. In extreme cases, subjects could be executed, but such power was infrequently used. This meant that conflicts between officials and others often festered and accumulated; refusing to give tribute was, after all, the quintessential way that persons proclaimed social status in Maale. Over time, up-and-coming kin groups may have been able to make good on their claims, to rise in the hierarchy, and eventually to assume new offices.

Such mobility was made rare, however, by conservative interpretations of bad times. When any large-scale misfortune intervened (and droughts and raids by enemies occurred too frequently) past transgressions of the established order, so-called gome, came to the center of public discourse: The misfortune occurred because of gome. During such times, it took an extraordinarily strong opposition to define a misfortune as the result of a past misordering of society – as for example the result of a chief's lack of power over fertility, the fact that he was not a "true"

A Maale subchief overseeing labor tribute in 1975. His necklace of heirloom beads, inherited from forebears, is an insignia of office. The horn under his arm was used to summon workers.

chief and had to be displaced by the "real" line. Instead, it was precisely during the beginning of bad times that belief in established chiefs and kings seems to have swelled strongest and tributes increased. Ironically, bad times appeared to many Maale as prime facie evidence of the power of kings and chiefs.

The dominant productive inequality in nineteenth-century Maale was, then, the relationship between the ritual king and chiefs on the one hand and commoners on the other. The king and chiefs quite literally lived on the labor of others. Although this kind of productive inequality cannot be described as domestic, it nevertheless built on and articulated with two other inequalities that resemble Meillassoux's formulation. One was the relationship between minimal lineage heads (Meillassoux's aînés) and others in and married into their lineage segments; the second involved the ties between household heads and their wives and coresident working children.

Lineages in Maale were constituted on the basis of what has been called conical clans.[7] That is, the entire group was hierarchized so that each member was either higher or lower in status, depending upon his relative closeness to one line – that of eldest sons descending from the founder. In Maale, the hierarchy was built not just on status differences but also on real productive inequalities. In order to describe these, let me begin with a hypothetical example of an old man, himself an eldest son, who has three sons – a group I shall call a minimal lineage.

When the old man dies, his property is functionally divided, with much the greatest share going to his eldest son (who, it should be remembered, had continued to live in his father's household while younger brothers had moved out). By that point, the three brothers, members of the same minimal lineage, each preside over their own household economies (I shall describe the inequalities involved in these below). But the two younger brothers do not yet have full control over the results of their and their dependents' labors, for the eldest brother "owns," according to the Maale way of thinking, the property of the entire minimal lineage – including that of his younger brothers.

But what "owning" means in this case is not control over productive powers as they are used in the process of production. Younger brothers carry out production independently of the eldest. Rather, ownership in Maale refers to the fact that only the eldest brother can carry out the

[7] Paul Kirschoff, "The Principles of Clanship in Human Societies," in Morton Fried, ed., *Readings in Anthropology*, 2d ed., vol. 2 (New York: Thomas Y. Crowell, 1968), pp. 370–81.

rituals that legitimate minimal lineage property and make it consumable.[8] The eldest brother does so by presenting first fruits to his ancestors, most immediately to his dead father. Only after the ancestors have been ritually presented with new grain, new honey, or fresh milk does the eldest brother ritually consume these products. And only after the eldest has tasted them can his younger brothers do with their crops, honey, or cattle what they would like. Before, this property is tabooed, and if a younger brother consumed or exchanged it, misfortune would surely befall him, according to the Maale.

The power of eldest brothers becomes clearer when we consider how minimal lineages segment. The eldest can grant his younger brothers the right to perform their own first fruits rituals. He does this by formally dividing the group's property, by, as the Maale say, making his younger brothers "go out." Even though he cannot take away cattle willed to younger brothers by his father, the eldest has wide latitude to take property that younger brothers have accumulated by their own or by dependents' labors. After this division, each younger brother becomes the head of his own minimal lineage, with new rights to propitiate his ancestors and new control over his own and dependents' labor.

As with the giving of tribute, we are in a very different world from capitalism. Does the Maale system described here represent real material inequalities, or is it, as they say, only ritual? To ask the question in this way misleads an analysis of Maale and, ironically, betrays a misunderstanding of our own society based on capitalism. The sources of capitalist inequalities also depend upon "beliefs": They are superstructural. That the sources of Maale inequalities are ritual, then, should be no surprise – even if Maale rituals are different from our own.

Why don't younger brothers resist the ritual control over their property by the eldest? The answer is that sometimes they do, and if younger brothers move far enough away, they sometimes manage to do so successfully. What happens in such cases is that the minimal lineage is effectively split, and any memory of old links between the two kin groups slowly dies out. There is good reason to believe that this is how most local lineages were in fact founded; myths of origin often mention conflicts between elder and younger brothers and movements to new areas.

If a younger brother who infringed the rights of his eldest continues

---

[8] The distance between capitalist and noncapitalist social orders can now be appreciated. As I argued in Chapter 2, historical materialism requires a definition of productive inequalities that will encompass both Maale notions of ownership and capitalist ones.

A younger brother, on the left, confessing (buts'ane) conflicts with his eldest to a diviner in 1974. The diviner is encouraging the young man to spit into the container in the latter's hand, a gourd that contains watery plants. This process is said to "cool" the young man's stomach and to remove any cause of misfortune.

to live in the same area, however, the whole load of social expectations will make it difficult for the breach between them to persist permanently. It is not, as in capitalist society, that the power of the state is used to set right contracts not fulfilled. The state does not exist. Rather, every misfortune in the younger brother's life (and given the material organization of Maale society, there will perforce be misfortunes) will be interpreted by those around him as a consequence of his resisting proper control by his eldest brother. In the end, as his child lies dying or as locusts destroy his field, an estranged younger brother will almost have to present a compensation payment to his eldest brother in order, as the Maale believe, to prevent further tragedy. And the payment may be greater than the value of the original bone of contention between the two.

To return to the specification of productive inequalities in traditional Maale: The relationship between eldest and younger brothers (with the latter's wives and children) was the second major productive inequality.

After eldest brothers made younger brothers "go out," this material inequality ceased, but status differences among brothers, and among all lineage mates, persisted.

I come finally to the last kind of productive inequality, that between household heads and their wives and working children. Unlike inequalities within minimal lineages that were articulated in relation to control over cattle, goats, and honey, the power relationships within households typically involved horticulture. The production of all crops was under the authority of the household head. Within households, men and boys performed a certain array of male tasks, women and girls female ones. Everyone in the household had a right to consumption by virtue of his or her membership, but it was only the mari ado, the "father of the house," who held the power to dispose of any surplus above what was consumed. Of course, a surplus did not just fall from the sky (in this sense, the word is misleading). Rather, surpluses were systematically created by heads who determined the size of fields, oversaw and paced the labor process, and husbanded granaries.

However a surplus was used, the mari ado, in part, controlled the fruits of others' labor. This is not to say that wives and children had no influence over matters of household decision-making. They did. Nor is it to assume that wives and children could not resist their husbands and fathers in certain ways. They could. Rather, the point is that social arrangements gave husband-fathers greater power in determining how to use household resources. At first approximation, then, a major opposition would appear to have existed between married men, on the one hand, and their wives and coresident, adult children, on the other. Most especially, men would appear to have been opposed to women.

Actually, productive inequalities were more complex. And the complexity resulted from shifts in roles as households moved through the developmental cycle. The Maale, as I have pointed out, had (and continue to have) a stem family developmental cycle. All daughters and younger sons move out of their parents' households soon after marriage to found new, independent economic units. Eldest sons, in contrast, continue to live and to work with their parents under the authority of their fathers, even after marriage.

Over the developmental cycle, the position of wives changes vis-à-vis their husbands. During the early stages, wives are indeed opposed to their husbands. But as more and more children are born, and as these children take up work roles within the household, the mother becomes a relatively more powerful figure. By the last and most expansive phase of stem family development, the configuration of household power has fundamentally changed.

Recall the composition of a typical household at this stage: an elder and his wife, their eldest son and the latter's wife and children, along with any unmarried daughters and younger sons. The household head, the elder, retains the formal authority to allocate household surpluses, but by this point, his wife has become so assimilated to the household and influential with regard to her children that the fundamental divide in economic interests occurs between the elder and his wife, on the one hand, and their coresident working children, on the other. Past menopause, the elderly wife becomes in some respects, more "male," and the elderly couple, together, supervise the labor of others – the man, his son, the woman, her daughter-in-law.

Finally, all inhabitants of Maale households occupied positions of relative power vis-à-vis outcastes. No Maale person blacksmithed, potted, or tanned; to do so was to accept outcaste status. Similarly, no outcaste gito or mani was allowed to cultivate the soil in Maaleland (this taboo was relaxed only in the 1960s and then unevenly). Maale consequently obtained craft products from outcastes in exchange for grain. But this exchange was conditioned by a systematic difference in power, and the terms of trade undoubtedly favored the Maale. Symbolic antitheses of ritual kings, outcastes were thought to have the inherent ability to bring not fortune, but harm. Outcastes were sometimes blamed for misfortunes and driven from the land. A final productive inequality obtained between all outcastes and all Maale.

So far, I have discussed tributary, lineage, domestic, and caste inequalities as if they operated separately. Obviously, they did not. Households and their changing productive inequalities were encapsulated within minimal lineages, and minimal lineages functioned within chiefdoms and kingdom as a whole. A household head who was himself an eldest brother and therefore the head of a minimal lineage – with some control over the results of the labor of his younger brothers and their dependents – was in a different structural position from others. His range of options was wider. He could add domestic to lineage surpluses in order to politick in various ways, or he could use lineage surpluses to increase consumption levels within his own household in order to smooth over contradictions there. Generally, it seems that wives and children were better off, in the widest social sense, in eldest brothers' households than in others.

The patterning of productive inequalities within households, then,

A mani woman putting the finishing touches on a clay pot, scraping it with a flint rock, 1974

depended on the operation of inequalities without. The same was true one step further up the hierarchy. Productive inequalities within minimal lineages were conditioned by the flow of surplus from commoners to the chiefs and to the ritual king. The organization of this flow depended on and reinforced the power of minimal lineage heads, for when subchiefs gathered tribute, either in kind or in labor, they did so from minimal lineage heads themselves. These men had the right to decide which member of their descent groups, whether of their own household or of their younger brothers' households, should be sent to work on the chief's or king's fields. Similarly, they had the right to decide whose cow, theirs or their younger brother's, would be sent for sacrifice. Any conflicts over these decisions were settled by local elders in the first instance and by subchiefs and chiefs in the second. Inequalities within households and minimal lineages were, therefore, reinforced by their placement within chiefdoms and the kingdom as a whole.

Indeed, it is not too much to say that inequalities reverberated one with the other in a single dominant chord. The effects of each were modified by the others. From this point of view, Maale households are not to be seen, as in Chapter 1, as so many simple units that can be added up to form a domestic mode of production – whether in Sahlins's or Meillassoux's formulation. Rather, it was more inclusive structures, particularly the way tribute was organized, that shaped households and, indeed, that conditioned the whole way of producing in Maale.

———

Productive inequalities in Maale having been located, the next step in our analysis is to understand how they are reproduced. When Marx posed a similar problem in regard to capitalism, he began his answer in *Capital* with an analysis of the concept of commodities. In capitalism, commodities appear to have a power that, in reality, they do not possess. This appearance, according to Marx, is not mere illusion; it is in fact generated by the social world just as, for example, mirages are created by atmospheric conditions. The particular aspect of capitalism that invests commodities in general (and capital in particular) with illusory powers involves the organization of production. When workers sell their labor power and the capitalist buys it to produce goods with machines, it appears as if the machines *in themselves* are responsible for a great increase in output, for the surplus produced at the end of the day. It seems natural, then, that the owner of the machines should be entitled to the surplus (just as the workers as owners of their own labor power had been entitled to their wages).

It is hardly an illusion that capital investments make workers' labor more productive. What is illusory is the discourse that abstracts machines from the labor process to speak of the "productivity" of capital – of "money making money." Capital, of course, produces nothing; in itself, it is only the product of past workers' labors. The only human element, the only active component of the production process, is labor. But this reality is inverted in social discourse, and capital seems to take on a life of its own. Ironically, the thing that men and women created with their own powers appears not as a result, a created thing, but as something endowed with creative powers of its own – powers that subsequently dominate men and women. As Marx put it in his early writings,

Just as in religion the spontaneous activity of the human imagination, the human brain and the human heart detaches itself from the individual and reappears as the alien activity of a god or of a devil, so the activity of the worker is not his own spontaneous activity. It belongs to another. . . .[9]

[9]Marx, "Economic and Philosophical Manuscripts," *Early Writings*, trans. Rodney Livingstone and Gregor Benton (New York: Vintage, [1934] (1975), pp. 326–7.

Exactly how this process of so-called fetishization occurs in capitalism is unique, but something broadly analogous occurred in Maale political economy. In Maale, *things* were not invested with an aura of creative power, but *persons*, living and dead, in certain social relationships. Maale discourse was dominated, in a phrase, by a fetishization of fertility. Whereas in reality the success of men and women in accumulating wealth and in bearing children depended on their own productive and procreative powers, the way that labor was organized in Maale made it *appear* as if that success depended on other people's fertility: that of the king and chiefs in the first place, that of descent-group elders in the second, and finally that of husband-fathers in the third. As it turns out, this appearance is the key to a number of Maale concepts – from ownership to gender to filiation.

In relation to the king and chiefs, fertility fetishism was grounded in the ordering of Maale horticulture and hunting. It was taboo (ketse) for anyone in Maaleland to plant his fields before the king. As the end of the dry season approached, each of the chiefs with his subchiefs brought tribute to the king. The king entertained them, and he prayed to his ancestors for rain. As the rains came, the chiefs sent labor tribute from their districts, and the king planted his fields. Only after the king had planted was it ritually permissible or shati (shati was the opposite of ketse) for the chiefs to plant, and only after the chiefs had planted was it shati for the subchiefs to plant. Finally, after the subchiefs had planted, commoners could begin. And among commoners, a hierarchical order was also maintained: first, the most senior elder of a local descent group (the eldest son of eldest sons) followed by successively more junior elders, down to heads of minimal lineages. Finally, within most Maale households, only men were allowed to place the seeds in the ground.

This ritual ordering was reversed when a man killed a large animal such as a buffalo or lion or an enemy man (such kills were the final mark of prestige for Maale men and were celebrated in numerous ways). After making the kill, a man took a trophy from the dead – the buffalo's hind leg or the lion's tail or the enemy's penis – and came dancing back to his minimal lineage head with it draped around his neck. The lineage head ritually made the kill again and presented the trophy to his ancestors, thus beginning the process that would make the killer shati or remove his state of taboo. (A killer was like a man who had planted his crops out of order; he had gotten out of line. Unlike the pattern in horticulture, however, the ordering of production in hunting had to be done after the fact rather than before.) The ritual was repeated at each step in the hierarchy over the killer, to his more senior lineage elders to his subchief to his chief to the king – near whose compound, in the case of killers of enemy men, the penis was finally deposited.

The conceptual scheme behind this ordering conditioned the very notion of "ownership" of things and, indeed, the concept of "persons" who did the owning. In capitalist society we think of persons as autonomous legal entities with power of control over things they own vis-à-vis other persons. In Maale the notion of personhood and the associated concept of control over property was different. No Maale man (I shall consider gender below) conceived of himself or was conceived by others as an isolated "individual" set against other individuals. Rather, each man was a constituent member of a lineage descended from an original founder, set within a particular chiefdom, set within the kingdom. And depending on his place within this array, each man exercised only relative control over his "own" property. To those to whom he was indebted for his very physical existence, to those who begat him – the ancestors along with living members of his lineage closer to the line of eldest sons of eldest sons, and the chiefs and king – a person was bound to defer various kinds of control over property that otherwise he referred to as his own. For it was the fertility and generative power of these others that was responsible, it seemed, for the property in the first place.

Consider the case of a younger brother who had managed to acquire a cow in trade for grain that he himself had grown. The man referred to the cow as his own, but his control over it was conditioned by claims of other persons located in the social hierarchy over him. The man's minimal lineage head could also say with justice that the cow was "his" (inasmuch as the head had the right to take the cow when the group segmented), as could the man's chief and the king (inasmuch as they had the right to take the cow in tribute). These claims rested on the notion that the cow was the result, not of the labors of the man, but of the generative powers of a hierarchy of persons, each one of whom had rights over what, according to Maale appearances, he had caused to come into existence.

The mystical endowment of others with one's own productive and procreative powers occurred at each level of social organization: from the kingdom as a whole to chiefdoms to lineages to households. It was, in fact, in households that the primary process of fetishization took place, primary in the sense that it provided the low note, the reverberating base for the system of ideas being discussed: namely, the creation of "men," as opposed to "women," and the endowment of "men" with peculiar powers over biological and social reproduction.

There were, as I have pointed out, three genders in traditional Maale: atinke, lali, and ashtime. Male, female, and transvestite. The first two were thought of as normal inasmuch as their combined sexual energies and productive labors were fertile and gave issue in children. But ashtime were considered abnormal, wobo or crooked. The one transvestite that I was able to interview in Maale presented himself in such terms: "The Divinity created me wobo, crooked. If I had been a man, I could have taken a wife and begotten children. If I had been a woman, I could have married and borne children. But I am wobo; I can do neither."

The intent of this self-presentation (no more pitiful condition existed, according to Maale standards, than not having descendants) was to deflect hostility and to invoke a certain acceptance. But this self-statement also reflected a central element in the fetishization of fertility: the identification, the misidentification, of social with sexual reproduction. In fact, the reproduction of Maale society had as much to do with labor as with biological generation; indeed, the transvestite mentioned above had raised three orphans, cultivating large fields by brewing beer and sponsoring dabo to obtain male labor. But no cultural vocabulary existed for talking about, for valuing labor in itself. Instead, social success – the result of a complex of real causes – was displaced onto and attributed to persons' fertility, and various kinds and amounts of fertility were codified into a set of gender concepts. In this semantic field, ashtime represented the paradigmatic lack of fertility. Silently pitied, partially feared, but generally accepted as part of the scheme of things that existed, ashtime were dead ends of ancestral lines.

What it meant to be a "man" or a "woman" was, in contrast, intimately tied up with generative power, good fortune, and the successful continuance of society. And everything was done to emphasize the complementary natures of men and women – that both were required for social reproduction. As we have already seen with respect to the sexual division of labor, the differences between men and women were exaggerated to the extent that no Maale man or woman could exist without access to the kind of labor that the other carried out. Similarly, with respect to Maale theories of sexual reproduction, it was believed that both males and females contributed to biological generation, men semen, women menstrual blood.

But if men and women completed each other, they were by no means

A Maale man and woman, 1974. The man, knees apart, in locally spun and woven cloth, is smoking a water pipe. The woman, legs crossed, wearing a leather skirt and skin cape, is grinding sorghum.

equivalent. Men were the cause of sexual and social generation. Men were the actors, the initiators, the ones who gave form and organization to life, whereas women were more passive and sometimes unreliable receptacles – as the Maale said, like the earth in which seeds were planted.[10]

Action and inaction were strictly enforced in customs surrounding sexual intercourse. It was considered wanton of a woman to initiate sex with a man (such behavior was gossiped about, particularly by women). And it was absolutely taboo for a woman to refuse to have sexual inter-course with her husband. A man so refused had either to beat his wife into submission (one husband in this situation slashed his wife's legs) or to divorce her instantly. A woman who exerted her will with respect to procreation upset a fundamental hierarchical relationship in Maale.

[10] The definition of men and women becomes clear in how the words were used as epi-thets: "lali!" "Woman!" was an insult, especially when addressed to a man but also, to a lesser extent, when said to a woman. A man thus insulted had few verbal defenses, but a woman taunted with her sex was likely to retort, "Whose ass do you think you dropped from?" On the other hand, "atinke ke" "is a male" – a phrase said with an entirely different inflection – was a compliment, even when half-admiringly applied to a woman.

Any man who continued to live in such an upside-down world faced sterility and death.

Maale marriage customs confirmed this image of men as active and women as passive. Young men looked for wives in a kind of dating called "pulling a girl out," lali gocane. At night, a young man went to a girl's father's compound, entered stealthily, and "pulled out" the girl. The two went outside and sat down together, the young man on the right, the girl on the left (right and left indicating higher and lower statuses in Maale culture), and it was taboo for the girl to get up and leave while the boy remained seated. Boys, then, roamed about at night, choosing girls to court, while girls remained at home waiting to be courted.

Once a girl had consented to marry, the process was organized by a discourse that portrayed the bride's father as "giving" her. Traditionally, Maale fathers accepted no gifts when their daughters married. Contrasting themselves with the neighboring Ari, who practiced bridewealth, Maale said that they did not "sell" their daughters. Rather, after consulting the intestine oracle to determine whether the union would be fertile, the father and his lineage "gave," ingene, the girl to the man and his lineage. In essence, the father saw himself as giving the girl's fertility, her capacity for bearing children. In one stroke, the girl's own procreative powers were made into a gift given by men, and her labor, just as crucial for successful reproduction as biological generation, was silently assimilated to this fetishized concept.

Unlike a process of buying and selling that has no further social consequences, this "giving" of fertility set up a long-lasting relationship of status inequality – between the groom and the bride's father and brothers and between successive generations of the descent groups of the two. In Maale culture, there was no way to repay a gift of fertility, so the husband and his descendants were permanently indebted to the wife's lineage. The indebtedness of the husband's lineage required them to respond to continual, if diminishing, demands for help – crops during bad years, a goat to slaughter when someone was sick, or occasional help with cultivation.[11]

---

[11] Ideally, the indebtedness lasted for four generations. At that point, if the original union had been successful and had produced a line of descendants, it was thought particularly auspicious to renew the relationship between wife-givers and wife-takers in a cross-cousin marriage. For such a marriage, Maale did not even consult the intestine oracle: Having produced descendants of descendants, the original link between the two lineages was obviously a fertile one, one to be repeated and reinforced in the present. If, after four generations, a cross-cousin marriage was not arranged, the two descent groups became alaga, nonrelatives.

If a girl's lineage "gave" her in marriage, the groom's "took" her. Indeed, there was no other way to express the fact that a man married except to say that he "took a woman," lali ekene. All the preparations for the wedding revolved around the young man's actions. In order to marry, he had to mobilize help from kinsmen and neighbors to provide a feast for the girl's female relatives and to give a cloth to the girl's mother. The girl's female relatives (but not her male ones) had to receive gifts because it was they who had done the hard work of raising her – it was the mother's cloth the girl had urinated on while she was a child. Interestingly, although such gifts appeared to recognize women's labors, what they actually did was to de-emphasize women's procreative powers. Everything was done to underline the fact that the bride's father's gift of future fertility could never be repaid, but the bride's mother received only a cloth to replace the one that her daughter had spoiled as a child.

Where was the bride in the discourse that defined marriage? In fact, she had a great deal of influence over whom she married. Fathers and mothers sometimes forbade certain marriages, but in actual practice it was difficult to prevent a determined girl from marrying whom she chose. But even if she chose, this fact did not appear in how the marriage was talked about. Whatever she did, a bride was "given" by her father and "taken" by her husband. To say that a woman married, one said simply that she "went," loene. This verb, which meant precisely to go along level ground, was one of a set of three that meant variously to go down in elevation, to go up, or to go at about the same altitude. No woman ever "took" a husband; she simply "went" – neither up nor down but from her father's compound to her husband's.

Households, once constituted, provided the context for the definition of the relationship between parents and children. And notions of gender and fertility conditioned the definition of filiation in Maale. This became clear in a conversation I had with a Maale elder. When I explained that some people practice matri-filiation and asked him why Maale children belonged to the lineages of their fathers – not mothers – the old man exclaimed, exasperated, "Well, it's the man who did it, isn't it?" In other words, it was the man's active fertilizing force that produced the child; it was he who planted the seed. Without him, there would have been no crop. The crop, therefore, belonged to the father.

I use the word "belong" advisedly, for in Maale the notion of filiation was intimately related to that of ownership. Indeed, one might say that ownership was a kind of filiation rather than the reverse; that is, owners of things were thought of as those persons whose force of fertility and

Children, the wealth of Maale, 1984. An elder sister, in the middle, is taking care of her younger brother.

fortune "begat" the thing. One of the principal ways of referring to possession (besides simple possessives such as "his" or "hers") was with the notion of parenthood. When, for example, a man saw an axe along a path and inquired who its owner was, he asked literally who the axe's "father" was. (For the smaller class of distinctively female things such as pots, a person would ask who the pot's "mother" was.) The act of begetting carried with it, then, a notion of an inherent right to control. In this respect, fertility fetishism in Maale inverted commodity fetishism within capitalism: Instead of things apparently having power over people, people appeared to beget things.

In this cultural world, wealth was ultimately a matter of descendants, not of things. For an adult, particularly a male adult, to die without children was the misfortune of all misfortunes. Maale said that such a person died "with a bad taste in his mouth," that is, he died tragically early, in the morning, as it were, before he had had time to rinse out his mouth. Almost everything was done to separate, indeed to obliterate, such misfortunes from memory and from continuing life. Fields of a man who died without descendants (fields designated by a special term, gabile) became ritually impure, and no one was allowed to take seeds from them. The dead person's name was tabooed, and anyone in the vicinity who happened to have the same name would change it. If pointedly questioned about such cases, Maale, depending on their distance from the person who had died, responded variously with information in lowered voices, awkward pauses, and evidently painful silences. In cultural terms, these deaths were almost too much to think about. Persons without descendants became black holes in genealogical space.

The opposite of these tragedies, indeed the kind of social success that made such cases *so* poignantly tragic, was the elder who died leaving many children and children of children. His funeral took on an air of celebration. Before his body was buried, the old man's eldest son knelt over the corpse and touched his forehead three times to the forehead of his father. (He would do the same four times when his mother died.) In this way, the eldest son – and only the eldest son – inherited his father's position, his force of character, his power to curse and to bestow fertility. The word for forehead in Maale, balliti, is the same one used to refer more generally to a concept of "fortune," "luck," "power" – in a word, fertility.[12]

To summarize, gender provided the ground for fetishization of fertility in Maale. To be a man was to generate. To be a woman was to reproduce, but in a way that entirely depended on a man. These categories motivated the hierarchy of persons in Maale from the ritual king to chiefs to subchiefs to senior lineage elders to more junior ones and finally to

---

[12] In his installation rituals, the king wore an iron phallus on his forehead. The symbolic connections between forehead, fortune, and male fertility were, then, explicit.

A funeral dance for a successful elder in 1974. The man's teapot, used to serve honey wine in Maale, is being held above the dancers' heads. It symbolizes the dead man's wealth and generosity.

wives. In an important sense, there were not just two genders, plus an anomalous third. There was in fact a continuous gradation of maleness from the ritual king to chiefs to subchiefs on down. This interpretation was made by the Maale themselves when they referred metaphorically to chiefs as the king's "wives." In relation to the king, the chiefs were more "female." And something similar appeared in the ritual of making younger brothers "go out"; there, eldest brothers put their right arm across the gate to their ancestral cattle corral and made younger brothers go out of the corral under their arm. Symbolically eldest brothers were asserting that their generative powers had produced the younger brothers and were now sending them into the world. In this sense, eldest brothers were more "male" than younger ones.

The ritual king, the kati, was the end of the continuum that anchored the whole system. He was the male principle incarnate. The taboos that surrounded the king's ritual residence, the so-called lion house, illustrated this in interesting ways. No woman of childbearing age could enter the king's compound, and most female domestic labor was done by ashtime, transvestites. Indeed, kings traditionally protected ashtime and gathered them into their compounds. The night before any royal ritual those taking part slept in the lion house because it was taboo to have sexual relations with women. But lying with an ashtime was not interdicted.[13] It was as if the king and the entirely male relationships that surrounded him in the lion house provided a nucleus that dominated and provided direction for the more female surrounding medium – everything else in Maale. Ironically here, ashtime, otherwise symbols of sterility, became part of the generativity of maleness in Maale.

After discussing the concept of commodities and of fetishism of commodities, Marx used these culturally specific notions to construct schemata to explain how productive inequalities are reproduced. And one of his major contributions in *Capital* was the explanation of why the continuance of class relations could never be an entirely smooth process but in fact required a certain dynamic, a certain cycle of booms and busts, set against a background of technological innovation and changes in class consciousness.

A comparable analysis of the laws of motion – to use too grand a phrase – of noncapitalist modes of production has barely begun. Instead, there has been a persistent tendency within Marxism, beginning with Marx himself, to assume that noncapitalist modes have no such dynamic. In this respect, as I pointed out in the Introduction, Marxist theory has borrowed from a long line of bourgeois scholarship that has portrayed technologically simpler societies as static instead of dynamic, as based on status rather than on contract, on tradition rather than modernity. In such views of so-called precapitalist societies, social reproduction hardly becomes problematic.

In the Conclusion, I shall return to the issue of why this image of non-Western societies arose. From the results of decades of ethnography (unavailable to Marx himself), it is clear that such a point of view is, quite simply, wrong. If so, what tendencies can be seen in the reproduction of Maale inequalities? What dynamic animated reproduction schemata?

As I have shown above, there were three main productive inequalities among Maale: household heads over their wives and coresident children; senior lineage elders over more junior ones and their dependents; and finally the chiefs and king over others. In maintaining their positions, the dominant men in all these relationships acted to maximize

---

[13] What Western societies would classify as homosexual behavior did not affect the gender identity of a man unless he assumed the receptive role. Consequently, men who had sexual relations with ashtime were hardly the less "male" for it.

not profits, but the number of persons who could be counted as dependent on their fertility. This strategy gave them access to control over the results of others' labor, and as I shall show below, such control could be used, in turn, to expand the range of persons who could be considered as dependent on their fertility.

In all three productive inequalities there were cyclical sets of patterns that interacted, within limits, to reproduce inequalities over time. Let me begin with households. Over the developmental cycle, there were definite changes in a domestic unit's ability to produce a surplus, accompanied by changes in the pattern of typical conflicts and coalitions. The early years of a new household were the most precarious, and the divorce frequency during the first five years of marriage was by far greater than at any other time. After especially bad arguments, particularly after beatings, a young wife often retreated to her parental home, and her father and brothers refused to return her until her husband showed contrition. Being in a position to take back his daughter, the father once again was able to emphasize that it was he who "gave" her and that consequently his son-in-law was eternally beholden.[14]

One Maale elder described newly-founded households in the following terms: "In Maale, young wives are their husband's 'enemies.' After they have borne us many children, they become our 'relatives,' but while they are still young, they are treacherous." He went on, with much disapproval, to tell a (probably apocryphal) story of a young wife who, while surreptitiously seeing a lover, murdered her husband. In other words, relationships between young husbands and wives were interpreted (especially by men) in relation to Maale gender concepts: men as orderly and responsible, pitted against women as unpredictable and irresponsible. It is ironic and perhaps noteworthy that young women's resistance to what was objectively an unequal relationship merely confirmed Maale gender ideologies. Women, particularly young women who questioned husbands' dominance, *were* quarrelsome and unpredictable.

As young wives had more and more children into middle age, the conflict between men and their wives usually subsided. There seem to have been a number of reasons for this transformation. Often with three to five children by the age of thirty-five, middle-aged wives probably found it more difficult to exit from unpleasant situations, and their parents may have been less willing to take on the support of many non-

---

[14] This line of argument was inspired by Jane F. Collier's *Marriage and Inequality in Classless Societies* (Stanford: Stanford University Press, 1988).

working children. Also by that time, wives had greater interests in preserving their husbands' households; children were women's future source of support and influence.

But as important as these reasons, I would argue, was the fact that the objective economic contradiction between men and their wives had lessened, if not disappeared. Remember that husbands controlled only surpluses above consumption. As Chapter 1 showed, middle-aged men's households had so many nonworking (but consuming) children, such a low supply of labor relative to consumption requirements, that they produced very little surplus. In other words, the household head's control of the product above consumption momentarily was of little social consequence. Inasmuch as both husbands' and wives' futures depended on their children, their interests began to coincide. A lull between two storms, middle-aged households were preoccupied with rearing the next generation.

When the oldest child began full-time work, the household's situation began to change. Specifically, its relative labor supply began steadily to increase. By the time that most men and their wives reached elderhood, their households possessed the greatest surplus potential of any phase of development. Not surprisingly, this economic strength correlated with status. No older man or woman with children was addressed or referred to by his or her own names; rather a man was known by the more respectful teknonym, "father of X," a woman by "mother of X," X being their first child.

The elder and his wife, then, partially controlled the fruits of others' labor, particularly the labor of their eldest son and his wife. The eldest son and his wife carried out much of the household's work while parents managed and decided how household surpluses would be used. The typical pattern of conflict that resulted was related to this pattern of economic contradictions, but the discourse of conflict in elders' households – how tensions were conceived and talked about – partially masked such structures.

The position of the eldest son was pivotal. As his younger brothers, lower in status and standing, moved out to establish their own independent households, he was expected to stay in his father's household, still subordinate to his parents' authority. Having remained, as the Maale said, "to feed his father and mother," the eldest son could expect to inherit most of his father's wealth and his ritual position. After his father died, the eldest son would continue "to feed his father" in first-fruit rites, not only for himself but also on behalf of his younger brothers. If an eldest son did not fulfill his obligations during his father's lifetime, he could be disinherited, at least of his father's material wealth. Elders had the right to dispose of their property however they saw fit, and when they could, old men personally divided their property in spoken wills, just before death.

The weight of Maale conceptions about social continuity and orderly male reproduction fell, then, upon eldest sons, and any expression of conflict between eldest sons and their parents was a serious matter. Eldest sons' wives, however, occupied a different role. The simplest (and Maale) way of putting the matter is that wives were, after all, women. And women were unpredictable. It is not too surprising, then, that conflicts in elders' households typically involved disorderly daughters-in-law and their husbands' parents, particularly their mothers-in-law. Being women, daughters-in-law were considerably freer to express the tensions that economic asymmetry produced in their and their husbands' experience. As long as conflicts could be attributed to the deficient character of the young wife – her very femaleness – notions of orderly male social reproduction were protected.

Often what happened was that the eldest son and his wife temporarily moved out of his father's house until no younger siblings remained "to feed their parents." The wife (less often, the mother-in-law) was blamed, and the eldest son was able, as the saying goes, to have his cake and eat it too. He retained his prospects for inheritance (the separation was not *his* fault), and, like his younger brothers, he could enjoy economic independence, at least temporarily.

These processes tended, then, to reproduce household inequalities over time. The typical experiences produced by these patterns made ideological concepts such of those of gender seem all too real. In turn, ideological notions, of male fertility for example, explained and informed recurrent kinds of social outcomes. Conflicts, at least the sorts described above, did little to call ideological notions into question. Just the opposite. They appear to have been crucial parts of the overall process of reproducing inequalities.

Like the reproduction schemata for capitalist firms, these patterns operated only within certain limits. Household heads, as I have said, had the power to control surpluses above consumption. This immediately made the level of consumption itself a political fact, and a variety of customs seemed almost designed to prevent "overexploitation" of wives and children. Although husbands had the right to open granaries one by one, wives had the right to decide on the day-to-day taking of crops

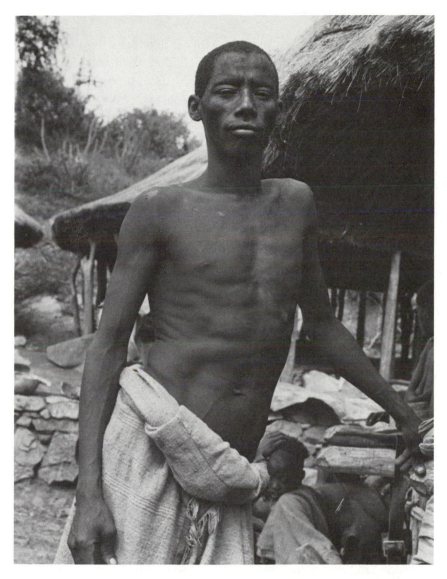

An eldest son in mourning, about to inherit his father's position, 1975

from whichever granary was in use. It was taboo for a husband to inter-
fere in this process, and his doing so was interpreted as a gome – a
transgression and a potential source of misfortune. Women, thus, were
given the power to ensure a decent level of support for themselves and
their children. This level was socially determined; it reflected patterns

of interaction throughout the economy, not just ones internal to productive units.

If this "reasonable" level of consumption was consistently compromised, wives had the right to divorce their husbands and to find new ones who would provide for them. While children were young, they accompanied their divorced mothers, and growing up in stepfathers' households, children were likely to be ritually filiated to descent groups of their mothers' new husbands. A husband, therefore, could go only so far. If he pushed his wife beyond a certain limit – using too much household production for reasons other than consumption – he risked losing everything.

Once socially defined levels of consumption were met, how did husbands use surpluses? In general, the principal goal involved the exchange of grain (perishable) for goats and cattle (which continued to reproduce). This was done in one of two ways. The first involved barter; whole granaries were bartered for cattle and goats. The second involved the establishment of a permanent kin-like relationship in which one partner gave crops (sometimes supplemented by goats or honey) and the other gave a young heifer or steer. In this way, the two became belli, bond kinsmen, and they addressed each other with "bee" – the greeting used between brothers and sisters.

So far I have deferred mentioning the wider lineage context within which men's households developed. Clearly, the same factors that shaped the development of stem family households (the prominence of the eldest son versus others and his inheritance of his father's ritual position and wealth) set the stage for the development of conical lineages. What other factors were involved in the reproduction of inequalities between eldest and younger brothers?

If a key material transformation in the reproduction of household inequalities was the conversion of grain into cattle, the comparable process for descent groups, at least those in the horticultural highlands, was the conversion of cattle into rights over land. In the nineteenth century, most of the highlands was divided into plots of land known as dini, and these were owned by individuals, usually by senior lineage elders. Ownership in this case was not focused on excluding others from one's land; just the reverse – dini owners attempted to attract as many followers as they could to cultivate their land. These followers were required occasionally to brew beer for the owner or to work in his fields. In other words, a quasi-tributary relationship existed between owners and others, a relationship justified, like all inequalities in Maale, by the notion that it was the owner's power over fertility that was partly responsible for prosperity and product.

This kind of tributary control over land was crucial for the development of large, coresident lineages. For despite the fact that household processes continually produced male sibling sets differentiated between eldest and younger brothers, no coercive power existed to require younger brothers to continue to live close to their eldest brothers and hence to subject themselves to various ritual demands for cattle. With some effort, any younger brother could move away from his eldest (even to other ethnic groups surrounding Maale), sever old lineage ties, and set up an independent descent group, as a new follower of a locally prominent man. Indeed, for younger brothers in descent groups without much wealth in land, mobility seems to have been the norm.

Senior elders within developing lineages were, then, in a delicate position. If they pushed juniors too far, if they took away too many cattle when making their younger brothers "go out," they risked their position of seniority. For seniors without juniors were not seniors. Being able to keep juniors in their place – and thus sending resources up the lineage hierarchy – depended on seniors' ability to dispense various kinds of favors. Support in cases of social conflict, help in marrying and sponsoring wedding feasts, and, perhaps most important, access to land on a basis guaranteed by kin ties were just some examples.

How did senior lineage elders build up the wealth necessary to found lineages in the first place? It is precisely here that the role of raiding and hunting becomes important. No more masculinizing acts existed in Maale – none more implicated in fertility and power over fortune – than raiding cattle from enemy peoples, killing a large game animal like a lion or buffalo, or killing an enemy. A man beginning a lineage, and descendants after him, who were successful in these connected pursuits were more likely to be able to gain control over land, for raided cattle or other animals received in exchange for buffalo or lion skins could be traded for land. And gaining control over land meant that succeeding elders would have more to offer followers and would be more likely to be able to keep juniors in their positions of dependence. That meant, in turn, that large, ramified descent groups would form.

The continuance of large lineage groups depended, of course, on more than wealth in land. In times of crisis (a serious drought may have occurred as often as every generation), those without crops or cattle had to trade land away. In time, lineages grew and declined, as senior elders were more or less successful in controlling wealth in its various forms.

Hunting and especially raiding were critical in maintaining wealth, since they tended to shift the burden of reproduction from within the group to without. In this context, the celebration of raiding and of hunting and the connection of these pursuits with maleness and fertility appear not just as aspects of Maale "culture." Rather, they make sense as motivated parts of the experience that men and women had in living in this particular political economy – in seeing certain lineage elders succeed and others fail.

From the reproduction of household and descent group inequalities, let me turn finally to those between commoners and the chiefs and king. At first glance, this relationship – tributary rather than based on descent or gender – seems qualitatively different from those discussed above. In fact, there are important continuities. Lineages, inasmuch as they depended upon land ownership, already operated on quasi-tributary relationships between senior owners and junior followers. What chiefship and kingship did in this context was to repeat and extend the same notions and relationships, as inequality was pyramided on inequality. The dynamics of this process was distinctive inasmuch as it involved new actors: heads of large lineages in competition with chiefs, and chiefs in competition with the king.

Chiefs were almost invariably the heads of large ramified lineages. Obviously, the causal relationship between office and lineage went in both directions; that is, holding chiefly office gave heads of local descent groups advantages in keeping juniors beneath them. But the opposite was also true. Heads of large lineages tended to become chiefs. The ideology of chiefship obscured this latter process to the degree that it denied the very possibility of replacing a chief (without the previous chiefly line in office the land's fertility would be destroyed). Replacements did in fact occur, however, and when kings appointed new lines to office, they looked to heads of large lineages. To the Maale, the wealth of these men, both in dependents and in possessions, proved their mystical powers over fertility and fortune. And, more mundanely, such men occupied an advantageous position in gathering tribute for the king; they had, first of all, a large following of kinsmen to call upon.

Even though replacements of chiefly lines were probably infrequent during most periods (actually the rate depended upon the king's power vis-à-vis important chiefs, and this, as I shall show below, waxed and waned), there was a continuous, if subterranean, competition between chiefs and the heads of other important lineages within their districts. If a chief alienated the king, if the tribute he brought was inadequate, ultimately he risked losing his position to others. For it was always in the interests of other lineage heads to advertise, as it were, their availability, by giving large tributes to the king. In this context, tribute was not so much something forced out of chiefs and lineage heads; it actually was in their own interests to give, since tribute validated givers' claims over fertility and thus over the labor of those beneath them.

Chiefs were only occasionally replaced, but the line that occupied the kingship appears not to have been changed since the founding of the kingdom. Again, it is difficult to separate the claims of ideology from actual historical processes (nowhere was there more at stake than with regard to kingship). But it seems unlikely that wholesale changes in the kingly lineage took place. What did change was the line within the royal lineage that was installed in office. Such changes were related to struggles between holders of the kingship and the occupants of the two most important chiefships in the center of Maale.

The chiefs of these two districts, Bola and Makana, could not be replaced by the king. They, along with the elders of Bola, chose the next king by consulting the intestine oracle, and they played primary roles in the rituals that installed and confirmed a new king in his office. In effect, the king and the chiefs of Bola and Makana were the three most powerful men in Maale, interconnected in a triangular relationship in which two were often allied against a third. If a king grew especially strong, he invited the opposition of the two chiefs, who could delay important rituals in his confirmation. Similarly, if one of the chiefs somehow grew too powerful, the interests of the king and the other chief made them natural allies in opposing any further usurpation of privileges.

The state of these triangular relationships influenced the process by which lines that occupied the kingship were changed. Whenever a king died, two alternatives presented themselves. The first, by far the most common, was to install the dead king's first son (in the nineteenth century and earlier, the king was allowed to have only one wife). But another possibility existed, one that had to be used when a king died without male heirs. That was to decide, in essence, that the deceased king had not been a "real" king at all; if he had, he would not have died without male issue. One of the dead man's brothers was then installed as king. If the brother had already died, his bones were dug up and ritually installed, after which the brother's living son was made to succeed. In this way, the perfect chain of connecting links that extended back to the first king of Maale was preserved, but the particular line within the lineage that occupied office was replaced.

The chief of Bola, 1974

If a king grew especially exploitative, if he alienated the chiefs of both Bola and Makana, this stratagem could be used even though he had produced sons to inherit. The Bola elders and the chiefs of Bola and Makana could decide that the country had been destroyed and that the land's fertility had dissipated. Rather than installing the dead king's son (who carried the same supposed lack of power over fertility and who, more mundanely, might be presumed to carry on the overweening ways of his father), the elders and the chiefs could install a brother of the dead man. Relationships within the royal lineage were then reformed and reordered. What had previously been a junior line was made into the senior one, and kinship terms were appropriately recast. This kind of reordering of royal relationships occurred once during the twentieth century after Maale had been incorporated into imperial Ethiopia, but it appears always to have been an option, in the nineteenth century and before.[15]

Inequality stacked upon inequality, each interacting with the other, Maale political economy was composed of an ensemble of reproductive patterns and cycles. Nothing was guaranteed about any of these processes. Some households failed. Husbands misjudged their possibilities and lost their wives and children. One man's loss was another's gain, and while some failed, others succeeded on an even larger scale.

One step higher in the hierarchy of inequalities, some lineages did not manage to stay together. Without the right mix of internal pressure on juniors and external sources of wealth, lineage seniors sometimes found themselves without juniors. That meant that other prominent men gained followers. Finally, some chiefs and kings did not keep or pass on their positions. Misjudging their rivals, whether heads of important lineages or brothers, or alienating their closest associates, some chiefs and kings were replaced.

Over the ups and downs of these processes, what stayed more-or-less the same was the way men gained power over others, the way that they thought about inequalities. In other words, what remained constant was the way of producing in Maale.

So far, I have analyzed Maale in itself, rather than as an instance of a more general mode of production. By doing so, I have postponed issues surrounding determination – determination of reproduction schemata by productive inequalities and of inequalities by productive powers. For it is only in comparisons between societies that determination becomes clear.

Here, as with the related problem of functional alternatives, I can only sketch possible answers. Too much depends upon kinds of research not yet done. Let me begin with the relationship between productive powers and inequalities, using the results and terms of reference established in non-Marxist anthropology. For the level of productive powers generally described by Meillassoux for his domestic mode of production and actually observed in Maale, what is the full range of compatible productive inequalities? The first source of information, approximate as it is, is

---

[15] For a study of this kind of reordering of royal relationships among the Tswana of southern Africa, see John Comaroff, "Rules and Rulers: Political Processes in a Tswana Chiefdom," *Man* 13 (1978): 1–20.

George P. Murdock's work on cross-cultural comparisons. Out of the 563 societies listed in Murdock's sample, 63 depended on extensive slash-and-burn cereal horticulture for significantly more than half of their subsistence. Of these, 22 were stateless, 39 were chiefdoms, and only 2 were classified by Murdock as states.[16]

It would seem that there is a strong association between the level of development of productive powers that we have been discussing and productive inequalities associated with so-called tribal societies (that is, ones in which inequalities are formulated only in kinship terms) and chiefdoms (societies that include, in addition, weakly developed tributary relationships). The question is whether tribes and chiefdoms are two variants of the same mode of production or whether they belong to different modes. So far, anthropologists and others have provided different answers. Both Marshall Sahlins and Gerhard Lenski, for example, lump tribes and chiefdoms together as "advanced horticultural societies" and "tribesmen" respectively, whereas Eric Wolf has recently taken the other tack of separating domestic modes of production from "tributary" ones (the latter category comprehending societies from Maale to feudal Europe to imperial China).[17]

There are several reasons for believing that the first alternative permits a better categorization of empirical materials. First, no study, as far as I am aware, has been able to show that the level of development of productive powers is higher in chiefdoms than in kin-based societies. Second, in world history there seems to have been a constant flux between tribes and chiefdoms; many tribes evolved into chiefdoms, and chiefdoms disintegrated into tribes. It is difficult to document these changes historically, but social anthropology has at least one well-analyzed example in Edmund Leach's study of the Kachin.[18]

Third and perhaps most important, the type of inequality between chiefs and their subjects is not radically different from that between, for example, fathers and sons or elder and younger brothers. Most of all, the power of chiefs is not backed by a monopoly of coercive force and does not, therefore, reach directly into the productive affairs of domestic groups beneath. Instead, inequality is stacked upon inequality, without

[16] George P. Murdock, *Ethnographic Atlas* (Pittsburgh: University of Pittsburgh Press, 1967).

[17] Marshall Sahlins, *Tribesmen* (Englewood Cliffs, N.J.: Prentice-Hall, 1968); Eric R. Wolf, *Europe and the People Without History* (Berkeley: University of California Press, 1982), chap. 3; Gerhard Lenski, *Power and Privilege: A Theory of Social Stratification* (New York: McGraw–Hill, 1966), chap. 7.

[18] Edmund Leach, *Political Systems of Highland Burma: A Study of Kachin Social Structure* (London: Athlone Press, 1954).

any radical change in the productive constitution of households. Only tribute – a varying amount of goods given not so much out of fear of punishment but for basically ritual and religious reasons – is sent up in hierarchy. According to Sahlins, a chief "is usually spokesman of his group and master of its ceremonies, with otherwise little influence, few functions, and no privileges. One word from him and everyone does as he pleases."[19] This description is perhaps an overstatement, but it vividly illustrates the contrast with more developed modes of production in which kings control access to land in such a way that tribute is backed by the coercive arm of the state.

If tribes and chiefdoms are only two moments of the same mode of production, what determines those moments and how is the transition made from one to the other? Jonathan Friedman's insightful analysis of the Kachin case provides an answer.[20] Below, I use his arguments to sketch a brief description of the dynamic of the mode of production of which Maale appears as a particular example.

Let me begin with a hypothetical case of conjugal family households in which productive inequalities oppose husbands to wives. Let me assume further that husbands' effective power is upheld by a system of patrilineal ancestor propitiation in which only married men are thought capable of interceding with ancestral spirits to assure fertility and social continuity. No doubt, there are other superstructural ways of stabilizing power differences in this mode of production; belief in ancestral spirits is just one such way.[21]

Now, imagine that something begins to encourage a concentration of power in the hands of particular men. We have already seen how competition over people – given the right conditions – could lead to such a result. This new degree of power can be stably reproduced – given the structure of the mode of production – in extremely limited ways. In the present case, there are basically two ways. Either productive inequalities can be expanded in scope (that is, fathers can keep married sons in their households to form stem or grand family household systems, for example), or inequalities can be stacked on top of each other. The latter alternative would maintain households as they are but bind certain

---

[19] Sahlins, *Tribesmen*, p. 21.
[20] Jonathan Friedman, "Tribes, States, and Transformations," in Maurice Bloch, ed., *Marxist Analyses and Social Anthropology* (London: Malaby Press, 1975), pp. 161–202.
[21] It is beyond the scope of this essay to analyze other superstructural arrangements that are functional equivalents to the Maale ones discussed here. It is, nevertheless, important to recognize that such equivalents appear to exist. I shall return to this issue toward the end of this chapter.

household heads in tribute-like relationships to others. Given the nature of kinship systems, there are only certain ways this can be done. One way that recurs in the ethnographic record involves the formation of conical lineages; that is, all younger brothers are made "tributary" to eldest ones.

I should emphasize that in my just-so story, the powerful *become* eldest brothers rather than eldest brothers becoming powerful (although once power has been institutionalized and defined by this particular kind of superstructural arrangement, the latter occurs to the degree that power is stably reproduced across generations). That kinship relations are reformed to fit the distribution of actual power is evident in many ethnographic reports.[22] The point here is that new power relations have to be legitimated somehow, and, given the pattern of kinship ideology, there are only certain ways of accomplishing this. One involves the formation of conical lineages with eldest brothers given the sole role of making sacrifices to the ancestors. The eldest brother becomes the only intermediary, the principal embodiment of control over fertility and fortune.

In this movement toward greater concentration of power, notice exactly what has changed. A new inequality has been instituted with regard to the production of a society's total product, and this inequality has been culturally defined and legitimated by a new mode of access to ancestral propitiation. But it would be a mistake to conclude in this case, as Maurice Godelier and Jonathan Friedman have done, that "religion" functions as a productive relation.[23] The new productive inequality, like every other one, is instituted materially; if the eldest brother had only status and no real control over division of the total social product, then we would not refer to a new productive inequality.

It is true that if the new inequality is to be stably reproduced over a period of time, the form of ancestral propitiation described above (or some other superstructural arrangement) is necessary. But to say that "religion" functions as a productive inequality is misleading, not least because it implies that when productive inequalities are "economic," superstructural ideas are materially unimportant.

The process of pyramiding productive inequality on inequality can be extended at least two or three steps further. Minimal lineage heads can be made subordinate to chiefs, and chiefs subordinate to paramount chiefs.

---

[22] For an example, see Comaroff, "Rules and Rulers," and Edmund Leach, *Pul Eliya: A Village in Ceylon* (Cambridge: Cambridge University Press, 1961).
[23] Friedman, "Tribes, States, and Transformations," and Godelier, *Perspectives in Marxist Anthropology*.

Subordination consists of two aspects: To qualify as a productive inequality, it must consist of some power to collect tribute in labor or in kind. And this raw power must be legitimated and culturally clothed, in the present case, by notions of the privileged and prior access of chiefs to power over fertility and good fortune.

Just how far the process of pyramiding may go is not clear, although there are obviously limits.[24] The more intervening links between the king at the apex and direct producers at the bottom, the more difficult it becomes to collect tribute. Consequently, as chiefdoms grow, they routinely segment. Unlike states, chiefdoms have no developed coercive power at their center to prevent segmentation. Each lower-level chief serves the same economic, political, and ideological functions as the one at the apex, so that relatively few organic ties bind the polity. Units at the periphery regularly secede. Tributes are no longer sent, and the king's mystical power over local fertility is no longer acknowledged.[25]

Segmentation depends, of course, on the availability of land. Let us assume for the moment that extra territory is not available. Assuming a fixed area of land, a dependence on extensive swidden horticulture, and the level of productive powers described above, total output should, as Friedman has argued, depend on labor input in the manner shown in figure 5 (overleaf).

Figure 5 is constructed on the assumption that each person works the same length of time so that population size (and density) is directly proportional to total labor input. The straight line, C, represents the fixed measure of consumption that every worker requires both for him or herself and for nonworking dependents. And the curved line T is the maximum possible total output.

Potential surplus – the difference between T and C – and how potential surplus relates to population density are the critical questions. There are three regions of the production function to consider: First, with population densities up to P_1, the addition of another adult at any point will

<hr />

[24] Henry T. Wright and Gregory A. Johnson, "Population, Exchange, and Early State Formation in Southwestern Iran," *American Anthropologist* 77 (1975): 267–89, define a state (the next most developed polity after chiefdoms in most typologies) as having three administrative levels: ". . . the highest level involves making decisions about other, lower-order decisions rather than about any particular condition or movement of material goods or people'" (p. 267). Traditional Maale had three distinct levels of political offices, but the highest level was not functionally specialized to any significant degree; decisions that the ritual king made were more or less of the same type as those of chiefs below him.

[25] On the so-called segmentary state, see Aidan W. Southall, *Alur Society: A Study in Processes and Types of Domination* (Cambridge: W. Heffer, 1956).

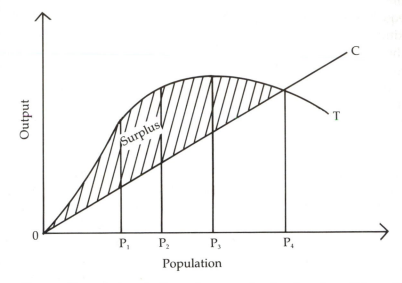

Figure 5: Theoretical production and consumption functions for swidden cultivators (after Friedman, "Tribes, States, and Transformations," p. 182).

result in a constantly increasing increment in potential surplus. This obviously is the region in which productive inequalities can be most easily
pyramided. A chief, by gathering around him more and more followers,
will be able to extract increasingly more tribute with every person added,
all other factors being held constant. Since most of the surplus will be
redistributed to the chiefs' followers, chiefship in this region of the production function may actually benefit many of the populace, even if it
does so unevenly.

The second region of population density, from P_1 to P_2, has different
characteristics. With each new person added to the territory, the total
surplus continues to rise, but it does so at a decelerating rate. That is, at
any point in this region, the potential surplus that an additional person
allows is always less than that added by the previous person. *Total* potential surplus nevertheless continues to rise with increases in population density. Since pyramiding is dependent on total surplus, it can continue to expand in this region, but its presence is obviously approaching
a limit, namely, P_2.

After P_2, a third portion of the production function commences, in
which total potential surplus decreases with each new person added.
This decrease results from well-known causes: An increase in population density requires a decrease in average length of fallow for swidden
fields. And with a decrease in fallow, and therefore of fertility of fields,

each unit of labor begins to produce less and less. Total output climaxes at P_3 and assuming, as we have done, that people continue to work the same length of time per day, total yield begins to decrease with increasing population density until the limit of P_4 is reached.

From P_2 to P_4, therefore, a certain amount of economic and political devolution must take place. The only way that chiefs could continue to appropriate the same amount of surplus would be to force subjects to work longer hours, and chiefs generally do not enjoy such powers. Presumably, in this context, chiefdoms tend to destratify and productive inequalities to "unstack" toward tribal organization. Either chiefs accept their fates and subside into mere figureheads, or they persist in pressing demands past what material conditions will bear, and revolts from below reestablish more egalitarian relationships.[26] Relatively high population densities – without a change in technology – lead theoretically to fewer productive inequalities. This is a process that Jack Goody, for example, has argued is supported by the ethnographic record.[27]

The conclusion to this line of thinking is that nineteenth-century Maale was apparently only one moment, one instance of a more complex set of possibilities circumscribed by its mode of production. Observed at a different point in time, Maale political economy might have looked quite different – even though productive inequalities remained broadly the same.[28] Within the possible variants of this way of producing, there operated a certain unitary dynamic. The competition in rights over people drove the social system toward greater complexity, toward tributary inequalities grafted onto domestic ones. Simply put, Meillassoux's domestic mode of production appears to involve considerably more than domestic inequalities.

Instead of a Sherlock Holmes mystery, this chapter and the one before it have turned into what Northrop Frye called an anatomy.[29] Anatomies

[26] For an example, see Leach, *Political Systems of Highland Burma.*
[27] Jack Goody, "Population and Polity in the Voltaic Region," in J. Friedman and M. J. Rowlands, eds., *The Evolution of Social Systems* (London: Duckworth, 1977).
[28] Even though technological sophistication remains constant in the scenario above, the level of productive powers changes with population size. As the mass of productive powers increases, productive inequalities at first increase, then decrease, as the size of the surplus increases and then decreases. In other words, there appears to be a certain equilibrium point around which the relationship between powers and inequalities may oscillate. This oscillation, for technologically less developed societies, is tied to population processes.
[29] Northrop Frye, *The Anatomy of Criticism: Four Essays* (Princeton: Princeton University Press, 1957).

are large-scale attempts to show how apparently disparate and uncon-
nected facts are parts of a single, articulated pattern. Essential human
nature; the sexual division of labor in Maale; the relationships between
husbands and wives, between fathers and sons, and between eldest and
younger brothers; the connections between Maale ideas of personhood,
of ownership, and of reproduction; the conferral of individuals' own
powers over fortune and fertility to a fetishized notion of a more "male"
other; the definition of kingship as the embodiment of male gender; the
placement of Maale as one moment in a series of possibilities that includes both tribes and chiefdoms: A historical materialist analysis has
required attention to all of these topics.

Why then were Maale households constituted as they were? By now,
it should be clear that there are a number of levels on which this question can be answered. Households were, first of all, shaped by the fact
that Maale occupied one particular moment in a series of possibilities
given by a larger mode of production. That moment involved other productive inequalities besides domestic ones – inequalities between lineage elders and juniors and between the king and chiefs and commoners. These latter relationships provided the context in which households
were formed, and, if they did not fundamentally reorder relationships
within domestic groups, higher-order productive inequalities nonetheless affected how households operated.

Within the context defined by kings, chiefs, and lineage elders, households were continually created by a set of recurrent, interconnected
practices. Households engendered children, "males" and "females," for
whom the concept of maleness was intimately tied up with mystified
power over fertility and with actual power over women and children. In
this way, political power in Maale was grafted onto biological sex; political economy became sexual, and sex, economic and political.[30] "Males"
and "females" produced by these practices married and re-created, in
turn, household structures in such a way that differences between "men"
and "women," atinke and lali, were confirmed by patterns of ordinary
experience.

All these processes were required to produce domestic units in Maale.
The neoclassical analysis of Chapter 1 assumed them as givens and pro-
ceeded to work out certain logical relationships among labor time, the
ratio of consumers to workers within households, and possible patterns

[30] Gayle Rubin, "The Traffic in Women: Notes on the 'Political Economy' of Sex," in Rayna
R. Reiter, ed., *Toward an Anthropology of Women* (New York: Monthly Review Press, 1975),
pp. 157–210.

of labor flow among households. But because what is assumed cannot at the same time be explained, Chapter 1 necessarily could not, I contended, deal with larger issues of history, power, and ideology.

How much further has the present Marxist inquiry progressed? I would argue that we have begun to bring power and ideology into focus. In fact, these two have been shown to be inseparably related. In order to be regularly reproduced, productive inequalities require certain sets of cultural discourses and practices that naturalize systems of domination; they require, in other words, ideologies. To the degree that people live within these discourses and practices, ideologies explain power. But Marxism asserts the reverse as well. Productive inequalities, as de facto distributions of power, "select" ideologies. Ideologies exist because they stabilize and secure a certain kind of power. Following out these connections in the relationships between kings and commoners, eldest and younger brothers, fathers and eldest sons, we have now, I suggest, a fuller understanding of power/ideology.

And yet some part of the analysis of these two is still missing, and that part relates to a lack of specification of the third master concept of this book – history. So far, I have constructed a set of reproduction schemata, a set of recurrent practices animated by a system of cultural understandings, in turn confirmed by repeated kinds of experience. These schemata show a certain internal dynamic, a tendency toward stacking inequality upon inequality, driven by an endemic competition in rights over people. But in no sense can the foregoing analysis, nor, for that matter, Marx's own reproduction schemata in *Capital*, be considered an explanation of particular events located in historical time. Both are schematic models of central tendencies in social orders, considered over whole epochs. It is for this reason that I have used the phrase "epochal structures" in the titles of this chapter and the last.

Implied in this phrase is the notion that societies can be placed into certain broad types and that history can be divided, at least roughly, into contrasting epochs. According to Marxist theory, the distinctive feature that demarcates social types and historical epochs is the nature of productive inequalities. Power differences grounded in material life define epochal structures. The polysemy of the adjective "epochal" is useful here, for productive inequalities are not only those patterns that delineate epochs. They are also those structures, according to Marxist theory, with particularly important consequences.

One of these consequences, according to the reproduction schemata constructed above (and in *Capital*), is that productive inequalities, once

in place, set up a certain pressure to persist. This indeed is what reproduction schemata set out to show: in outline, how inequalities are regularly reproduced. The difficulty with this kind of analysis – I shall call
it epochal analysis – is that it sometimes appears to set up a teleology, a
set of processes that go on behind the backs of social actors, outside
history.[31]

Indeed, according to one reading, reproduction schemata are no more
than orthodox functionalism in disguise. Only the terms of reference
have been changed; only what is reproduced is different – for Marxism,
inequalities, for functionalism, social units themselves. In this vein,
E. P. Thompson has written:

> . . . once capital has emerged on the page [in *Capital* and in the writings of
> structuralists like Althusser], its self-development is determined by the innate
> logic inherent within the category, and the relations so entailed, in much the
> same way as "the market" operates within bourgeois Political Economy, and
> still does so within some "modernization theory" today. Capital is an operative
> category which laws its own development. . . . This mode of analysis must
> necessarily be anti-historical, since the actual history can only be seen as the
> expression of ulterior laws. . . . This is an extraordinary mode of thought to
> find in a materialist, for capital has become Idea, which unfolds itself in his-
> tory.[32]

On these grounds, Thompson rejects epochal analysis and seeks to substitute for it what he calls the logic of historical method.

I have no wish to defend Marx (or Althusser) from Thompson's charges.
Implicit in my presentation, however, is a different reading of epochal
analysis, one that can be defended, I believe, in a way that ultimately
leads to, rather than away from, history. In order to illustrate my argument, let me return to the issue of the logic of functional explanations.

To recall, functional explanations are those in which the consequences
of a trait enter into the explanation of its persistence. In order for this
explanatory scheme to avoid a teleology (in which events later in time
are thought somehow to cause ones earlier), a feedback mechanism must
exist that connects the consequences of a trait with its persistence. In
modern Darwinian theory, for example, the generation of random genetic change, along with the operation of natural selection upon it, provides such a mechanism. No teleology is involved, then, in a statement

---

[31] I take the phrase "epochal analysis" from Raymond Williams, *Marxism and Literature*
(Oxford: Oxford University Press, 1977), pp. 121–2.
[32] E. P. Thompson, *The Poverty of Theory and Other Essays* (New York: Monthly Review
Press, 1978), p. 61.

such as "Birds have hollow bones because hollow bones facilitate flight." What this claim means is that genetic processes randomly created individual birds with lighter bones, and those birds consequently reproduced at higher rates.

Controversially, G. A. Cohen has argued that Marxism as a theoretical system can be defended even when feedback mechanisms cannot be specified.[33] In this respect, according to Cohen, functional explanations of biological traits were philosophically defensible *before* Darwin formulated the concept of natural selection. Even if Cohen is correct, it is clear (and he does not deny) that particular attempts to apply functional explanation can fall into a myriad of pitfalls. These have been described by many critics, among them Carl Hempel and Jon Elster. A consideration of some of these difficulties, in relation to the reproduction schemata above, will be helpful in establishing the limits of epochal analyses – of understanding exactly what they do and do not accomplish.

According to the presentation above, fertility fetishism existed in Maale from the late nineteenth century through the early twentieth because it instituted and upheld a certain degree of social inequality. This inequality existed because it was compatible with the level of productive powers and their further development. Let me consider some of the objections that could be raised against these "because" statements.

(1) Hempel has argued, as I pointed out in the previous chapter, that functional explanations have to consider the problem of what he called functional equivalents.[34] That is, other patterns of social thought could have fulfilled the same function as fertility fetishism, in which case we have not provided an explanation for the existence of the latter – even if it had the postulated effect of institutionalizing a certain degree of required inequality.

How one should distinguish functional equivalents is not clear.[35] In a trivial sense, every social trait may be said to be different from every other one. When should a difference count as "fundamental"? Is, for example, the productive inequality in capitalism different when workers

---

[33] G. A. Cohen, "Functional Explanation, Consequence Explanation, and Marxism," *Inquiry* 25 (1982): 27–56, was a response to Jon Elster's "Marxism, Functionalism and Game Theory," *Theory and Society* 11 (1982): 453–82; see also G. A. Cohen, "Functional Explanation: Reply to Elster," *Political Studies* 28 (1980); 129–35, a response to Elster's "Cohen on Marx's Theory of History," in the same issue of the journal, pp. 120–8.

[34] Carl G. Hempel, *Aspects of Scientific Explanation* (New York: Free Press, 1965), p. 311.

[35] G. A. Cohen has emphasized this point to me. I believe that he nonetheless minimizes the empirical problems posed by functional alternatives in *Karl Marx's Theory of History* (Oxford: Clarendon Press, 1978), pp. 274–7.

have the right to strike versus when they do not? A positive answer would seem to divide variants too finely, but it is not clear what general principle should be used to avoid such a result.

I do not propose to solve this conceptual problem. Rather, let me consider an example that, intuitively at least, appears to furnish a difference fundamental enough, on most any count, to constitute a true functional alternative to the Maale system described above: At broadly the same level of technological development, many highland New Guinea societies do not have chiefs but so-called big men, and the local idiom of power does not center on who begot whom but on who fed whom.[36] In these societies, notions of gender and of households are strikingly different from those in Maale. If such an alternative exists, we have not, in a strict sense, provided an explanation for the existence of fertility fetishism in Maale.

But, I would argue, this is not what epochal analyses attempt to do. In *Capital*, Marx did not provide an explanation of exactly why capitalist relations appeared in England. In Part VIII, he investigated some of the changes that logically had to occur – given the structure of the capitalist system. But, for the most part, Marx simply assumed the presence of capitalist relations and went on to explain how, once in place, they took on a certain momentum of their own. Similarly in the Maale case, we observed the presence of fertility fetishism and went on to explain how, once in place, it created a particular pressure in local social life. Hempel's point, therefore, does not invalidate epochal analyses but rather clarifies their explanatory claims. In the present case, why fertility fetishism, not some New Guinea equivalent, existed in Maale becomes a historical question – not one answerable in epochal terms.

(2) Elster has argued not only that a specification of feedback mechanisms between a trait's consequences and its persistence is required in valid functional explanations, but that such mechanisms are typically more complex than those involved in natural selection, at least as far as productive inequalities are concerned.[37] Human beings exist in cultural systems. Unlike genes, persons act intentionally. Therefore the feedback

---

[36] See J. A. Barnes, "African Models in the New Guinea Highlands," *Man* 62 (1962): 5–9; Andrew Strathern, "Kinship, Descent and Locality: Some New Guinea Examples," in Jack Goody, ed., *The Character of Kinship* (Cambridge: Cambridge University Press, 1973), pp. 21–33; Andrew Strathern, ed., *Inequality in New Guinea Highlands Societies* (Cambridge: Cambridge University Press, 1982); Marilyn Strathern, "Kinship and Economy: Constitutive Orders of a Provisional Kind," *American Ethnologist* 12 (1985): 191–209.

[37] Jon Elster, *Making Sense of Marx* (Cambridge: Cambridge University Press, 1985), pp. 27–9, and *Ulysses and the Sirens: Studies in Rationality and Irrationality*, rev. ed. (Cambridge: Cambridge University Press, 1984), pp. 28–35.

loops that occur in reproduction schemata typically involve a combination of intended and unintended consequences. Once unintended consequences are postulated, however, some link must be shown to exist
between them and actual intentions. According to Elster, this may be
accomplished by demonstrating that there are agents who (a) benefit
from the unintended consequences, (b) perceive that they benefit from
them, and (c) are able to reinforce the pattern in order to obtain those
benefits.[38]

The powerful in Maale – kings, chiefs, lineage elders, and husbands
– clearly benefited from fertility fetishism. They were also aware of this
benefit, I believe, even if their awareness was taken simply as the way
things should be. Finally, within limits, the powerful in Maale *did* act to
reinforce fertility fetishism. A woman who refused intercourse with her
husband could have her thighs slashed. A commoner who outraged Maale
customs could be ostracized, or in extreme cases, executed. In general,
the voices of the powerful influenced the formation of public opinion,
particularly in public forums like divinations and dispute settlements: in
which, for example, the misfortunes of a man who had defied his eldest
brother were decided to be the result of his transgression, or a drought
was said to be the result of the fact that commoners had not given enough
tribute to the chiefs and king.

Considering how functional explanations should be stated and defended helps to clarify two aspects of epochal analyses: on the one hand,
that they are limited in the sense that they do not give explanations of
history – of why what happened happened – and on the other, that
they nonetheless provide an essential prerequisite for historical understanding, a required first step.

With regard to the first point, this chapter began with an observation
that a set of productive inequalities was maintained roughly in the same
form in Maale from the late nineteenth century to the Ethiopian revolution. It then constructed a set of reproduction schemata that attempted
to explain some of the interconnections that gave rise to this persistence:
how Maale men and women continually acted in different structural
contexts to produce intended and unintended consequences, which in
turn had the effect of reproducing a certain system of inequality.

Nothing in this method of analysis implies that Maale inequalities *had*
to continue over this period of time. Instead of establishing any kind of

---

[38] Jon Elster, *Sour Grapes: Studies in the Subversion of Rationality* (Cambridge: Cambridge
University Press, 1983), p. 105.

teleology ulterior to history, Maale reproduction schemata uncovered a series of what Jon Elster has called filters, filters that selected certain outcomes and blocked out others.[39] Analyzing these filtering processes helped to explain what in fact happened in Maale, not what had to happen.

If the reproduction schemata themselves do not contain a sufficient explanation of why Maale inequalities persisted through the early twentieth century, do other parts of epochal analysis? To recall, the second "because" statement above was: Maale inequalities existed because they were compatible with the level of productive powers and their further development.

G. A. Cohen has offered a robust defense of the logic of this kind of statement, the so-called primacy of productive powers, and my exposition of Marxist theory has followed his. More accurately, my arguments have been based on one of Cohen's formulations of this thesis, for I believe that he has conflated two claims, one of which is true and the other not. The true version is:

> When relations [productive inequalities] endure stably, they do so because they promote the development of the forces. When relations are revolutionized, the old relations cease to exist because they no longer favour the forces, and the new relations come into being because they are apt to do so. Dysfunctional relations persist for a time before being replaced. During that time the character of the relations is explained by their suitability to a *past* stage in the development of the forces. . . .[40]

This way of stating the matter sets up no historical teleology for any particular society. Certain societies may not persist at all, and successful revolutions do not have to occur in every case of contradiction. Notice the different claim implied in the following statement:

> . . . with sufficient development of the forces the old relations are no longer compatible with them. Either they will have changed without lag along with productive development, or . . . there will now be "contradiction" between forces and relations. But if contradiction obtains, it will be resolved by alteration of the productive relations.[41]

These two statements appear to confuse (a) a certain pattern in evolutionary process that becomes visible only in retrospect and only over

---

[39] Elster, *Ulysses and the Sirens*, p. 30.
[40] Cohen, *Karl Marx's Theory of History*, pp. 160–1.
[41] Ibid., p. 158. Marx's statement in the preface to *A Contribution to the Critique of Political Economy* that "No social formation ever perishes before all the productive forces for which there is room in it have developed" is also objectionable if social formation is taken to refer to individual societies.

the sweep of epochal time with (b) what has to happen (according to the theory) in any particular society. These two different levels of inquiry also appear in Darwinian theory.[42] Over the entire sweep of biological evolution, more and more complex forms of life have evolved. But this (epochal) truth cannot be transferred to the particular (historical) trajectory of every species. It is in this sense, I argue, that epochal analyses are limited. Locally, they explain not what happened but, more generally, how things, if they happen, happen.

What occurred in Maale at any point was determined by a series of factors that we have not yet investigated, namely, the particular play of dominant power against local resistance. This historical causality operated whether productive powers and inequalities were in a state of compatibility or contradiction.[43] In either case, the local balance of power between groups was the proximate cause of whether productive inequalities were maintained in more or less the same form, were modified in ways that nevertheless preserved the same way of producing, or were fundamentally transformed. Weighing this balance between conflicting tendencies, at any particular moment, is what defines a historical, as opposed to an epochal, analysis. Hence E. P. Thompson's citation of Jean-Paul Sartre: "History is not order. It is disorder: a rational disorder."[44]

Since dominant power may be opposed and established ideology contested, discordant meanings and practices, ones that do not fit into Maale reproduction schemata, have to be considered: What were the forces that opposed dominant power? What kinds of consciousness escaped fertility fetishism? These issues will be examined in the next chapter.

[42] Stephen Jay Gould writes, "Does a land snail that is blown by a hurricane to a distant island, fertilizes itself, and becomes the progenitor of a new species fit in some predictable way into an overarching order of things? I don't know what to say about such an event except that it just happened. Nature produces some order by rejecting the ill-adapted, but we can hardly hope to specify an optimal arrangement of adapted species." *An Urchin in the Storm: Essays about Books and Ideas* (New York: W. W. Norton, 1987), p. 205.

[43] The position for which I am arguing is one that recognizes a hierarchy of levels of analysis and of "causes." G. A. Cohen in *Karl Marx's Theory of History*, pp. 148–9, calls attention to this hierarchy when he discusses the relationship between class struggle and mode-of-production explanations: "Now it is true that for Marx the *immediate* explanation of major social transformations is often found in the battle between classes. But that is not the fundamental explanation of social change. . . . why does the successful class succeed? *Marx finds the answer in the character of the productive forces.*" To the degree that more than one kind of reproduction schema is compatible with productive powers and their further development, the same complex hierarchy of causes operates in the case of successful social reproduction. The question of which level of analysis may be said to be "fundamental" seems answerable only in relation to what one wants to know.

[44] E. P. Thompson, *The Poverty of Theory*, p. 38.

I have emphasized the limits of epochal analyses. But I would like to conclude this chapter with my second point: Epochal inquiries, mode-of-production analyses, nevertheless provide the necessary beginning point for historical explanations. This is an aspect of Marxist theory that E. P. Thompson, for example, does not adequately acknowledge. The dice of history are loaded. Moreover, they are loaded differently in different modes of production. Without understanding the loading – something that is visible only over a span of epochal time – any student of history is apt to misunderstand why what happened happened in any particular place and time.

Epochal structures pinpoint the key sites in which social loading takes place. It is precisely there that something has to happen, as it were, for either reproduction to occur or change to be effected. Without a focus on these hinge points in interactional patterns, the study of history threatens to become a matter of the proverbial one-damn-thing-after-another. In contrast, disorder becomes rational – or at least understandable – when it is examined against the outlines of epochal structures, what Marx called ways of producing.

4. History at one point in time: "Working together" in Bola, 1975

Historical explanation is perhaps easier to perform than to analyze. Indeed, analysis often appears to lead away from, rather than to, the actual complexities of historical understanding. Thus historical materialists themselves have tended to divide into two more-or-less exclusive camps: social theorists concerned with models of ways of producing for whom the actual histories of particular societies rarely become much of a problem (for example, G. A. Cohen and Louis Althusser) versus mainly historians (Eugene Genovese and E. P. Thompson, among others), who interpret particular histories but who rarely discuss what they have done in relation to underlying issues in social theory.[1]

My goal in this chapter is to connect social theory with history. But unlike previous parts of this book in which I have found it relatively easy to move back and forth between abstract theory and Maale data, here I have discovered it difficult to rise very far above the "facts." For it is precisely something about the complexity of facts and how they interrelate that appears to be at the heart of historical explanation.

Raymond Williams has come closest to enunciating the kind of approach I wish to pursue:

In what I have called "epochal" analysis, a cultural process is seized as a cultural system, with determinate dominant features: feudal culture or bourgeois culture or a transition from one to the other. This emphasis on dominant and definitive lineaments and features is important and often, in practice, effective. But it then often happens that its methodology is preserved for the very different function of historical analysis, in which a sense of movement within what is ordinarily abstracted as a system is crucially necessary. . . . In authentic historical analysis it is necessary at every point to recognize the complex interrelations between movements and tendencies both within and beyond a specific and effective dominance. . . . We have certainly still to speak of the "dominant" and the "effective," and in these senses of the hegemonic. But we find that we have also to

[1] Eugene D. Genovese, *Roll, Jordan, Roll: The World the Slaves Made* (New York: Pantheon, 1974); E. P. Thompson, *The Making of the English Working Class* (Harmondsworth: Penguin, 1968). Thompson has considered issues of social theory in *The Poverty of Theory and Other Essays* (New York: Monthly Review Press, 1978), but there he attempts to put history in the place of theory rather than to join the two.

speak, and indeed with further differentiation of each, of the "residual" and the "emergent."[2]

Williams goes on to develop these categories, "dominant," "residual," and "emergent." What he designates as dominant and hegemonic is clear; residual and emergent, on the other hand, have specialized meanings that go beyond a mere reference to time. Residual cultural processes are not just archaic leftovers from previous time periods but are alternative, oppositional ways of living not captured by or included in the dominant hegemony. "Thus certain experiences, meanings, and values which cannot be expressed or substantially verified in terms of the dominant culture, are nevertheless lived and practised on the basis of the residue – cultural as well as social – of some previous social and cultural institution or formation."[3]

In empirical analysis, it is often difficult to distinguish precisely between dominant and residual, since actors within dominant traditions continually incorporate, interpret, and dilute important areas of the past in constructing their own sense of the present. For example, there is, according to Williams, little that is actively residual about the monarchy in modern Britain. Kings and queens have become integral parts of the dominant definition of British capitalism.

The same difficulty occurs on the boundary between dominant and emergent. The emergent is not merely the new, the novel. Emergent values and relationships, by Williams's definition, contain genuinely alternative or oppositional ways of living. As new practices are thrown up in any society, there is a continual struggle by dominant cultural actors to incorporate and to defuse the new. In modern capitalist societies, these processes have quickened as trade unions, working-class lifestyles, and a myriad of social movements have been variously and unevenly incorporated into hegemonic social and cultural patterns. "The process of emergence, in such conditions, is then a constantly repeated, an always renewable, move beyond a phase of practical incorporation: usually made much more difficult by the fact that much incorporation looks like recognition, acknowledgment, and thus a form of *acceptance*."[4]

These words – dominant, emergent, and residual – are cover terms.[5]

---

[2]Raymond Williams, *Marxism and Literature* (Oxford: Oxford University Press, 1977), pp. 121–2.
[3]Ibid., p. 122.   [4]Ibid., pp. 124–5.
[5]I have struggled, unsuccessfully, to find better terms than Williams's. The category "residual" is perhaps particularly open to misinterpretation, since it suggests a lack of real opposition to the dominant order. But the key notion is not lack of opposition but a

Like the notion of definitional maximization in neoclassical theory, they have no content of their own. Rather, they direct attention to variation in social and cultural practices, and they ground that variation in the flow of time and in the exercise of power. Any social moment is a complex intertwining of processes, some with a longer past, some with a more promising future, some intimately tied up with present hegemonies, some implicated in various ways of resisting dominant ways of living. With the analysis of the interaction of these processes – particularly as they relate to the balance of power between social groups – Marxism finally comes to terms with history.

If the epochal structures discussed in the previous chapter do not deal with temporal complexities, neither do they examine spatial ones. And just as Williams's time categories are necessary in making the transition to historical analysis, a similar conceptualization of space – with respect to power – is required. For political practices are patterned across space, as well as through time. What is needed, I would argue, is a categorization of space, like Immanuel Wallerstein's and G. William Skinner's, that highlights cores, semiperipheries, and peripheries.[6] These designations refer to zones of functionally integrated regional systems. Cores, semiperipheries, and peripheries interact, and they interact in ways determined by power differences.

Cores are, by definition, seats of dominant power; semiperipheries and peripheries are progressively farther removed. It will be immediately seen that heterodox social and cultural practices – both emergent and residual – are likely to be distributed across space in distinctive ways. Too little research has been done on what might be called the geography of domination, but in the case at hand, emergence in twentieth-century Maale took place mainly in the core, and it was there that the struggle to incorporate the new within dominant hegemonies took place, whereas residual social and cultural practices were concentrated in peripheries.[7] Such connections will no doubt vary from case to case, but given the

certain unworkability, given the drift of local history. For an additional difficulty, particularly with respect to the Maale case, see footnote 24 on page 176.

[6] Immanuel Wallerstein, *The Modern World-System: Capitalist Agriculture and the Origin of the European World-Economy in the Sixteenth Century* (New York: Academic Press, 1974), and G. William Skinner, "Regional Urbanization in Nineteenth-Century China" and "Cities and the Hierarchy of Local Systems," in G. William Skinner, ed., *The City in Late Imperial China* (Stanford: Stanford University Press, 1977), pp. 211–49 and 275–351. See also Carol A. Smith, ed., *Regional Analysis*, 2 vols. (New York: Academic Press, 1976).

[7] Somewhat similar patterns are discernible for imperial China; see G. William Skinner, "Mobility Strategies in Late Imperial China: A Regional Systems Analysis," in Smith, *Regional Analysis*, vol. 1, pp. 327–64.

dynamics of power contained within ways of producing, they will not vary randomly.

Regions are not just functionally interrelated into cores, semiperipheries, and peripheries; they are also, typically, hierarchically encapsulated within larger systems. Any one region with its own core-periphery structure may be, on a higher level, a constituent part of a more inclusive system. The notion of core or center is, then, relative. In most social systems, there is a hierarchy of centers that goes upward, step by step, in relation to successively larger functional regions. Again, exactly how such systems articulate, over what span, varies. Like the time-power categories of Williams, Wallerstein's and Skinner's space-power ones do not contain specific propositions; they only presume *some* patterning of economic and political practices across space.[8] These patterns must be recognized if we are to proceed from the epochal structures set out in the last chapter to the historical analysis attempted here – one of actual systems of power set in real space-time.

This last step toward history, or more accurately, toward historicity, involves not so much an analysis of change and transformation as an appreciation of each social moment as a fragile interaction of possibilities given by a set of structural alternatives.[9] With a slightly different weighting of such contending potentialities, any past historical moment could have turned out differently – sometimes dramatically differently. It is this contingency that I intend to examine below.

———

Let me turn for a last time, then, to the Maale vicinity, a section of which was analyzed in Chapter 1 – namely, Bola in 1975. I want to take up analysis by inquiring into the constitution of local factions in Bola (see map 1). What determined a household's membership in one versus another?

According to the argument presented in Chapter 1, neoclassical theory was able to accomplish its results by assuming many aspects of Maale political economy as givens and therefore making no attempt to explain them. One of these was household structure, a topic explored and ana-

[8] For another argument for the importance of space in social theory and in historical materialism, see Anthony Giddens, *A Contemporary Critique of Historical Materialism* (Berkeley: University of California Press, 1981), chap. 4.
[9] The critical feature of historical explanation, in the sense I am using the phrase, is not that it traces causes over a span of time (though this may be more or less required in particular analyses). What is crucial is a reading – set within a political context of a certain openness – of why things turned out as they did in particular places at particular times.

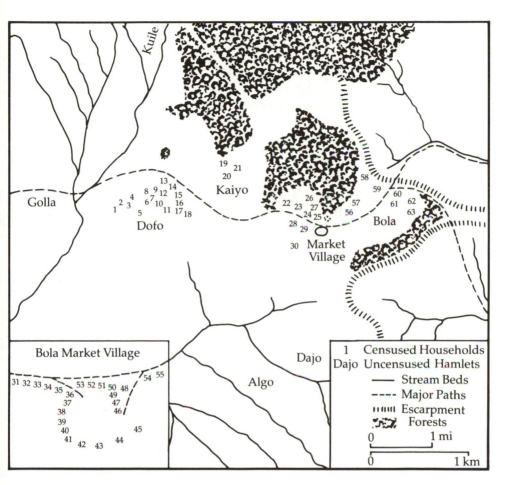

Map 1: Bola vicinity, Maale, 1975 (after Donham, *Work and Power*, p.75)

lyzed in Chapter 3. Yet another – one I want to consider in this final chapter – was community structure.

What made Bola, Bola, so to speak, is not yet clear. The transfer of labor from elders' households to those of more junior men obviously depended on how the interacting group was bounded and how it was defined.

Interestingly, the principal definition of community in Bola involved communal labor – who worked with whom. "Working together," wolla soofane, was a phrase that Maale everywhere used to describe and to make claims about fundamental sorts of political solidarity. Much more than a simple instrumental relationship, labor cooperation fused a variety of economic, political, and even religious concerns into one social form, one symbolic image.

This was brought home to me when I happened to be talking to Maale friends about changes wrought by the Ethiopian revolution – how the United States had supported Ethiopia before the revolution but had quit as its rival, the Soviet Union, had taken over that role. As I was struggling, not very successfully, to put the complexities of international relations into appropriate Maale terms, one young man interjected, "Oh, yes, it's like this. Before, Ethiopia and America worked together, but now Ethiopia and the Soviet Union are working together." Understood in the field of its particular Maale associations, wolla soofane, "working together" was just the phrase I needed.

There are two Maale verbs that can be translated as "working." The first, ma'dane, has the widest semantic range and is usually best glossed simply as "doing." A woman sweeping her house, an elder performing a ritual, or an anthropologist typing – all these people can be described as ma'dane, "doing" or "working." They all have "something to do," ma'do, the noun form of the verb.

The other verb, soofane, has a more restricted reference. To be described as soofane an activity must take place outside of the home. A woman taking care of a child or sweeping her house cannot be described as soofane, nor can an anthropologist typing his notes, unless this involves movement out of the place where he usually sleeps. Finally, even though an elder goes outside his home to accomplish the activity, propitiating the ancestors also would not count as soofane. In contrast to ma'do, any activity that can be described as soofane must be broadly related to some form of sustained bodily exertion. Thus a man or women who goes off to work in the fields, a woman who goes to the river to fetch water, a man who goes to the lowlands to check his beehives, and even cattle sent out to graze in the morning – all these can be described as soofane.[10]

The notion of "working together" is always expressed with this second verb, soofane, and so implies a range of assumptions similar, at least in some ways, to those made in English. In particular, it implies an opposition between domestic space, where one simply "does" things,

[10] It is perhaps significant to note that soofane, unlike ma'dane, does not have a noun form. People, therefore, do not talk about or make claims about the abstract notion of "working together," as I do in this chapter. Rather, they refer to and argue about people's actions of "working together."

Aratso, a Bola woman, working, ma'dane, in the courtyard of her compound. Bent over at the waist in typical female fashion, she is mixing flour and water to make beer, 1984.

and public space, where one "works." And it is cooperation in the public sphere that is marked as a key symbol of social solidarity. It is almost as if domestic groups described in the previous chapter, along with all the activity that they entail, exist isolated backstage while the show, the cooperative "work," in which actors find and form their political identities, unfolds center stage.

As might be expected, exactly who enters the stage is not an indifferent matter. Men, women, and children all work, soofane, at various jobs outside their homes, but they do so to varying extent. The roles of adult men are almost completely identified with public work, soofane; those of women and children are much more closely associated with domestic labor, ma'dane. "Working together," therefore, inevitably becomes entangled with gender ideology and with the Maale notion that men cooperate more successfully than women. Women themselves tend to interpret at least parts of their experience in these terms when they say that it is precisely in work, ma'do, that they cannot get along with one another, especially with mothers-in-law. Added then to the semantic overtones of soofane as public-and-male versus ma'dane as domestic-and-female, there is also a sense in which soofane is intrinsically group-building and socially integrative while ma'dane can be individualizing and socially divisive.

How is the notion of "working together" put into social practice? Two particular kinds of structural arrangements recur, not only in Maale but in many precapitalist economies over the world, and I shall call these blocs and webs. Both are particular kinds of networks.[11] For the purposes of illustration, imagine four households A, B, C, and D. As the name suggests, blocs are discrete groups in which relationships are transitive; that is, if A works with B and B with C, then A and C also work together. Webs, on the other hand, do not agglomerate into mutually exclusive groups; relationships are not transitive.

Bloc   Web

In Maale, there are, as I have pointed out, three types of arrangements in which persons combine to work cooperatively: helma, mol'o, and dabo. The first two are blocs – small blocs and large blocs as it were – and the third usually comprises a web. Maale describe cooperation in all of these arrangements as "working together," wolla soofane. Let me take up each in turn.

A helma is a small group of workers, usually three or four, who work in a set cycle of rotation on each other's fields. Each day that a helma assembles, the group works for about four hours, usually in the morning. Then workers go home and in the afternoon follow their individual pursuits. Very occasionally, the host of a helma provides beer, in which

[11] Since the present work follows a series of other network analyses in anthropology, it will be useful to clarify how the notion is used here in relation to what has been done before. Unlike Clyde Mitchell, I do not analyze networks from the point of view of individuals; see his *Social Networks in Urban Situations* (Manchester: Manchester University Press, 1969). Rather, I am interested in the social morphology of groups and quasigroups per se. In this regard, network analysis has become more lively of late in sociology than in anthropology (see, for example, Harrison E. White, Scott A. Boorman, and Ronald L. Breiger, "Social Structure of Multiple Networks: I. Blockmodels of Roles and Positions," *American Journal of Sociology* 31 (1976): 730–80). Sociologists, however, have not been sufficiently concerned with the cultural construction of social ties within networks – what such ties mean and how what they mean changes.

case work continues for a full day, about eight hours with time out for several rest stops.

Since horticultural tasks are to some extent apportioned on the basis of gender and age, helma groups are also usually differentiated along those lines. Adult men's helma are distinct from women's helma, and occasionally boys and girls (up to about eighteen years old) combine to form young people's helma. Men's helma are organized for all tasks in the horticultural cycle: clearing, cultivating, weeding, and harvesting both big-rains and small-rains fields. Women's helma form only for weeding and harvesting, and young people's helma mostly weed big-rains fields. In Bola, big-rains weeding makes the greatest demand for labor and calls forth the full work force from households.

Being small groups, helma do not have official roles for leaders who direct and coordinate the group's activities. Scheduling work days and making sure that everyone arrives on time are relatively easy matters for three or four people to accomplish among themselves. And without a differentiated structure of roles, helma work groups are relatively short-lived. Usually they are organized for one horticultural task, and after that task has been accomplished, the group dissolves. Sometimes a group survives two tasks in the horticultural cycle (about three or four months) but almost never for longer periods.

As I mentioned above, helma and mol'o, the next work group to be described, are blocs. Given their structural similarity, it is not surprising that successful helma sometimes evolve into mol'o. This transformation involves two interrelated processes. One is an increase in size. Larger than helma, mol'o vary in size from as few as six or seven members to as many as twenty-five. By the time a helma has increased in size to approximately seven, it is difficult to coordinate work informally; helma become mol'o when members choose a set of leaders, each with his own responsibilities. In other words, mol'o are minibureaucracies.

They are, however, minibureacuracies of a very special sort, for the titles of mol'o leaders and the symbolism that surrounds their functions are taken from the organizational structure of the Maale kingdom and its neighbors during the nineteenth century. Mol'o have "kings," "queen-mothers," "chiefs," and "outcastes." Each of these leaders has different duties. Like Maale notions of the kingdom as a whole, the mol'o's functioning is thought to depend on the harmonious union of these hierarchically arranged persons.

At the top of the hierarchy is the mol'o king. His essential function is to provide fair judgments in disputes among workers. In handling con-

Datso, a young Bola girl, at a weeding helma with other youngsters, 1983

flicts, the king has limited power to impose settlements, but he can order various fines and punishments. Such measures are rarely used and
depend upon support for the king's judgment by the majority of members. If someone continually offends the group (quarrels or arrives late
or does not do his share of work), he can be ostracized.

The choice of a mol'o king is critical. A good king, according to the
Maale, is a mild, good-natured man, slow to anger, not given to arguments and fights. If such a man is installed as king, then a mol'o can last
for decades. Under such favorable conditions, mol'o appear to have a
developmental cycle of their own: As a cohort of young men marry and
begin to work full time, they found a mol'o, continue to build social
solidarities, and "work together" until their sons begin full-time work.
Then the cycle begins again as their sons found a new mol'o. (Almost
no women work in mol'o. Households without working-age males
sometimes send an unmarried girl to these work groups, but as far as I
am aware, married women do not work in mol'o.)

After the king, the next most important position is that of outcaste.
He schedules days on which the mol'o works (this position is normally
filled by a Maale, not by a member of the real outcaste group of potters
and tanners, for the latter are not allowed to work with or eat with traditional Maale). Although a prescribed cycle of rotation is more or less
followed, a variety of circumstances interrupts its perfect unfolding. It
is the outcaste who keeps order in this system, who reconciles, as best
he can, competing claims, and who decides when and for whom the
mol'o will work next.

The outcaste, then, is required to take a more forceful and potentially
unpopular role than the mol'o king. Besides scheduling, the most dis-
ruptive issue, the outcaste also polices the work group during the first
half of the working day, punishing laggards and latecomers with whip-
pings to the leg. This aspect of his work, in fact, seems to account for
the outcaste's title. As I have pointed out, actual outcastes acted as
henchmen and executioners for the Maale king. Both feared and despised, associated with conflict and death, outcastes were symbolic in-
versions of the life-giving king. They performed services, sometimes
polluting, sometimes repugnant, that were nevertheless required for
social reproduction.

The roles of chief and queen-mother complete the array of mol'o offices. The chief is in charge of providing tobacco for the group (the Maale
are avid smokers), and during the last half of the work day, he takes
over the outcaste's role of policing the group. The queen-mother (usually

a male, of course, since few mol'o have female members) plays a principal role in the ritual beer drink at midday. Kneeling, the queen-mother offers a calabash of beer to the king. After the king has drunk some, the two of them, with their mouths side by side on the same calabash, drink the rest of the beer without stopping. The queen-mother repeats the same small ritual with the outcaste and then with the chief, after which the whole mol'o drinks. According to Maale thought, the union (in Maale weddings the bride and groom drink together from the same calabash) of hierarchically arranged persons guarantees the harmony of the work group and the fertility of fields.

The dabo, the final work group to be described, presents two contrasts to helma and mol'o. First, the dabo system of cooperation usually establishes a web, not a bloc. That is, sets of cooperating households are not discretely bounded. In sponsoring a dabo, a household brews beer – it is impossible to have a dabo without beer – and "begs" a number of its neighbors to come and work. The number of workers can vary from as few as two or three to as many as thirty and includes various mixes of men and women depending on the task at hand. Each household has its own circle of potential dabo partners, which overlaps to greater or lesser extent with the circles of neighboring households. Unlike the neatly bounded groups of helma and mol'o, the dabo work party system produces a more complex webbed pattern of relationships.

The second major contrast is that reciprocity in dabo labor given and received is not built into the system of cooperation – a fact established by Chapter 1. In helma work groups, each member receives back the labor he puts into others' fields in a matter of days; in mol'o work groups, in a month or two. But since dabo are sponsored only as the need arises and only if surplus grain exists to make beer, and since there is no set cycle of rotation, a much longer time may elapse before a household recovers the labor it puts into others' fields. Consequently, if certain households consistently have motive and means to sponsor more dabo than their neighbors, long-term debts can build up.

"Debt," however, is not quite the right word, for the Maale do not keep an exact accounting of labor given and received, at least not publicly.[12] Exact accounting would be a repudiation of how Maale define dabo cooperation in particular and "working together" in general – as a long-term, comprehensive relationship of mutual assistance. Coopera-

---

[12] From interviews at the end of a season, it was clear that people were generally aware of whether their net dabo balances were very positive or very negative. This was a subject, however, about which Maale did not like to talk.

Kaite, a young man in a Bola mol'o, pouring beer during a rest stop, 1974. Sitting in a tight semi-circle, others in the work group share a water pipe.

Bola men weeding with digging sticks in a dabo during 1983. The group moves along together, in rhythm.

tion is always more than an economic tit-for-tat. A dabo sponsor retains an obligation to help those who have worked for him, but that obligation can be discharged, as we shall see, in a number of ways.

Each of these three forms of "working together" must be understood against a background of the Maale definition of the units that came "together," for the very notion of coming "together" implies a prior separation. That separation was based first on household organization (domestic groups carried out about half of all horticultural labor on their own in Bola during 1975) and second on the structure of minimal lineages.

When members of households in the same minimal lineage cooperated in helma, dabo, or mol'o (to jump ahead, this happened only marginally more frequently in Bola in 1975 than if households had worked with neighbors only randomly), they could technically be described as "working together." But in these cases such a description had less political salience than in others, and it did not, for example, tend to appear in claims and counter-claims between descent mates during conflicts:

Rather than who worked with whom and what that implied, the key issues among descent mates were typically phrased in terms of shared blood and bones and the appropriate behavior that kinship required.

Understanding the meaning and pattern of "working together" requires, therefore, some reference to the structure of Maale kinship discussed in Chapter 3. For kinship – or more correctly, the cultural construction of marriage and parenthood that constituted households and the meaning of siblingship, particularly brotherhood, that constituted minimal lineages – defined the units that entered into labor cooperation. In "working together," it was as if households (and to a lesser extent minimal lineages) were already assumed to be solidary units, united by the strongest possible bonds. Through the social forms of cooperative labor and the cultural idiom of "working together," households coalesced into larger (but more weakly unified) political factions. Descent itself, even though it provided the strongest possible ties in Maale, did not ramify widely enough to define local political factions.

The task of defining and redefining each household's place in the local political world was accomplished by all three ways of "working together." In this respect, Maale work arrangements can be placed along a continuum different from the order in which I have just described them: a continuum from helma to dabo to mol'o. Helma were small groups and usually did not involve beer. Both dabo and mol'o, in contrast, were larger, and hosts did usually prepare beer. Finally, mol'o, but not dabo, involved the same persons working together over a period of time, a relatively tightly-knit group presided over by elected leaders. The mol'o seems to have instituted the greatest togetherness of any of the Maale ways of "working together."

It is important to notice that over this continuum the articulation between work groups and households changed; specifically, male labor grew in predominance as work arrangements served greater social and political ends. The proportion of male to female labor in helma was roughly equal; dabo were more heavily male; finally, mol'o were almost totally male. As work groups from helma to dabo to mol'o increasingly turned male and occupied center stage in local community life, more and more happened backstage. There, women's domestic labor, ma'do, specifically women's brewing of beer, was required for the very existence of male communal labor.

Brewing beer for a large dabo or mol'o was not a simple matter. First, finger millet had to be left in a damp pot to sprout and the resulting malt had to be ground. Other grain had to be stone ground, hour after hour

Aika'do and Halbo, two Bola women, preparing beer, 1983

of continuous work, and a large quantity of water brought from the stream about a mile away. Most women asked (and later gave) neighbors help with fetching water and sometimes with grinding, but these arrangements were not formalized and were not thought of as "working together." Finally, the malt and flour had to be mixed in a large pot of hot water and the brew poured into large gourds to ferment. If malt was on hand, this work, all of it women's work, could be accomplished in five days.

It was just these symbolically unmarked preparations that allowed dabo and mol'o to become such public forums. For, with beer, the character of a work party changed. The beer drink became the social focus of the day, not just for the workers, but for all those who were connected or allied with them. Of nonworkers, elders whose sons were working were most in evidence. They alternated between lending a hand here and there, shouting advice and supervision to the workers, and retiring to shade trees, companions, and calabashes of beer. Others who came to drink and to socialize were usually persons who otherwise cooperated with members of the work party, particularly with the host.

Women's individual labor in preparing beer was one backstage role. That of elders, "lending a hand here and there, shouting advice and supervision to workers" was another. To understand the role of elders requires some reference to previous discussions of household structure.

As I have already pointed out, the Maale in Bola had a stem-family household system. Within that system, the social construction of headship conditioned the way households "worked together." When a neighbor sponsored a dabo, he "begged" the household head, even though he might know beforehand that the head would send his son, daughter, or wife. In return, when the head sponsored his own dabo, it was he who decided when the work party should be convened, directed that beer be prepared, and "begged" neighbors to come and work. Finally, a husband-father influenced whether his wife and children entered into helma or mol'o, which group they joined, and how often beer was prepared. In sum, headship provided the other behind-the-scenes role in "working together": Besides wives who prepared beer, there were elders who directed.

Perhaps the best way to convey the role of elders and to illustrate what ties of "working together" meant in social practice is to recount an actual incident, a local flare-up, that occurred in 1975. The dramatis personae include Chore, an elder, and Sula, a middle-aged man. Chore's son and Sula worked in the same mol'o, and before that, Chore and

Cheka's father, a Bola elder, smoking a water pipe and observing the work of his son's mol'o, 1974

Sula's father, who was still alive, had worked together in the previous mol'o, by then defunct. One morning as cattle were being driven out to pasture, a heifer from Chore's herd wandered into Sula's house garden. In a temper, Sula ran out of his house to drive the heifer away and threw a rock that happened to hit her on a fatal spot. She fell down, instantly dead. As in other cases, there were wrongs on both sides. Chore's herd-boy should have been watching the cow; on the other hand, Sula should not have lost his head and thrown a rock. When he heard about the cow, Chore was furious – not only about losing the heifer but also because Sula had gone to work instead of butchering the animal. As it happened, the mol'o was working that morning. What could he do, Sula asked, he had no one to replace him in the mol'o; he had to go to work.

An elder who had worked with both Chore and Sula's father in the previous mol'o and whose son worked with Chore's son and Sula in the current one intervened and finally managed to soothe Chore's anger and persuade him not to demand compensation. When I wondered at the fact that Sula gave nothing to Chore, the elder who had helped settle the case protested, "But aren't they neighbors? They work together."

It is noteworthy that he did *not* claim that the two men were kinsmen, even though Sula had in fact married Chore's sister's daughter and could therefore have been counted as Chore's relative, iginni. Instead, the elder pointed out that the two men belonged to the same local community, they "worked together." Perhaps tomorrow the tables would be turned and Chore would require Sula's forbearance and goodwill.

Had Chore pressed his claim in the local court, where adversaries are described as "enemies," it would have been tantamount to repudiating his long relationship with Sula's family and with their common mol'o. Chore's legal claim was a strong one, but had he advanced it and alienated Sula's family and refused the mediation of other mol'o members, he would have isolated himself. He would have had to establish new friends, to gather a new set of work partners, and to collect new supporters in local affairs. Thus "working together" had a momentum of its own in this case, a momentum that elders not directly involved in the work process promoted and channeled.

Labor cooperation appears, then, to have been the most salient way that Maale households publicly established and continually reestablished their local social and political identities, the local boundary between "us" and "them." Lines of social solidarity were drawn in various social forms in which young and middle-aged men, whom I shall lump together as juniors, tended to predominate. This was particularly the case with mol'o groups presided over by junior men playing the roles of king, queen-mother, chief, and outcaste. But behind the publicly marked activities of junior men stood two backstage roles, one filled by persons less powerful than junior men – namely their wives – and the other by persons more powerful – elders. Wives brewed and elders directed. Neither participated directly in "working together," but the roles of both have to be taken into account in understanding what communal labor meant and how it accomplished its wider social effect.

How did the different work groups that I have described interrelate in Bola during 1975? Were helma, for example, strictly subsets of larger mol'o, or did households tend to cooperate with one group of neighbors in helma, another in mol'o? Did households draw dabo workers from the pool of their mol'o partners or from outside? How were the boundaries of local communities drawn?

The patterns that the various ways of "working together" can take when added together range over a number of possibilities. It will be intuitively clear, I think, that in most cases a web added to a web will result in another, composite web. (The only exception obtains in those rare cases in which one web exactly fills the holes of another to yield a composite bloc.) Blocs, on the other hand, can form either webs or blocs when they are added. Overlapping blocs produce a composite web, a web of rather special configuration in which households that belong to more than one bloc act as bridges between otherwise separate portions of the total network. Only blocs that do not overlap or that exactly superimpose yield blocs again when they are added.

These patterns are of more than formal interest, for they characterize a social continuum from an economic-political landscape built up out of separate, composite blocs to one linked together by a continuous, seamless web. Sociologically, these two cases may be thought of as closed versus open, respectively: closed groups being, just as the name suggests, tightly knit and very solid groups, poised jealously to guard their interests vis-à-vis outsiders; open webs resting on more relaxed forms of linkages in which boundaries are fuzzy at best and political relationships always messy.

There is no reason to assume that one of these, or an approximation to it, was characteristic of Maale political economy per se. For the past three-quarters of a century that helma, dabo, and mol'o have coexisted in Maale, it may well be that the economic and political designs of particular Maale regions have successively opened and closed.[13] And at any

[13] G. William Skinner has analyzed how local communities appear to have opened and closed in synchrony with the dynastic cycle in imperial China in "Chinese Peasants and

particular time, there probably has been variation over space: one local political economy composed of closed blocs just at the moment when an adjacent area, enjoying more relaxed local conditions, formed its political economy via an open web.

It is methodologically important to be aware of the family of possibilities contained in any congeries of institutional arrangements, even when one analyzes a fairly small locale, as I am about to do. For it trains attention where it should be: on distinctly local matters and conditions rather than *the* structure of Maale political economy (or *the* pattern of Nuer kinship or whatever). Bola, the area that I am about to describe, was by no means a typical settlement of Maale households. In fact, for as long as Maale could remember, Bola had been a local political center, the residence of Maale kings. To appreciate the particularity of Bola requires some attention to the wider spatial structure of Maale and how that structure changed during the twentieth century as the way of producing described in the previous chapter was transformed.

In the nineteenth century, Maaleland was presided over by the ritual king, who lived in the heart of the country at Bola, and by chiefs who supervised the thirteen surrounding districts. Districts were not, however, natural social units; that is, district boundaries did not define human interaction systems. Typically, the borders of districts simply followed dry stream beds. The rugged mountains in the center of Maale and the river Woito that curled around Maale territory (see map 2, overleaf) were much more critical geographical features. Taken together, they defined the four regions of Maale: a central highland valley core (favored horticulturally, and the seat of kings) surrounded by three lower and drier peripheral valley systems (that included Maale along one mountain wall and neighboring ethnic groups along the opposite wall). These peripheral valleys held good grazing areas and were often the scenes of cattle raids back and forth between Maale and their neighbors.

Each of the four regions was a partially bounded social unit; for example, a typical person was more likely to know people from, more likely to have stock partners from, and more likely to marry within his or her own region compared to others.[14] Regions 2, 3, and 4 were, then, focused on the highland core, region 1. The ritual king, the sacred em-

the Closed Community: An Open and Shut Case," *Comparative Studies in Society and History* 13 (1971): 270–81.

[14] To some extent, Maale cultivated social ties precisely because they went against the grain of this regional pattern. That is, men looked for stock partners or in-laws in other regions so that when disasters of various sort hit their own areas, they had "relatives" who could help.

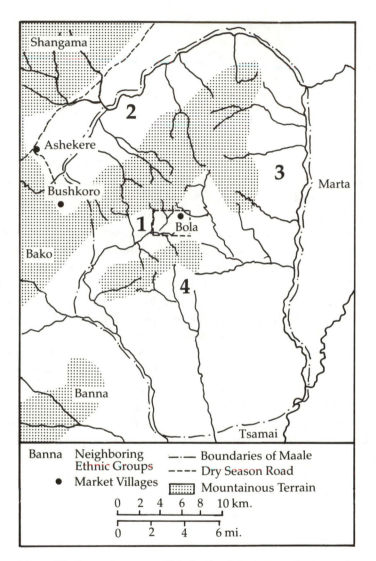

Map 2: The four subregions of Maale (the dotted rectangle shows the extent of map 1, p. 143). The administrative center at Bako was roughly twenty kilometers east of Ashekere.

bodiment of the polity as a whole, lived in the core, and it was there that peripheral Maale were forced to retreat when they were badly defeated in war, there similarly that they went in bad years to exchange cattle for grain, and there that they had to render labor tributes to the king.

By the early twentieth century, this spatial patterning was changed by the conquest and incorporation of Maale into the expanding Ethiopian empire. Indeed, the whole of Maale political economy was transformed as a series of garrison towns were set up in the area, as Maale chiefs and kings were brought into the imperial bureaucracy, and as patterns of tribute and land rights were slowly but fundamentally changed.[15] By 1975, the mode of production described in the previous chapter, although still relevant to many aspects of Maale life, no longer furnished the independent dynamic of local political economy. Rather, Maale production was increasingly conditioned by the mode of production characteristic of the northern empire that encapsulated and dominated it.

How are we to understand, then, twentieth-century Maale society? Specifically, what is the relevance of the old way of producing discussed above? And how does it interrelate with the new mode of production that increasingly affected Maale life – an expansionary political economy, like many African empires, that continually incorporated frontier groups into the dominant ethnic identity associated with imperial power?[16]

For problems of this sort, most frequently discussed in relation to the expansion of capitalism, two analytical answers have been proposed of late. The first, associated with the work of Wallerstein, insists that local political economies, as they are incorporated into the world system, became "capitalist." There is only one way of producing, that characteristic of the widest, encapsulating social system.[17] The second answer, inspired by the work of Althusser, speaks of the "articulation" of modes of production. It is said that the process of articulation can even preserve a noncapitalist mode of production, inasmuch as it serves certain needs of the dominant capitalist mode.[18]

---

[15] For a fuller analysis of these transformations, see "From Ritual Kings to Ethiopian Landlords: the Maale Case," in Donald L. Donham and Wendy James, eds., *The Southern Marches of Imperial Ethiopia: Essays in History and Social Anthropology* (Cambridge: Cambridge University Press, 1986), pp. 69–95.

[16] I have discussed the political economy of traditional empires in the north of what became the modern state of Ethiopia in "Old Abyssinia and the New Ethiopian Empire: Some Themes in Social History," in Donham and James, *Southern Marches*, pp. 3–48.

[17] Immanuel Wallerstein, *The Modern World-System*.

[18] Pierre-Philippe Rey, *Colonialisme, neo-colonialisme, et transition au capitalisme* (Paris: Maspero, 1971) and *Les alliances de classes* (Paris: Maspero, 1973). See also Harold Wolpe, ed.,

Neither of these ways of proceeding appears entirely adequate. The problem with the first, often pointed out by anthropologists, is that it has no way of analyzing the variety of economic and political systems located at the periphery of the world system.[19] If everything is capitalist, there are no other models to capture the reality of local political economies that look very different from the wider system in which they are embedded.

The recourse, I would argue, is to recognize the relativity of ways of producing – a relativity dependent on the actual spatial system being analyzed. For example, twentieth-century Maale political economy continued to be dominated by the way of producing described in the last chapter, while Ethiopia was influenced by another, imperial mode of production, while finally the world system was undoubtedly capitalist. Each of these spatial systems, one encapsulated in the next, had a different dynamic and was dominated by a different class.

This vision of a hierarchy of modes of production is not completely unlike that contained in the notion of articulation. What is different in the approach taken here is an insistence that the way any larger system conditions a local one is a historical problem – not an epochal one. By this, I mean that the connections between levels cannot be explained functionally but must be seen as the outcome of contingent, historical processes.[20]

In Maale, higher-level political economies increasingly affected local life during the twentieth century. Historical processes pressed old realities into new molds, as people used old practices in new ways, but the basic inequalities in Maale remained largely the same – even as they were redefined and given new meaning. In the process, each of the productive inequalities described in Chapter 3 became, to varying degree, a site of strain and stress: between chiefs and commoners, between minimal lineage heads and their younger brothers, and between household heads and their wives and coresident working children.

The Articulation of Modes of Production (London: Routledge & Kegan Paul, 1980). Aidan Foster-Carter, "The Modes of Production Controversy," New Left Review 107 (1977): 47–77, gives a helpful review.

[19] Eric R. Wolf, Europe and the People Without History (Berkeley: University of California Press, 1982), p. 23; Sidney W. Mintz, "On the Concept of a Third World," Dialectical Anthropology 1 (1976); 377–82.

[20] The notion of articulation, in contrast, implies that one mode fulfills the functional requirements of another. For an example of this approach, one to which I shall return in the Conclusion, see Claude Meillassoux, Maidens, Meal and Money: Capitalism and the Domestic Community (Cambridge: Cambridge University Press, [1975] 1981), part II.

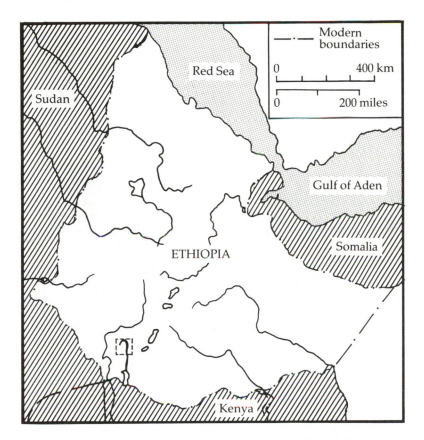

Map 3: Modern Ethiopia (the dotted rectangle toward the lower left shows the extent of map 2, page 160.

Of all Maale inequalities, kingship and chiefship – if one can continue to use these terms – had changed most fundamentally by the 1970s. During Maale's existence as an independent polity in the nineteenth century, the power of kings had rested materially on their ability to gather tribute from all of Maale, tribute in labor and in kind. Such tribute was justified by the notion that the king was responsible for the fertility and well-being of fields, people, and animals. Gradually and unevenly over the course of the twentieth century, the tributary political economy of Maale was replaced by one based on land ownership backed by the force of the Ethiopian state and on political positions within the imperial bureaucracy.

Bailo's son, the young landlord king of Maale, with his entourage on the eve of the revolution. Well-dressed, riding a mule, surrounded by mani retainers, one of whom is carrying his gun, the "king" resembled landlords in other parts of rural Ethiopia at the time. The tin-roofed house in the background was one of the very few in Maale in the 1970s.

Kings, most of the chiefs, and a few northern soldiers who settled in Maale thus became landlords or, perhaps more accurately, tax-farmers. They gathered tributes from their lands (now delimited by the state), kept most for themselves, and passed on a little to the imperial treasury. Many in this group, particularly the king, also occupied the lower levels of the imperial bureaucracy, overseeing law and order and settling local disputes. In time, this nascent class of lords, even the Maale kings, took on more and more of northern Ethiopian culture. The king was among the first to send his children to school to learn Amharic (the national language), to build a tin-roofed house, and to give up old taboos (against outcaste potters and tanners, for example). The ideological message was no longer a celebration of the king's control over fertility but an advertisement of a rough sort of power and influence designed to protect and expand lords' and their clients' landholdings and revenues.

Since kingship was the material and ideological linchpin of the traditional way of producing, the other inequalities in Maale could not help
but be affected, even if they were less dramatically and more unevenly
transformed. The processes analyzed in the previous chapter that un-
derlay the formation of large lineages began to be disrupted: the transformation of surplus grain into cattle into traditional rights over land
that could, in turn, be used to keep junior lineage mates tied to their
natal homes. By the middle of the twentieth century, the state bestowed
land rights, and although it was mainly senior lineage elders who were
given these rights, this was not always the case. When land was distributed and redistributed in Maale in the 1950s and '60s, much depended
on political ties of clientage to the new lords, whether to the erstwhile
king or chiefs or to northern settlers. Occasionally, a relatively junior
elder used such ties to gain land rights, and this began to disrupt relationships within conical lineages.

These changes reverberated one step downward to households. There,
a combination of the advent of Protestant Christianity, an increase of
cash-cropping, and the beginning of education (processes discussed more
fully below) combined, in some places, to transform the stem-family developmental cycle. These changes, particularly Protestantism and education, gave sons new sources of power, and some parents had to live
out their later years without coresident children. Husband-fathers, in
the new context of kings who were really landlords and lineage elders
who were really lords' clients, began to occupy a different place in local
thought and practice. At the very least, husband-fathers found it increasingly difficult to play the role of miniature kings who brought fertility and social order. Other ideologies began to appear, ones that glo-
rified a kind of individual realpolitik, of persons using ties to others
more highly placed to rise in the imperial system defined by rights to
land.[21]

All of these transformations in productive inequalities occurred unevenly over space. In the nineteenth century all of Maale had, as it were,
stood facing the center of the country, those farther away occupying more
and more peripheral positions. By the 1970s, the economic and political
center on which Maale life focused had moved from the highlands of
Maale itself to a successor of the garrison town located outside Maale at

---

[21] Donald N. Levine, *Wax and Gold: Tradition and Innovation in Ethiopian Culture* (Chicago:
University of Chicago Press, 1965), describes these cultural themes common to northern Ethiopia.

Bako. Now all Maale faced, as it were, westward. Region 2 (see map 2 on p. 160) was in the process of becoming the new core, while region 1 was declining into the role of semiperiphery. Regions 3 and 4 were still peripheries.

As might be expected, region 2 underwent the greatest number of transformations in the twentieth century. It was mainly there that tax rights over land were given to northern settlers. These northerners became powerful enough to displace Maale chiefs, and by 1975 none of the chiefs in core region 2 – unlike their counterparts in semiperipheral and peripheral regions – owned much land or played important roles in the imperial bureaucracy. It was also in region 2 that the only road in Maale territory was eventually built, and by the 1970s cultivators there were beginning to produce a surplus of grain to feed the town of Bako. Transport costs precluded any such development in other regions of Maale.

Finally, religious transformations followed in the new core. After the Italian occupation, a Sudan Interior Mission station was founded at Bako, and by the 1960s native evangelists from Welaita began proselytizing in Maale, mostly in region 2. Trained by foreign missionaries, the evangelists taught Amharic, and they preached the gospel. Besides exhorting belief in Christ, they taught hard work, honesty, bettering one's lot, and a certain contempt for traditional ways. In particular, evangelists preached against the consumption of beer. Converts, giving up beer, thus gave up their old work partners, and Protestant communities developed into rigidly demarcated and highly solidary blocs in which believers "worked together" only with other believers. They even developed a new structure of work called maddo, "helping," in which members of a church worked for those of its number who were in particular difficulty.

On the eve of the revolution, then, almost every aspect of Maale political economy varied systematically across space. In the new core, region 2, Maale were increasingly drawn into the market, northern tax farmers had replaced the Maale political elite, Protestant communities were winning adherents, and there were few stem-family households. In the semiperiphery, region 1, the Maale political elite, lineage organization, and traditional household structure remained more-or-less intact, but all were coming under increasing pressure. Finally, in regions 3 and 4, nineteenth-century Maale structures of economics and politics remained most undisturbed.

What these changes meant in people's lives, particularly in local politics, can be illustrated by considering Maale's social drama par excel-

Two Protestant boys painstakingly reading the Bible (in Amharic) in a Maale
church, 1984

lence, the story of the succession to the kingship in the decades just
before the revolution. Matters came to a head in the early 1960s when
the incumbent king, Yebirka, a traditional, mild-mannered man, was
accused in government court by his brother's son, Bailo, of unlawfully
taking office. Bailo, an up-and-coming man with strong ties to the new
landlord elite, was able to win the court case by a variety of stratagems.
For the first time in Maale history, it was said, the kingship was transferred to a successor before the incumbent had died.

Winning the court case, however, did not settle the transition, for
Bailo died suddenly and unexpectedly in 1971. Until 1975, when the
kingship was abolished by the Ethiopian revolution, no successor was

installed. Bailo's educated son took over administrative duties in relation to the state but was not installed as ritual king. Two factions were
deadlocked: traditionalists who argued for recalling Yebirka, shown opposite (Bailo's death was a sign that he was not meant to rule in the first
place and so neither was his son), versus those connected with the landlord elite who favored Bailo's "northernized" son, pictured on p. 164.

Besides the split between traditionalists and landlords, there was a
third basis on which political loyalties were cast in 1975: Protestantism.
Maale Protestants, given their religious differences and their commitment to taking advantage of economic opportunities, inevitably came
into conflict with Bailo and others over land. And in several of the cases
that developed between Protestants and encroaching landlords in Maale,
the Protestants were able to win. The network of co-believers that
stretched over the entire province, the resulting ease of travel to appeal
cases to the provincial capital, the ability to use Amharic, and finally the
direct intervention of foreign missionaries in court in a few cases – all of
these factors contributed to the success of Protestants and helped to gal-
vanize their opposition both to traditionalists and to rich assimilationist
landlords.

In sum, there were three major segments in Maale politics by the mid-
1970s: (1) traditionalists, concentrated in the peripheries and semiperiphery, who wanted to bring back Yebirka, who chafed under the ex-
ploitations of northern landlords but viewed the similar exactions of the
Maale king as legitimate, (2) rich landlords and their clients, in the core
and semiperiphery, most of whom were adept at dealing with imperial
courts and most of whom supported Bailo's educated son, and finally
(3) Maale Protestants, mostly in the core and semiperiphery, who were
opposed both to the existence of traditional kingship and to the en-
croachments of landlords, whether by northerners or by the Maale elite.

These three segments – more than political factions, almost whole
ways of living – rested on residual, dominant, and emergent forms of
consciousness. Given wider Ethiopian society in 1975, there was something distinctly anachronistic, at times oppositional, about traditionalists; in using the rhetoric and core symbols of the nineteenth century,
they refused to come to terms with the conquest and incorporation of
Maale into Ethiopia. Landlords and their clients, on the other hand, were
very much a part of the wider dominant culture in Ethiopia; they were
much more attuned (in hindsight, perhaps too narrowly attuned) to the
present. Finally, Maale Protestantism represented, to some degree, an
oppositional and emergent consciousness, one out of line with current

The deposed king of Maale, Yebirka, telling his story in 1974

reality, not a survival from the past, but a form of culture pregnant with possibilities of future transformation.[22] When the revolution did come to Maale, Protestants were its main supporters, and they dominated the leadership of the new peasant associations established to take the place of the king and others.

———————

Bola, in region 1 in what had once been the core of Maale, was a point at which many of these contradictory political forces came precisely into collision. By 1975, residual and dominant factions populated the vicinity; the absence of the emergent group was not the result of mere chance, as we shall see. The 63 households of the vicinity (see map 1 on p. 143) were peopled by Maale horticulturalists, by immigrant non-Maale horticulturalist-traders, and by outcaste potters and tanners who were cultivating fairly large fields by 1975.

The Maale horticulturalists who lived in the vicinity of Bola had traditionally occupied a special place within the kingdom. Bola elders, along with two chiefs who lived nearby, had determined the line of royal succession. In addition, they had served as middlemen between the king and the surrounding populace, collecting tribute, enjoying part of the largesse themselves, and relaying messages and orders. By 1975, these Bola elders and their households grouped rather strongly toward the traditionalist pole of politics. They did not do so very openly, however, for they were living on land owned by Bailo's son (and most had lined up on the wrong side in the dispute of the 1960s, that is, with the young man's father's opponent, Yebirka).

The non-Maale immigrant traders all lived in the market village situated in Bola, one founded along with a new weekly market in about 1963 by Bailo shortly after he had won his court case and had taken over the office. The traders, who in addition cultivated fields, were either Muslims from Jimma, an important trading center in southern Ethiopia, or Orthodox Christians from various locales outside Maale. All spoke Amharic, and a few were minimally literate. By 1975, these few literate traders were taking over the middleman role between the king and the populace. They collected taxes, kept rudimentary records, and acted as judges during the king's absences. Literate traders had become more useful to the king than traditionalist elders in the changed circumstances of the

[22] When I analyze Protestantism as a part of emergent consciousness in 1975, I am concerned only with that historical moment. Even though Maale Protestants played a critical role in the early years of the revolutionary period, they were swept aside by the 1980s.

twentieth century. And from the other side of the relationship, traders needed the king. With no kinsmen nearby nor traditional rights of occupation, traders had only the king as a protector.

Besides the traders, the seven households of outcaste potters and tanners in Bola were also clients of the new king. When he took over in the 1960s, Bailo allowed outcastes to begin cultivating fields on his land. The women of the group continued to make pots for the local market, but as imported cloth replaced skins in local dress and as hides were increasingly exported from Maale via the Bola market, outcaste men turned from full-time tanners to part-time cultivators. The king exempted these new cultivators from rents, in contrast to the surrounding Maale. Instead of extracting rents, he dropped old taboos against outcastes entering his house and made them into his personal servants. Outcastes carried the king's guns, they accompanied him on mule trips, and they served in his house.

If most of the Maale in Bola fell into a residual group of traditionalists whereas traders and outcastes were associated with the dominant faction of the new landlord king, the third political segment, Protestants, were wholly missing from the Bola landscape. This was not accidental, for all of Bola was owned by the king. As the opposition between landlords and Protestants grew ever stronger in the 1960s, Bailo forbade Protestants to settle on his land and instructed Maale living in Bola to withdraw their children from Protestant schools (at that time, the nearest government school was a six-hour walk away). This the Maale did.

Maale, immigrant traders, and outcastes were, then, the inhabitants of the Bola area, and they lived in a number of hamlets and villages. Only the market village, occupied entirely by immigrants, was an agglomerated settlement; the rest were dispersed hamlets. Close to the market village was Bola hamlet (Bola was the name both for the whole area that I am describing and for the particular hamlet). Bola hamlet was occupied by the king, by outcastes who lived nearby, and by traditional Maale. The other two hamlets, Kaiyo and Dofo, were occupied only by Maale, often by relatives of those living in Bola, since both Kaiyo and Dofo had been established by Bola people beginning in the 1950s. These three Maale hamlets – Bola, Kaiyo, and Dofo – will recur in the description of events below, along with the Bola market village. How did people in Bola, Kaiyo, and Dofo "work together" in 1975?

Mol'o. I begin with the mol'o because it was the principal form within which political solidarities were formed in Bola vicinity. Two mol'o groups worked in Bola during 1975, one populated by Maale households in Dofo

Napise, a mani man in Bola

and Bola hamlets and the other mainly by immigrant traders and out-castes. The first, I shall call the "residual" mol'o for ease of reference, the second the "dominant" mol'o. These terms should not lead to confusion. Residual and dominant refer not to mol'o themselves but to the type of political commitments around which mol'o were formed.[23]

The residual mol'o was founded in about 1964 by a group of young men in their twenties. Previously, the only mol'o in the vicinity had been one organized by the young men's fathers in the 1930s. Thirty years later, many of the men in the mol'o, elders by then, had begun to retire from full-time work as their sons matured. At first, children simply replaced their fathers in the old structure; the mol'o king's eldest son became king, the outcaste's eldest son became outcaste, and so forth. Elders advised their children to continue with the old group, but their admonition went unheeded in the early 1960s when a group of young men, many of them younger brothers, organized a new mol'o with officers of their own choosing. The new mol'o prospered and attracted additional members while the old one, increasingly plagued by disagreements, eventually disbanded.

The founding of the dominant mol'o, rather than a phase in a regularized developmental cycle, was an innovation in local history. As I pointed out above, outcastes had not traditionally cultivated crops in Maale. Only after the new king came to office did outcastes start their own fields, and by about 1971 they were involved enough to found a mol'o. Gradually market villagers joined the work group as they too turned more and more to cultivation. When the market was first established, profits made from buying in Bola and reselling outside the area were fairly high, since local Maale did not have much information about outside prices. By the 1970s, however, profits had been pushed downward, mainly by Protestants who were beginning to enter trade themselves. Consequently, Bola traders had to turn to cultivation.

The split between traders and outcastes on the one hand and the surrounding Maale on the other was sharp: No trader or outcaste belonged to the residual mol'o, and no Maale household in Dofo or in Bola hamlet belonged to the dominant mol'o. There was only one apparent anomaly:

---

[23] At first glance, it is odd that the dominant faction in Bola did not crystallize in a type of work group more obviously related to its own cultural vision. In contrast, both residual and emergent factions in Maale "worked together" in groups constructed around their own particular cultural values – the residual faction in mol'o groups presided over by ritual kings, the emergent faction in Protestant maddo groups, animated by the notion of Christian charity. Only the dominant faction coalesced in a work group that culturally was not its own, at least originally. I shall return to this apparent paradox below.

Harmiza, a young Bola man, during a mol'o rest stop, 1983

All three of the Maale households of Kaiyo hamlet belonged to the dom-
inant mol'o. They were, in fact, its only Maale members. Why did Kaiyo
Maale "work together" with traders and outcastes rather than with their
Maale neighbors?

In most ways, Kaiyo Maale were no different from their Maale com-
patriots. The three household heads, all members of the same minimal
lineage, had grown up in Bola and had served Maale kings just as their

neighbors had. By 1970, however, all three had congregated in a settlement of their own, Kaiyo, because of a series of quarrels with surrounding Maale. Dofo and Bola elders explained these quarrels by the fact that
one of the Kaiyo men had a "bad-mouthed wife." She continually caused
trouble.

Whatever the effects of a possibly sharp-tongued woman (certainly a
convenient explanation for elders), structurally it is important to understand that the head of the Kaiyo lineage was the one Maale in the Bola
vicinity who actively supported Bailo as he took over in the 1960s. The
other elders, still loyal in spirit to Yebirka, carried out their duties to the
new man but apparently remained rather cool. Describing the political
situation at the time, one man said, ". . . people just sat still." The head
of the Kaiyo lineage was an exception. He and Bailo became bond friends,
and the king even built a house for his favorite wife in Kaiyo.

Whether Kaiyo men's political commitments to the king led somehow
to everyday quarrels with their neighbors, or merely reverberated with
them, is not clear. In any case, Kaiyo Maale became estranged from their
Maale neighbors; separate residence was one indication of this estrange-
ment, and choice of work partners was another. Kaiyo Maale dropped
the observance of taboos against eating with outcastes (as their landlord,
Bailo, had taken the lead in doing), and they joined the new dominant
mol'o along with the other clients of the king.

The overall result of these local conflicts and confrontations was that
the dominant mol'o, and the political faction from which it crystalized,
stood completely on its own. No trader, outcaste, or Kaiyo Maale worked
in any other mol'o. The dominant bloc was an encysted, closed community surrounded on all sides by sharp boundaries in regard to who
worked with whom in mol'o. Various other mol'o – the residual mol'o
in particular – existed around the closed dominant bloc, but they, unlike the latter, tended to overlap and to grade into one another. As mentioned above, overlapping blocs produce a web. The residual mol'o reported on here was only part of a much larger web, one that extended
well beyond Bola.

These formal patterns emphasize what might not be so clear otherwise, namely, just how tenuous the dominant form of rule in Maale was
and how robust residual social forms and cultural values were. By 1975
Maale had existed as a part of imperial Ethiopia for more than three-
quarters of a century, but its placement within the state rested more on
coercive power than on actual cultural integration. Residual Maale culture retained much of its local position, and dominant Ethiopian culture

had not yet crystalized into a local hegemony.[24] In other words, the process of constructing a new structure of dominant power in early twentieth-century Maale had not involved a revolutionary rupture with the previous way of producing. Rather, old institutions and meanings were incorporated into imperial culture and given, finally, new functions and meanings (not unlike, for example, the monarchy during the development of capitalism in Great Britain).

This aspect of twentieth-century Maale is perhaps best indicated by the fact that even the dominant faction coalesced organizationally in the mol'o, a structure redolent of nineteenth-century Maale traditionalism. What the mol'o meant by 1975, however, was being renegotiated. The dominant faction was in the process of incorporating part of traditional Maale culture and in doing so was transforming and even neutralizing its essential point: The hierarchy that culminated in the king was no longer being justified by claims to inherent control over natural fertility but to land ownership as defined by the imperial state. The whole notion of kingship, both of Maale as a whole and of local mol'o groups in particular, was changing. And the change was taking place because the dominant faction was using kingship and the mol'o in new ways.

The overall result was one of small dominant blocs centered on the landlord king and a few others, surrounded by an expansive and quietly resistant residual web. The blocs were dominant only because they enjoyed the backing of the state's coercive apparatus, and the web residual only because the cultural values on which it was built were inadequate for life in *any* version of modern Ethiopia. Outside the study area, the expanse of residual web was broken here and there by a different kind of bloc – oppositional Protestant communities. Committed to education, beginning to produce cash crops and to trade, Protestants were poised to capture leadership from the dominant coalition.

Helma. Mol'o established the overall pattern of "working together" within which both helma and dabo were organized. Although there was some degree of overlap between dominant and residual factions in helma cooperation, most people chose helma partners from the same pool of households that made up their mol'o or that was allied with it (see figure 6). For example, Dofo and Bola Maale chose 81 percent of their helma

---

[24] What I have designated as "dominant" is, then, somewhat different from Raymond Williams's usage. In particular, it does not imply hegemony. Imperial culture occupied a hegemonic position at the center of the Ethiopian empire, but not at the southern periphery that included Maale. Although not hegemonic, imperial ideals were certainly dominant in Maale by the 1970s, inasmuch as they were more closely tied to forms of extant power than any others.

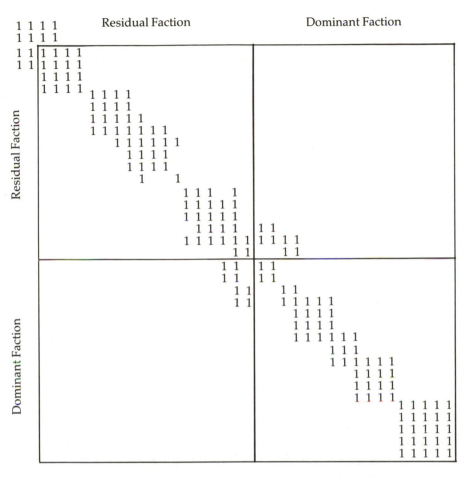

Figure 6: Helma in Bola during 1975 in relation to mol'o. (This is a matrix in which Bola households who worked in helma are arrayed against each other. Blanks indicate the absence of a helma tie; 1 indicates the presence. The pattern above shows that most helma were discretely contained within mol'o-defined factions, the exceptions being a limited amount of overlap shown in the middle and in the extreme upper left-hand corner of the figure. The latter occurred because one helma combined households of the residual faction with ones outside the study area.)

partners from their own numbers or from the immediate area of the next overlapping mol'o. And traders, outcastes, and Kaiyo Maale associated with the dominant mol'o chose 77 percent of their helma partners from inside their group.

These percentages mean that of the fifteen helma established in the seven-month period from planting big-rains fields to clearing small-rains ones in 1975, only two were of mixed membership. One of these was composed of two Bola Maale households plus two trader households from the market village (one of these traders was courting a Bola widow and later incorporated himself into Dofo–Bola work patterns when he married her). The other mixed helma was composed of two Dofo Maale households plus two Kaiyo Maale ones (as I have mentioned, Kaiyo and Dofo inhabitants had lived and worked together before their split in the 1960s). Both these helma can be thought of as bridges – the only points of contact between two otherwise separate networks.

Bridges, apparently, were just the points at which local tensions often built up and were sometimes acted out. Strikingly, no dispute in 1974–75 that reached the king's court involved persons of the same mol'o faction; as I have already pointed out, there was a great deal of pressure to settle disputes among those who "worked together" in the same mol'o before tensions ramified and rigidified into actual court cases. The two court cases that did occur during this time period involved not only members of different factions but precisely the bridging members between the dominant and residual groups. Further data would be required to verify the connection, but it seems that bridges, those relatively weak ties between two otherwise separate and fairly dense networks, tended to be links through which local conflicts were often expressed.

Dabo. Besides the pattern established by helma, dabo cooperation added a third and final layer to "working together" in Bola. And like other forms of cooperative labor, dabo took their structure from the outline laid down by mol'o. Broadly, dabo divided rather neatly into two webs almost exactly associated with dominant and residual factions, as figure 7 shows. Only two households were an exception: one Maale widow from Bola who, as I have already noted, was being courted by a Bola trader and who worked in market-village dabo more than in residual ones, and one Dofo man who had quarreled with his neighbors and was currying new dabo partners in the opposite, dominant faction. In the residual faction, 84 percent of households' dabo partners came from within the faction; the comparable figure for the dominant faction happened to be exactly the same.

The matrix shown in figure 7 is clearly asymmetrical. If the graph is folded along the diagonal, each square does *not* touch another of exactly the same value. This formal property is a result of how dabo are organized. As I have already noted, in dabo household A can work for B without B, in turn, working for A. This potential social asymmetry means that dabo matrices can also be unbalanced. At the extreme, one house-

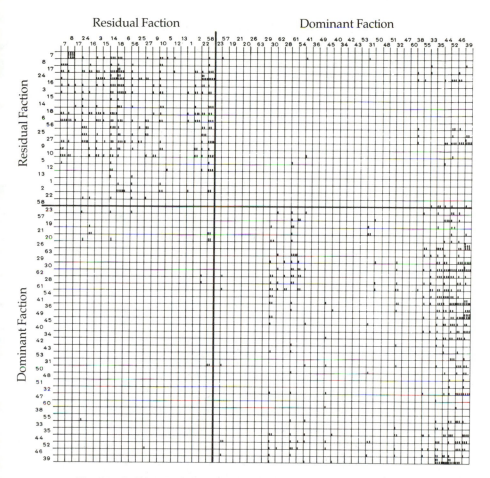

Figure 7: Dabo in Bola during 1975 in relation to mol'o (after Donham, *Work and Power*, p. 154). Household identification numbers (see map 1, p. 143) are shown along the sides of the matrix. Each row of the table – left to right – indicates the number of days that a particular household worked for others, and the corresponding column – up and down – shows the number of days others worked for it.

hold in the Bola vicinity experienced a net deficit of 28 dabo work days over the four months of most intense work that figure 7 covers, while another experienced a net surplus of 54 dabo work days. It turns out that asymmetries not only existed, they were patterned. And the pattern offers an additional source of information about how "working together" worked in Bola in 1975.

Let me take the residual faction first – precisely the group of households analyzed in Chapter 1. Maale hamlets, to recall the discussion above, were composed of households with different relative supplies of domestic labor. Elders' households were generally large and possessed of ample supplies of labor, middle-aged men's households were typically short of labor, and finally the households of young men and their wives (along with others like widows) were neither labor-rich nor labor-poor. Figure 8 (another way of representing the data shown in figures 2 and 7) shows that the imbalances in dabo labor given and received in the residual faction were related to these stages in the developmental cycle of domestic groups. As chapter 1 showed, there was a net transfer of dabo labor from elders' households (with two notable exceptions) to more junior men's households.

For the dominant faction (not discussed in Chapter 1), dabo labor flows were even more dramatic. There, however, the phase of household development did not correlate with the pattern of labor flows. Household size among Bola market-villagers varied little with the age of household heads, and there is even some (inconclusive) evidence that household size tended to vary with wealth – the greater the wealth, the larger the household. Wealth, in fact, seems to have been the prime variable in establishing the pattern of asymmetry in the dabo web of the dominant faction.

Figure 8 shows that there were large transfers of dabo labor from poorer to richer households in the dominant faction. Market-villagers were obviously the core of the dominant faction, since even middle-level market households were able to garner a net surplus of dabo labor, often from other middle households in the same faction. The four richest households enjoyed a remarkable total surplus of 146 dabo work days during the four-month study period, while at the other extreme, the seventeen poor households of the dominant faction experienced a collective deficit of 121 dabo work days.

It is clear that to "work together" did not mean that the households that came "together" were equal. Exactly the opposite; labor flows in the dabo system of cooperation were directly involved in generating and regenerating differences in wealth and power. To some extent, the centrality of beer-drinking in dabo organization covered up this fact. For, at the same time that some dabo hosts were garnering extra labor from others, the etiquette of the beer-drink emphasized hosts' generosity. Exactly as they would have given beer to guests who came to their houses, dabo sponsors "gave" beer to those who came to their work parties. But of course being a worker was not the same as being a guest, and dabo labor flows were intimately tied up with inequalities within political factions.

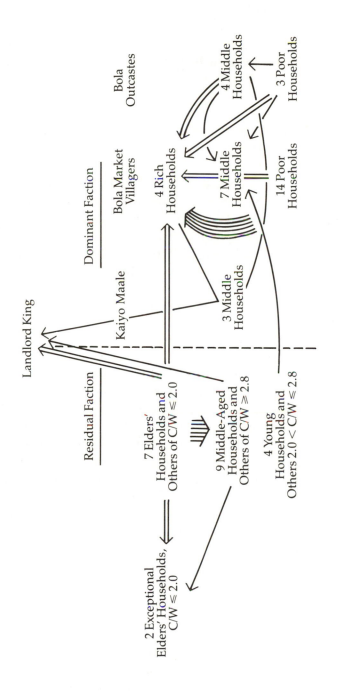

Figure 8: The total pattern of dabo labor flows in the Bola area during 1975 (after Donham, *Work and Power*, p. 161). Each arrow represents ten days of dabo labor during a four-month period.

When people were free to choose to work in dabo or not (one informant explained, "When someone begs me to work in his dabo, I go if I want to; if not, then I don't go"), why did such labor flows take place?

————————

Within the dominant faction, the most politically influential men were three of the four richest market-villagers who enjoyed a large surplus of dabo labor. Their influence and, to a great extent, their wealth derived mainly from their relationship to the landlord king. Two of the four had been scribes for Bailo or his son, presiding over court cases in the king's absence, collecting rents, and serving as intermediaries between Bola and the local subprovincial capital. A third man had served from time to time as the king's representative in collecting rents. And all of the three men, much more than middle-level men in the market village or surrounding Maale, were regularly involved in settling local court cases. (Only one of the four men who enjoyed such a surplus of dabo labor had no special relationship to the landlord king.)

Rich market-villagers were able to gather labor from poorer households for a number of reasons. Economically, rich market-villagers found no difficulty in providing beer for their work parties; roughly half of what they needed they simply bought in the weekly market, already prepared. Poor households, on the other hand, very often did not have the extra grain needed to make beer and thus to sponsor a dabo. When I asked one such man why he continued to work in others' dabo when he had no hope of receiving help in return, he explained that he expected gradually to accumulate enough grain to sponsor dabo in the future. Whether this hope was reasonable, in strictly economic terms it is clear that his dabo deficits – labor deflected from his own fields – actually delayed the time when the poor man would be able to recoup his losses (even if beer temporarily provided some of his subsistence).

But there were other, political reasons that poorer households continued to "work together" with the leaders of the dominant faction. To "work together" was fundamentally a matter of choosing sides in Bola. Had poor market-villagers refused to work in the dabo of their richer neighbors, such a refusal would have been taken as a social breach, a declaration of social separation. Such a step would have been difficult for at least two reasons. First, poor immigrant traders would have found it difficult to establish many supporters among the surrounding traditionalist Maale. And, second, they would have cut themselves off from the favors that rich market-villagers could afford to give. Goodwill at

A Bola market-villager, drinking beer on market day, 1974

rent time and support in a court case were just two of the ways in which the properly disposed wealthy could help.

Let me turn to the residual faction. The pattern of dabo labor flows there was diametrically opposed to those analyzed above. In the residual faction, most politically influential households, namely those of elders, experienced deficits of labor in dabo work parties, not surpluses. There were only two exceptions, as figure 8 illustrates; one of these was an elder who was by far the richest of any Maale in the Bola vicinity (otherwise the Maale of that area were remarkably homogeneous in wealth). The other was a trader long integrated into Maale society, his mother having been Maale. These two exceptions aside (both seem to reflect the wealth-related pattern above), there was a net transfer of labor from most elders' households to junior men's households, as Chapter 1 showed. Why did most elders give away labor?

Elders in the residual faction found their traditional position of special influence in Maale challenged from two social blocs in the 1970s. On one side, they came into conflict with immigrant traders in Bola who were taking over their old role as middlemen between the king and the surrounding population. Literate traders, not elders, were becoming more effective in dealing with and profiting from the new system of landlords, rents, and local court cases. On the other side, another threat grew – that of the Maale Protestants. More than one informant pointed out that it was mainly junior men who were converting to Protestant Christianity by the 1970s – in particular, younger brothers who stood to inherit little when their fathers died. In Protestant blocs, junior men with a few years of education were gaining a great deal of influence that they would not have enjoyed under the old Maale system. For traditionalist elders, then, Protestant communities threatened to lure away their young men, to undermine the loyalty of their closest following.

Caught between the immigrant traders in Bola and the Maale Protestant communities nearby, elders in the residual faction fought to keep alive the old system and their special position in it. It was in this particular context – aggravated by all of the unease and upset caused by the progress of the Ethiopian revolution in the north during 1975 – that elders transferred labor to households of junior men.

Simply stated, elders appear to have transferred labor to middle-aged men in return for support and for deference. It was elders' gift of labor that obligated and subordinated junior men. If middle-aged men did not reciprocate dabo labor, then at least they were under some compulsion not to offend. After all, elders' labor support could be withdrawn, as the case of one middle-aged man named Bereha shows. After being thrown out of the residual mol'o and after quarreling with his neighbors in Dofo, Bereha did not receive any more dabo labor than he contributed to others in 1975. Dissatisfied and isolated, he eventually moved away.

Looked at together, the pattern of asymmetries in the dabo webs of the residual and dominant factions were arguably interrelated. Neither would have taken the pattern it did during 1975 without the other. Given the boundary between the two factions, poor market-villagers almost had to work for their rich neighbors. And given the threat to traditionalist elders from dominant and oppositional blocs, elders had to preserve their political following by some means, "giving away" labor being perhaps the readiest means at hand. If somehow the boundary between residual, dominant, and emergent factions could have been erased or at least blurred, then it is reasonable to assume that the pattern of dabo labor flows analyzed above would have been changed.

Along with the pattern of dabo asymmetries, the structure of internal solidarities of each faction was also interrelated. As I have already noted, conflicts within either faction were muted and rarely reached public expression. Internal solidarity went hand-in-hand with the sharp boundary between residual and dominant networks. It was the increasing incorporation of Maale into Ethiopia along with Bailo's policies to found a market village and to bring immigrants into his administration that established and maintained this boundary. And if the policies of the landlord king were partly the cause of the cleavage, he himself performed the function of settling the conflicts that were generated.

When the revolution finally arrived in Bola in late 1975, traditionalist elders asked rhetorically, "How can we survive without a king? Even bees have a king [what we call queen bees Maale call king bees]. Termites have a king. Cattle have a leader. Without a king, we will kill each other off." In a sense, the elders were correct – but correct only as long as previous realities, previous patterns of "working together," were assumed to hold.

As far as I can tell, stem-family households, helma, dabo, and mol'o have coexisted as social forms in Maale for at least the past eighty years. And the cultural concept of "working together" seems to have remained broadly the same, at least insofar as it is "about" political solidarity. A great deal can be said about each of these social and cultural elements as constants, as structures. But such constants cannot provide an explanation of who worked with whom in Bola in 1975. Disembodied social and cultural forms, they radically underdetermine the meaning and social organization of "working together" that I have just described. And without this last level of specificity – of practices set within a particular historical context – one gets little sense of how local people actively produced their own society and culture, "not just as they pleased," yet with some measure of freedom. With exactly the same social and cultural elements, the same mode of production, local political economy could have turned out differently in Bola during 1975, much differently.

With respect to the social organization of "working together," I have emphasized the importance of the boundary between dominant and residual factions. Both dabo and helma stacked neatly within mol'o-defined groups. But this particular outcome was not automatically given; mol'o could have overlapped one to the next, and dabo and helma could have bridged and connected mol'o into one more-or-less continuous web. Such a pattern (with, one would expect, different structures of dabo labor flows) could have resulted in a more relaxed political environment in which actors did not have to choose sides in quite the same way. In other words, the social patterns I discovered in Bola were the result of an array of factors peculiar to that place and time; they cannot necessarily be assumed to have held in Bola in 1925 or in other Maale locales in 1975.

The same methodological point can be made with respect to the meaning of "working together." Although this notion seems to have been focused on political solidarity for as far back as I can determine, the identity of actors addressing one another on the same stage, making claims back and forth, quite simply conversing, was different over time. I have mentioned the change in meaning that accompanied the dominant faction's use of the mol'o. For another example, consider what it meant to a Maale person to work in a mol'o before Protestant missionaries arrived compared to afterward. Before, working with beer had little political significance. Beer made work parties into larger and more social gatherings, and it was always associated with a certain amount of prestige. But providing beer did not entail a political statement in itself. After Protestant communities were organized and after beer was tabooed and new ways of "working together" were organized by church officials, sponsoring a work party with beer, particularly a mol'o, meant something different. It meant a rejection of Protestantism and a rejection of Protestants' own rejection of the traditional Maale political hierarchy – kings, queen-mothers, chiefs, and outcastes.

Yet another switch occurred after the revolution in Maale in late 1975. Until then, both residual and dominant factions used the mol'o, with its notions of inherent hierarchy among persons, as an organizing form.

Kaiyaro, the Bola woman shown as a frightened child on p. 93. By December 1983, she had given birth to her ninth child, a girl. The passage of time – and the transformation of historical contexts – is perhaps most graphically illustrated by reference to the succession of generations.

After the revolution, new forms of "working together" were organized not only at the level of the peasant associations that were organized to take over the functions of the king but also at the local level that included mol'o. Some people spontaneously gave up mol'o and organized new kinds of work groups presided over by "chairmen," "judges," and "policemen." But some mol'o carried on, even though revolutionary cadre agitated against them. "Working together" in mol'o during the postrevolutionary period indicated an incomprehension of or, at the strongest, a rejection of new egalitarian ideologies and forms of organization.

It is this last level of actual practices set in particular space-time that analyses of modes of production, such as that of the previous chapter, can never capture. But, equivalently it can be argued that an understanding of epochal structures is a necessary prerequisite for the kind of historical analysis that I have just completed. For it was precisely the state of play within productive inequalities that determined how Maale "worked together" in 1975. By that time, the Ethiopian revolution had begun to unfold in the north of the country. Emperor Haile Selassie had been imprisoned in September 1974, and about a month later, fifty-seven of his top-ranking men had been executed.[25] As Maale began to clear new fields at the beginning of 1975, they realized that local changes might well follow. An air of uncertainty hung over local events until July 1975, when "red guard" students arrived in Maale and arrested Bailo's son, along with the richest northern landlords living in the area.

The pattern of "working together" analyzed in this chapter and the labor flows discussed in Chapter 1 took place precisely during this period of uncertainty. The revolution, with its slowly increasing stress on socialist egalitarianism, began to threaten the very basis of Maale productive inequalities – the notion of an inherent hierarchy between kings and chiefs on the one hand, and commoners on the other, between eldest brothers and younger ones, and between household heads and their dependents. These inequalities interlocked one with the other, and all depended (I have argued) on a particular complex of ideas about gender.

At the end of the weeding season in 1975, kingship and chiefship were finally and irrevocably abolished in Maale. The productive inequality that had dominated and encapsulated all others was suddenly swept away, and of the formerly empowered, only household heads were left standing – naked. Partly in anticipation of such an outcome, partly as a last-ditch effort to preserve the old order that had conferred a privileged position upon them, Bola elders in 1975 turned their local community inward, demarcated boundaries with adjacent peoples, and shored up their closest followers by transferring labor to more junior men's households.

[25] Many Maale, even though they resented northern landlords to some degree, viewed Haile Selassie as a distant ritual king on the model of their own kati. Haile Selassie's imprisonment in the fall of 1974 was therefore a momentous event for Maale.

Maale students in Bushkoro, the only school in Maale at the time, marching to welcome a new representative of the revolutionary government in 1975. The sign in Amharic celebrates the land reform: "The land you till has become your security."

How Maale inequalities were modified during the twentieth century is a complex story, but at each moment, the state of play within productive inequalities conditioned what happened. By the 1960s, the landlord king, backed by the imperial state, was able to use traditional symbols and offices to accomplish new ends. He was able, in fact, to dominate traditionalists in Maale. But the king's power was not complete. He could not prevent the formation of oppositional Protestant blocs nor eradicate the quiet resistance of traditionalists. Below the landlord king, lineage heads and husband-fathers also continued to occupy positions of some power. Despite sporadic opposition from angry brothers, unfilial children, and "bad-mouthed" wives, they directed the day-to-day operation of the local political economy.

On the eve of the revolution, then, the Maale produced a good deal more than sorghum when they "worked together." They produced the social groups and cultural discourse that defined, in part, who they were. It is this last level of actual practice – of living men and women using social forms and cultural notions in historical context – that completes a historical materialist analysis.

"Gift," Man Ray, 1921

Conclusion

> *As for what motivated me, it is quite simple; I would hope that in the eyes of some people it might be sufficient in itself. It was curiosity – the only kind of curiosity in any case, that is worth acting upon with a degree of obstinacy: not the curiosity that seeks to assimilate what it is proper for one to know, but that which enables one to get free of oneself. After all, what would be the value of the passion for knowledge if it resulted only in a certain amount of knowledgeableness and not, in one way or another and to the extent possible, in the knower's straying afield of himself?*
>
> Michel Foucault

How does one summarize arguments such as these? Perhaps the best way is to attempt to restate them in an entirely new way. I have argued that culture, the style in which things are done, is a consequential matter. I would like to try to apply that insight to my own analyses in this book in order to specify more clearly what critical theory is and what makes it "critical."[1]

Some time ago, Edmund Leach, following Ludwig Wittgenstein, wrote, "Logically, aesthetics and ethics are identical. If we are to understand the ethical rules of a society, it is aesthetics that we must study."[2] Using that intuition with respect to social theory itself, let me consider the contrasting moral visions of neoclassicism and Marxism via the rhetorical structures of my previous chapters. In other words, let me look at what I have done as a set of stories, as a collection of narratives.

Hayden White, influenced by Northrop Frye's typology of Western literature, has argued that the same modes of emplotment appear among historians as among literary writers: romance, tragedy, comedy, and sat-

---

[1] The epigraph to this chapter, by Michel Foucault, refers to the role of knowledge in permitting the knower to stray afield of himself; see *The Use of Pleasure*, trans. Robert Hurley (New York: Pantheon, [1984] 1985), p. 8. Marxism's central tenet is that this process depends on more than individual knowledge. As long as society is organized in such a way that one group's existence is coercively supported by the labor of others, individuals cannot, in the end, get free of themselves. Critical theory is devoted to making these supraindividual connections more visible and, once more visible, an object for contest.

[2] Edmund Leach, *Political Systems of Highland Burma: A Study of Kachin Social Structure* (Boston: Beacon Press, 1954), p. 12.

ire.[3] These forms, and meditations upon them, have an ancient history in Western thought, and although any attempt to construct a typology with them is bound to result in a certain crudeness, questions of rhetoric nevertheless appear to delineate – in a way I have found difficult to express otherwise – the manner in which all social theories proceed from particular moral assumptions.

If Frye's four are taken to represent the archetypical stories that anthropologists tell, then Chapter 1 of this book may be said to be a "comedy." The conflict I focused on – the fact that high dependency ratio households did not seem to work longer hours – was shown, finally, to have an almost obvious explanation. In the end, the conflict turned out not to be a conflict at all, and as the curtain went down, we in the audience had the feeling that all was right with the world.

> The reconciliations which occur at the end of Comedy are reconciliations of men with men, of men with their world and their society; the condition of society is represented as being purer, saner, and healthier as a result of the conflict among seemingly inalterably opposed elements in the world; these elements are revealed to be, in the long run, harmonizable with one another, unified, at one with themselves and the others.[4]

Comedy, not as joke of course but as plot, appears to be a persistent feature of neoclassical analyses, so-called Pareto optimality typically providing the healthy resolution to apparent contradiction.

Chapters 2, 3, and 4, as steps in a historical materialist analysis, formed different kinds of stories. In Chapters 2 and 3, the conflict that drove the narrative was *not* overcome. Instead, the reproduction of the tension between kings and commoners, elder and younger brothers, and husbands and wives provided a ground against which social facts turned out to mean something different from what they seemed. This constant "irony" – that people acted in terms of categories that had unintended consequences – provided the master trope of the story. The plot was not so much a retelling of events as a synchronic piling of detail upon detail, from one area of life to another, in one reduction of Maale cultural categories to power differences.

If the plot of Chapters 2 and 3 were all there was to historical materialism, the story contained therein would not be recognizably Marxist – perhaps Nietzschean or Weberian, but not Marxist. For, placed across

---

[3] Hayden White, *Metahistory: The Historical Imagination in Nineteenth-Century Europe* (Baltimore: Johns Hopkins University Press, 1973); Northop Frye, *Anatomy of Criticism: Four Essays* (Princeton: Princeton University Press, 1957).
[4] White, *Metahistory*, p. 9.

irony, there is a romance in every Marxist story, a "romance" of oppositional consciousness and of future hope.

The Romance is fundamentally a drama of self-identification symbolized by the hero's transcendence of the world of experience, his victory over it, and his final liberation from it – the sort of drama associated with the Grail legend or the story of the resurrection of Christ in Christian mythology. It is a drama of the triumph of good over evil, of virtue over vice, of light over darkness, and of the ultimate transcendence of man over the world in which he was imprisoned by the Fall.[5]

Chapter 4 did not end in a triumph, but it was nevertheless guided by glimpses of the spirit necessary for such a conclusion: a spirit of resistance, whether by backward-looking traditionalists or restless Protestants. Like neoclassical stories that tend to end in comedy, Marxist analyses characteristically combine irony and romance – "irony" because of the unmasking of the present and "romance" because of future hope. One might almost say that irony is put at the service of romance, for unmasking is a critical first step toward future emancipation.

My point is not, of course, that Marxism is "only" a trope. Neither is the cultural construction of labor power or of Maale descent "only" superstructural. Such an interpretation betrays a misunderstanding (ensnared in capitalist ideology) that this book has sought, at some length, to dispel. Rather, my claim is that romantic irony goes some distance toward defining an essential aspect of Marxism, namely, its commitment to a certain set of assumptions about human nature: succinctly put, that power is deeply ambivalent. It at once promotes human development and progress and, at the same time, contradicts and grates against universal human needs.

This assumption cannot be "tested" in the same way as a scientific proposition; rather, like other assumptions in other social theories, it allows scientific propositions to be formulated. Once formulated, propositions can be shown to be better and worse representations of social reality, but they nonetheless retain a certain imprint from their point of origin.

A strictly neutral social science – or, what amounts to the same thing, a tropeless rhetoric – is, I assume, as impossible as jumping over one's shadow.[6] The only reasonable response to this predicament, it seems to

---

[5] Ibid., pp. 8–9.
[6] Leonard P. Wessell, Jr., argues that Marxism's "mythopoetic" origins invalidate it: *Karl Marx, Romantic Irony, and the Proletariat: The Mythopoetic Origins of Marxism* (Baton Rouge: Louisiana State University Press, 1979). In contrast, I assume that all social theories con-

me, is to examine and to choose one's rhetorical assumptions, not to pretend that they do not exist.

———

Given this stance, a prominent theme of preceding chapters has been the relationship between de facto power and culturally encoded ideology – between base and superstructure. I believe that it is accurate to say, as Perry Anderson has done, that G. A. Cohen's interpretation of base and superstructure "supersedes virtually all previous discussion."[7] In my exposition above, I have sought to build on Cohen's insights. But I have found his interpretation lacking in one respect, namely, in formulating a definition of relations of production (or as I have called them, productive inequalities) that applies equally across different modes of production. As a preface to a summary of my arguments, let me quote Cohen:

If production relations [or productive inequalities] require legal expression for stability, it follows that the foundation requires a superstructure. This seems to violate the architectural metaphor, since foundations do not normally need superstructures to be stable. We must be careful if we are looking for a visual image to go with the metaphor. One slab resting on another would be inappropriate. One correct picture is the following: Four struts are driven into the ground, each protruding the same distance above it. They are unstable. They sway and wobble in winds of force 2. Then a roof is attached to the four struts, and now they stay firmly erect in all winds under force 6. Of this roof one can say: (i) it is supported by the struts, and (ii) it renders them more stable. There we have a building whose base and superstructure relate in the right way.[8]

This way of putting the matter, although clearly an advance over the notion of two slabs, is still not entirely adequate. The difficulty is that (already existing) productive inequalities do not simply "need," as Cohen

tain mythic elements, at least in the way the phrase is being used here. The choice between theories involves a complex intersection between considerations of how far each alternative allows one scientifically to understand social reality and politically to make sense of one's own life. For a more complex discussion of the varieties of "romantic irony" – from what nowadays might be called modern to postmodern – see Meyer Abrams, *Natural Supernaturalism: Tradition and Revolution in Romantic Literature* (New York: W. W. Norton, 1971); Anne K. Mellor, *English Romantic Irony* (Cambridge: Harvard University Press, 1980); Kathleen M. Wheeler, ed., *German Aesthetic and Literary Criticism: The Romantic Ironists and Goethe* (Cambridge: Cambridge University Press, 1984); Lilian R. Furst, *Fictions of Romantic Irony* (Harvard: Cambridge University Press, 1984).
[7] Perry Anderson, *Arguments Within English Marxism* (London: New Left Books, 1980), p. 72.
[8] G. A. Cohen, *Karl Marx's Theory of History: A Defence* (Oxford: Clarendon Press, 1978), p. 231.

says, superstructures for stability. They cannot exist without superstructures.

Granted, it is necessary to define and to locate, as Cohen has expertly demonstrated, productive inequalities in a way that is independent of superstructures. We may even attempt to develop a superstructure-free typology of inequalities in which producers are said to control "all," "some," or "none" of the productive powers they use.[9] But such an exercise will not furnish an *analysis* of modes of production, for productive inequalities are never maintained simply by force. As systems of regularized social interaction, inequalities are inextricably embedded in superstructural meanings and practices. Cohen realized this when he wrote: ". . . might frequently requires right in order to operate or even to be constituted. Might without right may be impossible, inefficient, or unstable."[10]

But if Cohen is correct, then the image of four struts that are subsequently stabilized with a top should be replaced by what it otherwise resembles: an already-built table. Of the table top, one can say: (i) it is supported by its legs and (ii) its existence is required for the legs to be legs. Without the top, the legs do not stand upright. They become only sticks of wood of such-and-such a length.

Why is this modification important? Because it prevents a misunderstanding of Marxism as an economic determinism, in which economics – the four struts – is understood in capitalist (superstructural) terms. For example, in the typology mentioned above, Cohen assumed that control over productive powers is a universal desideratum in defining productive inequalities.[11] But, as I have argued, immediate control over economic resources is not the basis on which all systems of domination are cast. Rather, "control" over productive powers becomes an omnibus analytical concept only in the presence of a certain superstructural definition of personhood – one that defines the labor of men and women as a thing, a commodity, to be bought and sold like all other things.[12]

---

[9] Ibid., p. 65.　　[10] Ibid., p. 231.
[11] Ibid., p. 65.
[12] Marx wrote: "The capitalist epoch is therefore characterized by the fact that labour-power, in the eyes of the worker himself, takes on the form of a commodity which is his property; his labour consequently takes on the form of wage-labour. . . . it is only from this moment that the commodity-form of the products of labour becomes universal," *Capital*, vol. 1, trans. Ben Fowkes (New York: Vintage, [1867] 1976), p. 274, fn. 4. In fact, far more attention needs to be paid to the cultural construction of labor power within various capitalist societies. Max Weber may, perhaps, be said to have begun this task in *The Protestant Ethic and the Spirit of Capitalism*, trans. Talcott Parsons (New York: Charles Scribner's Sons, [1904–5] 1958).

In Maale, such ideas were nonexistent. As I have shown, the relevant notions centered on fertility and fecundity, gender and lineage priority, chiefly and kingly position. Even though such concepts may strike us as strangely noneconomic, they powerfully organized and maintained material inequalities in Maale. We would have overlooked them had we begun analysis with a definition of the base that was, in fact, encumbered by capitalist categories.

The notion that poor people have to "sell" their labor power to rich people in order to survive is no more economic than the idea that Maale women have to "marry" men in order to enjoy fertility. Both are superstructural systems of meanings and practices that institute and uphold (different) bases. On this view, the analysis of modes of production becomes a matter of (1) locating effective power differences over material production as these are reflected in differential control over the total product and (2) analyzing the meanings and practices that tend to reproduce such powers. There should be no presumption that (2) conforms to our notions of what is economic.

On this reading, ideology is not something that simply legitimates power (the top that stabilizes the four struts). Rather, it provides the very terms in which power regularly becomes power (the tabletop that makes legs legs).

———————

I have illustrated this revised notion of base and superstructure in an analysis of Maale. But such a position has consequences for the examination of other modes of production – including capitalism, that heartland of Marxist theory. Once one starts with the realization that all empirical analysis must be carried out in particular superstructural terms, then the goal is not somehow to escape those terms in order to get down to the really real, the hard "economic" facts. Just the opposite: The task becomes one of interpreting and, in fact, deconstructing the cultural categories that are implicated in the continuance of productive inequalities – wherever they can be found. In this sense, Marxist analysis resembles, in some ways, surrealist art.

In Maale, the same institutional structures accomplished both the production of material goods and the reproduction of laborers: households grouped in chiefdoms under the authority of the ritual king. In this respect, prerevolutionary Maale resembled many technologically simple societies. When a household completed a cycle of production – enough to provide for its own subsistence, tributes to the chiefs and king, and the necessary extra in seeds and tools for the next cycle – it simultaneously accomplished the task of reproducing future labor, both biologically and socially. In this sense, the organization of production did not depend upon other structures for continuity; in producing, Maale household enterprises produced both product and people.[13]

The same is not true of capitalism. In capitalism, to a degree perhaps unprecedented in world history, the organization of production is institutionalized separately from that of the reproduction of labor. This separation defines the split between so-called public and private realms in capitalist societies.[14] In the public sphere, "civic society," free individuals meet and contract to carry out production. In the private sphere, men and women marry, bear and educate children, and pass on family property.

Marx's great achievement in *Capital* was to show that the formal freedom of the public sphere is illusory inasmuch as it is founded on a prior inequality between those who own capital and those who do not:

The sphere of circulation or commodity exchange, within whose boundaries the sale and purchase of labour-power goes on, is in fact a very Eden of the innate rights of man. It is the exclusive realm of Freedom, Equality, Property and Bentham. Freedom, because both buyer and seller of a commodity, let us say of labour-power, are determined only by their own free will. They contract as free persons, who are equal before the law. Their contract is the final result in which their joint will finds a common legal expression. Equality, because each enters into relation with the other, as with a simple owner of commodities, and they exchange equivalent for equivalent. Property, because each disposes only of what is his own. And Bentham, because each looks only to his own advantage. The only force bringing them together, and putting them into relation with each other, is the selfishness, the gain and the private interest of each. Each pays heed to himself only, and no one worries about the others. And precisely for that reason, either in accordance with the pre-established harmony of things, or under the auspices of an omniscient providence, they all work together to their mutual advantage, for the common weal, and in the common interest. When we

[13]Some of the pitfalls involved in analyzing the reproduction of labor are discussed in Olivia Harris and Kate Young, "Engendered Structures: Some Problems in the Analysis of Reproduction," in Joel S. Kahn and Josep R. Llobera, eds., *The Anthropology of Pre-Capitalist Societies* (London: Macmillan, 1981), pp. 109–47.

[14]Some degree of differentiation between public and private spheres also occurs in many noncapitalist societies, but how this differentiation is instituted and what it entails is different. The issue of how to analyze the public and the private in different modes of production has a complicated history in recent feminist anthropology. See Michelle Z. Rosaldo, "The Use and Abuse of Anthropology: Reflections on Feminism and Cross-Cultural Understanding," *Signs* 5 (1980): 389–417. John L. Comaroff has reviewed the issue in "*Sui generis:* Feminism, Kinship Theory, and Structural 'Domains,' " in Jane F. Collier and Sylvia J. Yanagisako, eds., *Gender and Kinship: Essays Toward a Unified Analysis* (Stanford: Stanford University Press, 1987), pp. 53–85.

leave this sphere of simple circulation or the exchange of commodities, which provides the "free-trader *vulgaris*" with his views, his concepts and the standard by which he judges the society of capital and wage-labour, a certain change takes place, or so it appears, in the physiognomy of our *dramatis personae*. He who was previously the money-owner now strides out in front as a capitalist; the possessor of labour-power follows as his worker. The one smirks self-importantly and is intent on business; the other is timid and holds back, like someone who has brought his own hide to market and now has nothing else to expect but – a tanning.[15]

Thus Marx constructed a theory – a critical theory – that cut through the ideology of equality in the public sphere to lay bare an underlying system of domination.

By limiting his analysis in *Capital* to the public realm, however, Marx appears to have unconsciously accepted part of capitalist ideology.[16] According to capitalism's own self-definition, the private sphere is noneconomic. It is simply naturally given: Men and women naturally marry in the way they do, women naturally nurture children, and men naturally pass on property to their biological offspring.

Whether in fact the private sphere is simply biologically determined is an important issue. For it is clear that the public realm – given form by Marx's reproduction schemata in *Capital* – actually depends on the organization of the private for its continued existence. This is evident from the fact that labor power itself is not produced as a commodity; that is, capitalists do not hire men and women to bear and to educate future workers. Rather, children are born and raised in the private realm dominated not by the selfishness of the cash nexus analyzed by Marx but by affection, by "love." As the saying goes, love is something that money can't buy. In general, it is love – unconditional, diffuse, and enduring – that provides the distinctive defining feature of the private, as it contrasts with the public world of work – the latter being, as Marx pointed out, self-interested, specialized, and time-limited.

If processes within the private realm are socially constructed in culturally specific ways and if, moreover, these cultural terms are implicated in forms of power just as real as class and, indeed, on which the continuance of class depends – then *Capital* is, as many feminists have pointed out, a seriously incomplete analysis of the capitalist mode of produc-

[15] Marx, *Capital*, vol. 1, p. 280.
[16] It will become clear below not only that Marx limited himself to the public sphere; within that sphere, he also limited himself to "economic" structures – neglecting issues such as race and nationality.

tion.[17] In order to advance critical theory, a method of analyzing capitalism must be developed that takes into account the interrelationships between the public and the private. To accomplish this, we are required to confront a series of new, "noneconomic" issues. I believe these include, at a minimum, gender, sexuality, race, and nationality.[18]

The first three of these – gender, sexuality, and race – are intertwined in the inner constitution of the private realm, and the last – nationality – establishes the outer boundaries of the public. All are aspects of how persons are constituted as natural beings in Western European capitalism: black, American male. White, British female. Within the bounds of the public sphere, each individual is said to have the same right to contract, to buy and sell, to voice opinions, and so forth. But this stress on public equality is contained within a set of definitions of natural differences. Women, blacks, homosexuals, and illegal aliens – to name a few – have not, at various points, enjoyed the same rights as others, to the degree that they have been constituted as naturally (or unnaturally) different.

Marx and Marxists have long discounted these aspects of personhood

---

[17] After confronting anthropological materials, Engels wrote: "According to the materialist conception, the determining factor in history is, in the final instance, the production and reproduction of immediate life. This again, is of a twofold character: on the one hand, the production of the means of existence, of food, clothing, and shelter and the tools necessary for that production; on the other side, the production of human beings themselves, the propagation of the species. The social organization under which the people of a particular historical epoch and a particular country live is determined by both kinds of production: by the stage of development of labor on the one hand, and of the family on the other . . . ," *The Origin of the Family, Private Property, and the State* (London: Lawrence & Wishart, [1884] 1972), pp. 71–2. Unfortunately, this insight, published in 1884, was never applied to the analysis of capitalism itself, Marx's major work, volume 1 of *Capital*, having been published first in 1867.

[18] A certain amount of prejudice appears to have prevented Marx and Engels from fully examining these issues. It is noteworthy that utilitarian precursors of neoclassical theory like John Stuart Mill and Jeremy Bentham developed more critical views of the private realm than did Marx and Engels. On women, Engels's *Origins of the Family* does not compare with Mill's *The Subjection of Women* (Cambridge: MIT Press, [1869] 1970). And on the question of sex, Bentham held considerably more independent views than Engels. In notes unpublished at the time, Bentham attacked laws against same-sex sex as "barbarous." See Louis Crompton, *Byron and Greek Love: Homophobia in Nineteenth-Century England* (Berkeley: University of California Press, 1985), pp. 38–53. In contrast, Engels referred to sodomy as "abominable" in *The Origin of the Family*, p. 128, and when Marx sent his friend Engels a then-current book on homosexual behavior, Engels lightly replied, "The pederasts are beginning to count themselves and find that they form a power in the state . . . it is only by luck that we are personally too old to have to fear that at this victory we will have to pay bodily tribute" (translated from *Marx Engels Werke*, vol. 32, pp. 324–5, and cited by Gary Kinsman, *The Regulation of Desire* (Montreal: Black Rose Books, 1987), p. 59, n. 74).

as secondary to class in capitalism and as fated to disappear as the public sphere expands, inwardly into the private realm and outwardly to erase national boundaries. According to Marx and Engels:

The bourgeoisie has torn away from the family its sentimental veil, and has reduced the family relation to a mere money relation.[19]

The working men have no country. . . . National differences and antagonisms between peoples are daily more and more vanishing, owing to the development of the bourgeoisie. . . .[20]

Surely, few aspects of orthodox Marxism are further from the truth of actually existing capitalism. In our century alone, how many people have sacrificed their very lives "for their country"? And in North America alone, how much more deeply has sexuality become the essence of individual beings, "love" the very bulwark of private lives?

A full consideration of this problem is beyond my objective and indeed my competence. Let me merely outline some extant works of others, as they relate to a fuller analysis of capitalism, beginning with the issue of nationalism. To start with a definition, nationalism is a doctrine that holds that humanity is naturally divided into nations, that each nation is constituted principally by a common language and/or culture, and that each such unit – characterized by what Benedict Anderson has called a "deep horizontal comradeship" – has a right to its own state.[21] One culture, one state, one public realm.

For those of us who swim in these ideas as fish swim in water, it is difficult to realize that they are relatively recent inventions in world history, roughly coincident with the rise of the world capitalist system: "A man must have a nationality as he must have a nose and two ears. . . . All this seems obvious, though, alas, it is not true. But that it should have come to *seem* so very obviously true is indeed an aspect, or perhaps the very core, of the problem of nationalism."[22]

[19] Marx and Engels, "Manifesto of the Communist Party," *Collected Works*, vol. 6 (London: Lawrence & Wishart, [1848] 1976), p. 487.
[20] Ibid., pp. 502–3.
[21] Benedict Anderson, *Imagined Communities: Reflections on the Origin and Spread of Nationalism* (London: Verso, 1983), pp. 15–6. Nationalism in the sense being discussed here apparently originated in the late eighteenth and early nineteenth centuries. For an attempt to link nationalism with the uneven development of capitalism, see Tom Nairn, *The Break-Up of Britain: Crisis and Neo-Nationalism* (London: New Left Books, 1977). Ernest Gellner, *Nations and Nationalism* (Oxford: Basil Blackwell, 1983), makes his arguments in relation to the requirements of industrialism in general, not capitalism in particular. See also Elie Kedourie, *Nationalism* (London: Hutchinson, 1961).
[22] Gellner, *Nations*, p. 6.

"Motherland." "Fatherland." "My country right or wrong!" It is clear that notions of the nation build, in turn, on the kinds of enduring solidarity that characterize the private realm.[23] In his study of American kinship – the center of what I am calling the private – David Schneider pointed out that there are two kinds of love that recur in two kinds of relationships: "love" between parents and children based on a natural tie of blood, and "love" between husbands and wives based on a relationship entered into under the law.

At the very center of this classificatory structure, combining nature and law to create "love," is the capitalist family. Its master symbol, according to Schneider, is sexual intercourse – or as it is appropriately phrased, "making love."

Father is the genitor, mother the genetrix of the child which is their offspring. Husband and wife are in sexual relationship and theirs is the only legitimate and proper sexual relationship. Husband and wife are lovers and the child is the product of their love as well as the object of their love; it is in this sense that there are two kinds of love which define family relationships, one conjugal and the other cognatic, and it is in this sense that love is a synonym for sexual intercourse.[24]

Again, for those of us who swim in these ideas, it is difficult to see them as merely one way of looking at the world. Sexual intercourse between men and women is, one presumes, a human universal.[25] But intercourse does not universally mean "love," and "love" does not universally constitute a private realm, in opposition to a public world of impersonal

---

[23] On the connections between notions of nationality and kinship see David M. Schneider, "Kinship, Nationality and Religion in American Culture: Toward a Definition of Kinship," in Robert F. Spencer, ed., *Forms of Symbolic Action* (Seattle: University of Washington Press for the American Ethnological Society), pp. 116–25.

[24] David M. Schneider, *American Kinship: A Cultural Account*, 2d ed. (Chicago: University of Chicago Press, 1980), p. 24. For a critique of Schneider's analysis in relation to whether American kin terms contain a core reference to biologically constituted relationships, see Harold W. Scheffler, "The 'Meaning' of Kinship in American Culture: Another View," in Keith H. Basso and Henry A. Selby, eds., *Meaning in Anthropology* (Albuquerque: University of New Mexico Press, 1976), pp. 57–91. The issue of whether or not notions of kinship universally contain a biological element does not affect, as far as I can see, any of the arguments I make below.

[25] With the emphasis on heterosexual "love," the category of the homosexual as a deviant type evolved during the nineteenth century. Before, homosexual behavior had been a sin like others that anyone might fall into. Afterward, homosexuality – and heterosexuality – came to be thought of as parts of the "natures" of persons. See Michel Foucault, *The History of Sexuality*, vol. 1, trans. Robert Hurley (New York: Pantheon, [1976] 1978); Robert A. Padgug, "Sexual Matters: On Conceptualizing Sexuality in History," *Radical History Review* 20 (1979): 3–23; and John D'Emilio, "Capitalism and Gay Identity," in Ann Snitow, Christine Stansell, and Sharon Thompson, eds., *Powers of Desire: The Politics of Sexuality* (New York: Monthly Review Press, 1983), pp. 100–13.

contracts, of "work." Schneider does not inquire into the historical development of the pattern he analyzed.[26] Had he done so, he would have found, I believe, that these notions of the private – what historian of England Lawrence Stone has called the closed domesticated nuclear family – developed in broad conjunction with the rise of capitalism.[27]

Once the split between public and private realms is constituted as it is in capitalism, it provides fertile ground for the encouragement of various kinds of racism.[28] According to the ideology of the public sphere, each person is "free"; he or she has the same chance. Differences in wealth, then, can result only from natural differences among persons. This common sense of the public realm takes on peculiar power when it is combined with private notions that collapse, as Verena Stolcke has argued, social inheritance with biological heredity: Children naturally "take after" their parents. They share the same "blood." Once wealth is

[26] Schneider's ahistoricism, like much of recent North American cultural anthropology, stems from two theoretical presuppositions: (1) that society can be analyzed as a system of norms, analytically separable from culture, which is taken to be a set of core symbols, and (2) that patterns of culture can be examined by analogy with the structures of language. Historical materialism contests both of these assumptions. Something of its ability to encompass other modes of analysis is illustrated in this reinterpretation of Schneider's work. Reinterpreted as ideology, as implicated in power relations, and therefore subject to historical transformations, Schneider's cultural patterns take on new significance.

[27] This is not Stone's point, of course, nor should the relationship between changes in economy and family be seen in any simple unilineal or functionalist way. According to Stone, ". . . the four key features of the modern family – intensified affective bonding of the nuclear core at the expense of neighbours and kin; a strong sense of individual autonomy and the right to personal freedom in the pursuit of happiness; a weakening of the association of sexual pleasure with sin and guilt; and a growing desire for physical privacy – were all well established by 1750 in the key middle and upper sectors of English society," The Family, Sex and Marriage in England 1500–1800 (London: Weidenfeld and Nicolson, 1977), p. 8. See also William J. Goode, World Revolution and Family Patterns (Glencoe: Free Press, 1963), and Edward Shorter, The Making of the Modern Family (New York: Basic Books, 1975). Controversially, Alan MacFarlane has argued that "individualism" was an ancient, rather than a relatively recent, part of English society and culture; see The Origins of English Individualism: The Family, Property, and Social Transition (Cambridge: Cambridge University Press, 1979).

[28] I am not suggesting that capitalism invented racism. Various kinds of color prejudice have helped to organize systems of domination in noncapitalist societies, particularly those in which conquest or slavery are prominent forms of local experience. But something distinctive seems to have been created by the conjunction of color prejudice with egalitarian ideologies. Eugene Genovese makes this point with regard to the American South: The only way to justify slavery in a society that affirmed the absolute value of individual liberty was to "exclude its victims from the community of man," in Elizabeth Fox-Genovese and Eugene D. Genovese, The Fruits of Merchant Capital: Slavery and Bourgeois Property in the Rise and Expansion of Capitalism (New York: Oxford University Press, 1983), p. 403. See also Oliver Cromwell Cox, Caste, Class and Race: A Study in Social Dynamics (New York: Monthly Review Press, [1948] 1959); St. Clair Drake, Black Folk Here and There: An Essay in History and Anthropology (Los Angeles: Center for Afro-American Studies, University of California, 1987).

linked with "blood," racial and ethnic differences can be powerfully valorized.[29] By the late nineteenth century, according to Eric Hobsbawm, the bourgeoisie thought of itself as distinctly racially superior:

Racism pervades the thought of our period to an extent hard to appreciate today, and not always easy to understand. . . . it is perhaps best explained as a mechanism by means of which a fundamentally inegalitarian society based upon a fundamentally egalitarian ideology rationalized its inequalities, and attempted to justify and defend those privileges which the democracy implicit in its institutions must inevitably challenge.[30]

The form and degree of racism have of course changed over time. Still, there has been a continuing tendency within capitalist societies to collapse notions of social and biological reproduction.[31]

As Stolcke has argued, this collapse has a number of other important consequences, most particularly for women:

If social inequalities are thought of as natural differences, genetically transmitted, and if inheritance follows the dictates of heredity, then monogamous marriage, i.e., the exclusive right of the husband over his wife's sexuality, becomes a critical social mechanism to ensure that reproduction occurs between socially, and thus supposedly genetically, equal partners.[32]

Women become defined by their reproductive capabilities: nurturant and loving, mothers presiding over domestic spaces, private havens in an otherwise heartless world.[33]

Notions of gender, sexuality, race, and nationality interrelate in complex ways, and together they constitute a system of power, in both the private and public realms of capitalism: Lines of gender, race, sexuality,

---

[29] Verena Stolcke, "Women's Labours: The Naturalisation of Social Inequality and Women's Subordination," in Kate Young, Carol Wolkowitz, and Roslyn McCullagh, eds., *Of Marriage and the Market: Women's Subordination Internationally and Its Lessons*, 2d ed. (London: Routledge & Kegan Paul, 1984), pp. 159–77. See also the same author, Verena Martinez-Alier, *Marriage, Class and Colour in Nineteenth-Century Cuba* (Cambridge: Cambridge University Press, 1974).

[30] Quoted in Stolcke, "Women's Labours": E. J. Hobsbawm, *The Age of Capital, 1848–1875* (London: Weidenfeld and Nicolson, 1975), pp. 267–8.

[31] Social and biological reproduction take place synergistically, but that does not mean that one is reducible to the other. See Stephen Jay Gould, *The Mismeasure of Man* (New York: W. W. Norton, 1981). Gould begins with a quote from Charles Darwin: "If the misery of our poor be caused not by the laws of nature, but by our institutions, great is our sin."

[32] Stolcke, "Women's Labours," p. 168.

[33] The intersection between Marxist and feminist theories over the past decade has been both vexed and productive. Gender is a category, after all, that crosscuts *every* other axis on which inequality is built in capitalism. In this sense, it is potentially a privileged entryway into the more complex analysis of capitalism that I am advocating. Nancy C. M. Hartsock, *Money, Sex, and Power: Toward a Feminist Historical Materialism* (New York: Longman, 1983), and Michèle Barrett, *Women's Oppression Today* (London: Verso, 1980), are recent examples of these strands of work.

and ethnicity divide and redivide the working class, divide and redivide the household. This process of fractionation takes place in more varied and complex ways than I have been able to indicate so briefly here. Only one of the simplifications of the discussion above is that it draws on mostly North American examples; modern Japanese notions implicated in the construction of power would, no doubt, offer instructive contrasts.

However that may be, the theoretical point I wish to make remains: that productive inequalities in capitalism are not limited to ones of class. Indeed, inasmuch as the public sphere depends on the private for its very continuity, one could say that it is impossible to conceive capitalism as a mode of production except as the intersection of a number of class and nonclass inequalities. Just how many such axes will be required in an expanded epochal analysis of the public and private is unclear, but it is difficult to imagine that gender and nationality will not be on the list.

If this way of proceeding be accepted, it will immediately be clear that an influential version of Marxism – that class is "economic," whereas ethnicity reflects "cultural" factors, that class resides in the base for capitalism, whereas gender and race are the result of superstructural factors – is wrong. All of these inequalities occupy the same analytical level. All are constituted in superstructures, sets of meanings and practices that tend to reproduce productive inequalities. It may be that all are actually required in order to reproduce capitalism, even if one – class – provides the dominant inequality, the low note that anchors the chord.

In this light, it is wrong, I believe, to identify the capitalist mode of production with only one of its faces: liberal and benign, eradicating racial, gender, and sexual discrimination in the public sphere. Nazi Germany should count as the other extreme. On this reading, Auschwitz becomes a horrendously simplified illustration of the interior logic of the private sphere: the extermination of racially inferior Jews and Gypsies and of unnatural homosexuals, the cult of women as mothers, and the aggrandizement of the Fatherland.[34]

In closing this line of thought, let me speculate on the difference that it would have made had the first "Marxist" analysis been done not of

[34] The problems of explaining the Holocaust are exceptionally complicated. Here, I am concerned only to point to its relevance for the themes I am discussing. See Claudia Koonz, *Mothers in the Fatherland* (New York: St. Martin's Press, 1987); Gisela Bock, "Racism and Sexism in Nazi Germany: Motherhood, Compulsory Sterilization, and the State," *Signs* 8 (1983): 400–21; George L. Mosse, *Nationalism and Sexuality: Respectability and Abnormal Sexuality in Modern Europe* (New York: Howard Fertig, 1985).

capitalism, but of a technologically simpler mode of production such as that of Maale. From such a beginning, it would, no doubt, have been difficult to develop *Capital*'s abstract analysis of the public sphere. But it would have been far easier to understand the private realm, to realize that "love" is just as much a secret of capitalism as the "commodity." The intensity of the first depends on the abstractness of the second.

<hr />

If the relationship between power and ideology – base and superstructure – has provided one master theme of this book, the connection between epochal analyses – reproduction schemata of various forms of power/ideology – and the actual contours of history is another.

Within anthropology, a concern for history has a long past. Ever since F. W. Maitland, nearly a century ago, asserted that anthropology would have to choose between being history and being nothing at all, the nature of historical explanation has been a recurring theme: at the birth of functionalism during the 1930s,[35] of transactionalism and structuralism in the 1960s,[36] and of poststructuralist approaches at present.[37]

Clearly, what history has been taken to be – why anthropologists must study it or why they may ignore it – has varied. In this book, I have argued for a particular view of historical explanation, one that makes it the final goal of a stepped analysis. It should be clear that what I mean by historical explanation is not simply an account of the connections between events over a period of time. A leads to B leads to C. Rather, the historical view that I have sought to develop places a central emphasis on power in the reproduction of society and consequently on an investigation of the particular encounters of differently empowered groups

---

[35] Both Radcliffe-Brown and Malinowski criticized aspects of past evolutionary theories as mere historical conjecture: A. R. Radcliffe-Brown, *Structure and Function in Primitive Society* (Oxford: Oxford University Press, 1952), p. 3; Bronislaw Malinowski, *A Scientific Theory of Culture* (Chapel Hill: University of North Carolina Press, 1944), pp. 28–9.

[36] For transactionalist readings of history, see Fredrik Barth, "On the Study of Social Change," *American Anthropologist* 69 (1967): 661–9, and I. M. Lewis, "Introduction," *History and Social Anthropology* (London: Tavistock, 1968), pp. xx–xxv. On structuralism vis-à-vis history, see Claude Lévi-Strauss, *The Savage Mind* (Chicago: University of Chicago Press, [1962] 1966), chap. 9.

[37] I use the category poststructuralist only in the loose sense of some (present) reaction against the (various) structuralisms of the past: See Renato Rosaldo, *Ilongot Headhunting 1883–1974: A Study in Society and History* (Stanford: Stanford University Press, 1980); Richard Price, *First Time: The Historical Vision of an Afro-American People* (Baltimore: Johns Hopkins University Press, 1983); Gerald Sider, *Culture and Class in Anthropology and History: A Newfoundland Illustration* (Cambridge: Cambridge University Press, 1986).

in specific contexts. In sum, historical analyses must be located *in* time. They must capture what might be called historicity, but they do not necessarily have to deal with large-scale changes *through* time.

That this kind of analysis – of possible divided interests, of uneasy compromises, of unpredictable conflict – is necessary in order to understand capitalism nearly everyone, Marxist and non-Marxist, has assumed. (There is much less agreement, of course, on how such an analysis should be carried out.) That a similar approach is necessary in order to comprehend the social structure of technologically simple societies is a possibility only recently and incompletely entertained in anthropology – whether by Marxists or by non-Marxists. What accounts for the difference? What makes our society appear "hot," but so-called primitive ones appear "cold"?[38]

Extrapolating from a number of recent arguments, I suggest that part of the answer rests on a persistent tendency of Western scholars to project capitalist notions of the public and private onto other societies.[39] According to the ideology of the public sphere, the dynamism of capitalism results from its "economics," whereas notions of the private sphere define its constancy: "kinship" as naturally given. Examined from this point of view, so-called kin-based societies indeed appear "cold" – for economics in such societies is virtually missing, and kinship is vastly expanded. Since kinship is, in this view, biologically based, kin-based societies are by definition historically static.[40]

---

[38] These are Lévi-Strauss's phrases in *The Savage Mind*, but the conceptual opposition they imply between "historical" and "nonhistorical" societies has been employed by anthropologists of widely varying theoretical commitment. The exception is, interestingly, transactionalist or neoclassical work. In the latter strand of anthropology, Edmund Leach's *Political Systems of Highland Burma* is a critical text. What Marxist theory adds, as Jonathan Friedman has shown, is an analysis of the connections between political strategy and economic organization.

[39] David M. Schneider, *A Critique of the Study of Kinship* (Ann Arbor: University of Michigan Press, 1984); Sylvia J. Yanagisako, "Family and Household: The Analysis of Domestic Groups," *Annual Review of Anthropology* 8 (1979): 161–205; Jane F. Collier, Michelle Z. Rosaldo, and Sylvia J. Yanagisako, "Is There a Family? New Anthropological Views," in Barrie Thorne and Marilyn Yalom, eds., *Rethinking the Family: Some Feminist Questions* (New York: Longman, 1981); Rayna Rapp, "Toward a Nuclear Freeze? The Gender Politics of Euro-American Kinship Analysis," in Collier and Yanagisako, *Gender and Kinship*, pp. 119–31.

[40] In what is probably still the leading textbook on kinship – an indication of the pervasiveness of these ideas – Robin Fox introduces his analysis with four principles: (1) women have the children, (2) men impregnate the women, (3) men usually exercise control, and (4) primary kin do not mate with each other. See *Kinship and Marriage* (Baltimore: Penguin, 1967), p. 31. The first and second are biological facts; they universally apply to people in all societies. The third and fourth are social facts that depend on cultural constructions; how men exercise control, even if it is assumed that they universally do so, indeed what "control" means, varies from society to society. It varies, in part, because

I have attempted to develop an alternative view, one that establishes history as a key word in the analysis of any mode of production, whatever its level of technological development. In order to do so, I have argued for a stratigraphic notion of causation, one that recognizes and connects different levels of analysis:

Chapter 1 was an analysis of strategic conduct. Labeled neoclassical in economic theory, transactional in social theory, this method of analysis showed that high-dependency households in Bola did not work longer hours in 1975 *because* low-dependency households, presided over by elders, transferred labor to them. Chapters 2 and 3 argued that Bola elders were able to transfer labor *because* of a fundamental inequality within Maale households. This inequality existed as part of an ensemble of relations between chiefs and commoners and between lineage elders and juniors. These inequalities existed *because* they were compatible with the productive powers in Maale. Finally, Chapter 4 examined the particular configuration of political blocs in Bola. In 1975, Bola elders, dependent on the king for their special position within the polity, were threatened by the same forces that threatened the king – local Protestants and the revolution rumbling ominously in the north. *Because* of these particular conditions, Bola elders transferred labor to younger men's households in their community.

These *because* statements occur on contrasting levels of analysis; they can perhaps be made in a different order from the one I have chosen. But a central argument of this book is that different levels of causality must be connected in any robust version of Marxism. How does one level relate to the others? What are the limits of each? To what degree does one logically lead to another? These are some of the questions I have sought to clarify, in relation to what I have called epochal and historical modes of analysis.

The position I have taken contrasts with both that of G. A. Cohen (who has argued, in effect, for the self-sufficiency of epochal analysis) and that of E. P. Thompson (whose rhetoric, at least, suggests that historical explanation can be self-sufficient). Cohen and Thompson have discussed these matters in theoretical terms.[41] But the same contrasts

power is always open to contestation in human societies. Hence kinship is, in a fundamental sense that Fox's exposition misses, a historical subject. Even if, as Fox asserts, male dominance is "rooted in" our primate natures (p. 32), my point remains. Even if the biological requirements of reproduction under certain technological regimes select a range of power inequalities between men and women, these cannot be understood in the same way as biological facts.

[41] G. A. Cohen, *Karl Marx's Theory of History* (Oxford: Clarendon Press, 1978), and E. P.

appear in the empirical analyses of many anthropologists: for example, in Claude Meillassoux's notion of articulation between modes of production in South Africa and in Marshall Sahlins's study of Hawaiian contact with European explorers in the late eighteenth century.[42] In my terms, Meillassoux has attempted to construct an epochal explanation without examining history, and Sahlins has attempted to build a historical explanation without grounding it in epochal structures. A brief consideration of these contrasting approaches will be helpful in summarizing arguments made above.

During the 1970s, it became almost an article of faith among Marxists that any social formation was organized by more than one mode of production – often capitalism in articulation with some other way of producing.[43] In this interaction, the capitalist mode was usually said to be dominant; that is, it subjected the other modes to its own requirements rather than the reverse. In this way it was claimed capitalism could actually preserve so-called precapitalist modes on the periphery of the world system. Articulation became thereby an explanation for underdevelopment.

Meillassoux's model of how the domestic mode of production articulates with capitalism is an example of this argument and is aimed at explaining systems of circulating labor migration, the most notorious example of which is South Africa. So-called tribal areas, noncapitalist enclaves, are so ordered that a substantial portion of male workers have to work as migrants in the capitalist sector, at wages that do not pay for the full costs of reproducing future laborers, that do not support the men's wives and children in the reserves. According to Meillassoux, this system results from the process of articulation and from the overall pressure of the capitalist mode to keep wages as low as possible:

It is by establishing organic relations between capitalist and domestic economies that imperialism set up the mechanism of reproducing cheap labour-power to its profit – a reproductive process which, at present, is the fundamental cause of underdevelopment at one end and of the wealth of the capitalist sector at the other.[44]

Thompson, *The Poverty of Theory and Other Essays* (New York: Monthly Review Press, 1978).

[42] Claude Meillassoux, *Maidens, Meal and Money: Capitalism and the Domestic Community* (Cambridge: Cambridge University Press, [1975] 1981), part II; Marshall Sahlins, *Islands of History* (Chicago: University of Chicago Press, 1985).

[43] Aidan Foster-Carter, "The Modes of Production Controversy," *New Left Review* 107 (1977): 47–77, gives a useful review; see also Harold Wolpe, ed., *The Articulation of Modes of Production* (London: Routledge & Kegan Paul, 1980).

[44] Meillassoux, *Maidens*, p. 95.

In other words, Meillassoux offers an epochal explanation, based on the general logic of capitalism, for migrant labor, a system that contains noncapitalist elements. According to this line of argument, the function of migrant labor is to keep wages low and profits high. The fulfillment of this function is a fundamental aspect of capitalism.

This argument accomplished a great deal in confronting anthropologists with issues they had tended to neglect, but there are two ways in which I believe it is misleading. First, capitalism has no epochal "need" for labor that is somehow below cost. For capitalist reproduction to occur, class inequalities must be preserved, it is true, but this requirement sets up no uniform need for cheap wages. Some capitalists, those who produce goods consumed by workers, actually benefit from higher wages. Therefore, how wages are determined is a complex historical, not epochal, problem, one that requires an examination of a number of particular factors, from class fractions and how they are involved in production, to the actions of the state in relation to these groups. The postulation of the fulfillment of a simple epochal need short-circuits the kind of historical analysis that is required at this point.

The second difficulty involves the very attempt to use the notion of multiple modes of production to describe aspects of social reality not covered by a single mode. I have argued that the concept of a way of producing is, ab initio, an abstract model of how a dominant form of power functionally interlocks with an organization of production so that the resulting structure characterizes a whole epoch of time.

It is certainly true that any particular society in real space-time is a considerably more complex and heterogeneous reality than such a model. Wage labor, for example, may exist as a subsidiary form in feudal societies, as migrant labor exists in capitalist South Africa. But if so, these contingent connections must be analyzed historically – that is, in a way that acknowledges and explains the contingency. This cannot be accomplished by adding the functional requirements of one epochal system to another to produce a still grander articulated structure. It is more accurate to say that the analytical problem at hand involves "disarticulation," the conditional coupling of social traits, traits in some ways compatible, in some ways contradictory.[45]

[45] In the South African case, the fact that the economy is dominated by a gold mining industry faced by internationally fixed prices and high costs of deep-level, low-grade ore is probably important. See Frederick R. Johnstone, *Race, Class and Gold; A Study of Class Relations and Racial Discrimination in South Africa* (London: Routledge & Kegan Paul, 1976). The relevance of Johnstone's thesis is pointed out by Shula Marks, "White Supremacy," *Comparative Studies in Society and History*, 29 (1987): 385–97.

In other words, there is *always* some distance between empirical reality and models of ways of producing. Moreover, the relationship between these two changes as the spatial unit being considered changes. As G. William Skinner has shown, smaller social units nest, in various ways, into larger ones, and different social processes become visible at different levels of social integration.[46] I have analyzed a relatively small unit, Maale, a former chiefdom become an administrative district of an African empire. The model of its dominant inequalities, the relevant mode of production, was the one constructed above. But I might have focused on larger units, including Ethiopia itself, in which case a different mode of production would have become relevant, one resembling in some ways European absolutism.[47] Finally, it would have been possible to consider the dynamics of the world system in which Ethiopia was located. As Eric Wolf has recently shown, the relevant mode in that case would surely have been capitalism.[48] In sum, how one bounds time to create epochal structures depends on how one bounds space and vice versa.

Let me turn from the issues raised by Meillassoux's analysis to those posed by Sahlins's. If Meillassoux may be said to expand epochal analysis into the proper preserve of historical explanation, Sahlins does the reverse. In a dramatic account of Hawaiian cultural categories and how they changed on contact with Europeans, Sahlins makes many of the points I made in Chapter 4. Indeed, that chapter was inspired by his analysis:

Taken together, the set of transformations mediated by tabu suggests a permanent dialectic of structure and practice. Revised in practice, in relations of the conjuncture, the categories return to the cultural order in altered relationships to each other. But then, responding to structural change in the cultural order, the relations of the conjuncture change from one historical moment to the next.[49]

Sahlins uses the dialectic between structure and practice – on the model of Saussure's analysis of language into langue and parole – to show how the categories male and female, commoner and chief, Hawaiian and

---

[46] G. William Skinner, "The Structure of Chinese History," *Journal of Asian Studies* 44 (1985): 271–92.

[47] Donald L. Donham, "Old Abyssinia and the New Ethiopian Empire: Themes in Social History," in Donald L. Donham and Wendy James, eds., *The Southern Marches of Imperial Ethiopia: Essays in History and Anthropology* (Cambridge: Cambridge University Press, 1986), pp. 24–37.

[48] Eric R. Wolf, *Europe and the People Without History* (Berkeley: University of California Press, 1982).

[49] Marshall Sahlins, *Historical Metaphors and Mythical Realities: Structure in the Early History of the Sandwich Islands Kingdom* (Ann Arbor: University of Michigan Press, 1981), p. 54.

British, changed as the taboos and interdictions that were critical in defining them were broken and used in new ways.

But why were just these categories and not others central to the history of the period? In transferring a model of language (a system of communication with few material constraints) to the very different object of society (a system of action necessarily embedded in the material world), Sahlins has no way of analyzing the critical role of power in answering this question.[50] Structure, according to Sahlins, is definitionally severed from any relationship to material reality. Language considered as langue is a self-contained and interrelated set of symbols with *no* necessary relationship to anything outside itself.

If the concept of structure is cut free from power, the opposite occurs with respect to the second concept – parole or practice. For practices are inherently political: "In the cultural system, the sign has a conceptual value fixed by contrasts to other signs; whereas, in action the sign is determined also as an 'interest,' which is its instrumental value to the acting subject."[51] Put into action, at particular conjunctures, symbolic structures are to some degree revised and reordered. But what kinds of conjunctures promote change and which do not? Change to which parts of the structure? Without a theory of how "relations of the conjuncture" affect structure – and Sahlins offers none – this scheme becomes tautological. Anything that happens can be recounted in its terms. Lévi-Straussian structuralism is perhaps saved from stasis thereby, but whether history is explained remains another question.

Sahlins is forced into this impasse by a determination to accord symbols their due place in social theory. It is this, also, that conditions his rejection of Marxism: "These practical notions of culture [Marxist and utilitarian] would offer us a history on the model of a physics. Symbols are symptoms, direct or mystified, of the true force of things."[52] I have attempted to construct a different reading of Marxism. Productive powers, productive inequalities, bases, and superstructures – all of these depend on cultural interpretation. The only part of historical materialism that is independent of local symbols is its starting point – the very definition of what constitutes an inequality. Inequalities, to count as such, must be located in material reality. What regularly constitute them,

---

[50] See Perry Anderson's discussion of this issue in *In The Tracks of Historical Materialism* (Chicago: University of Chicago Press, 1984). According to Saussure himself, language is a "human institution of such a kind that all the other human institutions, with the exception of writing, can only deceive us as to its real essence if we trust in their analogy," quoted in Anderson, p. 2.

[51] Sahlins, *Islands of History*, p. 150.   [52] Sahlins, *Historical Metaphors*, p. 7.

however, are precisely complexes of meaning and practice. This way of understanding Marxism does not require a notion of symbol as symptom nor a construction of history as physics.

To conclude, I have argued that historical materialism requires both epochal and historical analysis – not just both, but more precisely, a motivated transition from the first to the second. For such a transition to be possible, epochal analysis must be understood as incomplete, and historical analysis as conditioned.

Locating the proper boundaries between these two analytical projects is not often easy.[53] Antonio Gramsci, always sensitive to the implications of theory for practice, called attention to the difficulty when he wrote:

A common error in historico-political analysis consists in an inability to find the correct relation between what is organic and what is conjunctural. This leads to presenting causes as immediately operative which in fact only operate indirectly, or to asserting that the immediate causes are the only effective ones. In the first case there is an excess of "economism," or doctrinaire pedantry; in the second, an excess of "ideologism." In the first case there is an overestimation of mechanical causes, in the second an exaggeration of the voluntarist and individual element. . . . The dialectical nexus between the two categories of movement, and therefore of research, is hard to establish precisely. Moreover, if error is serious in historiography, it becomes still more serious in the art of politics, when it is not the reconstruction of past history but the construction of present and future history which is at stake.[54]

As Gramsci warned, magnifying the contingent leads to idealism, minimizing it to economism. Getting things into focus is an exacting and always contested task, in social science as well as in life.

It is often thought that Marxism emphasizes determinism. The reverse is also true. For the final object of historical materialism, that for which the analysis of causes is only a prerequisite, is locating contingency – and thus being able to act upon it.

I began this book with Walter Benjamin's description of the angel of history: "His eyes are staring, his mouth is open, his wings spread. . . . The angel would like to stay, awaken the dead, and make whole what has been smashed. But a storm is blowing from Paradise; it has got caught

[53] For a discussion of this problem in relation to arguments made in this book, see the Appendix.
[54] Antonio Gramsci, *Selections from the Prison Notebooks*, ed. and trans. Quintin Hoare and Geoffrey Nowell Smith (New York: International Publishers, [1948–51] 1971), p. 178.

in his wings with such violence that the angel can no longer close them. The storm irresistibly propels him into the future to which his back is turned. . . ."[55]

"Romance." A utopian moment. Without them, Marxism is not Marxist, critical theory is not critical. But, I have argued, romance must be combined with irony. United in tension, romantic irony contains its own notion of emancipation. Instead of any final transcendence (as might be suggested by a one-sided romanticism), liberation becomes a social asymptote: possible to approach but, given the tragic finitudes of human existence, impossible finally to reach.

Benjamin's point of view contained its mixture of irony. But notice the way the romantic moment is formulated in his thought. Benjamin's angel — like many an anthropologist — looks backward for redemption, backward to traditions endangered by capitalist progress.[56] I have argued that this vision is fundamentally flawed. What capitalism has fractured was, quite simply put, never whole. Tradition only stabilized and inculcated a set of other inequalities — even if it is difficult for us, set as we are within capitalist ones, to see them as such.

The ability to transcend the present comes not from a redemption of the past but from a decentering of the present that results from juxtaposing radically different ways of living. This (anthropological) decentering must be applied not only with respect to capitalist norms but, in some measure, with regard to the theory that calls those norms into question — Marxism itself. Not only with respect to Marxism as science but in regard to the basis on which that science rests.

In the end, what historical materialism depends on, its Grundlage, its base, is a certain shape of the moral imagination.[57] This is true in two

---

[55] Walter Benjamin, *Illuminations*, ed. Hannah Arendt, trans. Harry Zohn (New York: Harcourt, Brace, and World, [1955] 1968), pp. 259–60. For a copy of the Klee watercolor that inspired Benjamin's epigram – less impressive than Benjamin's description – see O. K. Werckmeister, "Walter Benjamin, Paul Klee, and the Angel of History," *Oppositions* 25 (1982): 103–25.

[56] Why have anthropologists so persistently located romantic wholeness in the past rather than in a struggled-for future? The answer is no doubt complex. Part of the explanation may lie in the greater contemplative safety of doing so. If wholeness is located in the past, the present becomes an elegiac study of decay or, at most, of resistance to decay. In contrast, when wholeness is located in the future, the present encapsulates a politically charged existence.

[57] Marxist moral theory has developed in conversation with liberalism, just as Marxist economic theory did the same with respect to neoclassicism. Throughout, the project of liberal moral theory has been to develop universal principles to define individuals' rights and obligations.

As with neoclassicism, the exact terms on which Marxism locates itself with respect to liberalism are critical. In my view, Marxism should incorporate and transcend liberalism

"Lunch in Fur," Meret Oppenheim, 1936

senses – both for the analyst and, in the long term, for those he or she analyzes. As G. A. Cohen has written, insofar as the course of history is inevitable for Marxists, it is inevitable not despite what men and women may do but because of what, being human, they will predictably do.[58]

Hence a final reason that liberalism and Marxism should be understood together: If all of the structures that prevent human freedom were somehow smashed – from class to gender to sexuality to race to ethnicity – comedy would indeed become a master plot. Liberal rights would come into their own. It is this asymptotic ideal of an emancipated future – not of a harmonious past – that properly animates historical materialism. As Gramsci said: Optimism of the will. Pessimism of the intellect.

rather than simply rejecting it. As Steven Lukes in *Marxism and Morality* (Oxford: Clarendon Press, 1985) has shown, however, there has been a tendency within historical materialism to insist that *all* concern for individual rights is ideological, that consequently any means can be used to promote the transition to equality, and that under the highest stages of communism, there will be no need for "rights" since all contradictions will have disappeared. This (what can only be called) one-sided romantic view has had fatal consequences. By not inquiring into certain questions, this version of historical materialism has disabled its followers from anticipating and perhaps preventing Marxism's disasters during the twentieth century – from Stalin's Soviet Union to Pol Pot's Cambodia.

[58] Cohen, *Karl Marx's Theory of History*, p. 147, fn. 1. This claim has been elaborated in chap. 4 of Cohen's new study, *History, Labour, and Freedom: Themes From Marx* (Oxford: Clarendon Press, 1988).

Appendix: Predicting the past from the future

In this book, I have attempted to present both epochal and historical analyses. Given the constraints of anthropological fieldwork – data collection over a relatively brief span of time, the virtual lack, in the Maale case, of written historical records, the consequent difficulties of interpreting oral historical materials – I have faced a number of difficulties.

This was particularly true with respect to measures such as household labor time and net flows of labor among households. In order to separate out what was epochal – relatively stable and indeed characteristic of the Maale way of producing – and what was historical – responsive to particular local configurations of events – I ideally needed data over a long span of time. The realities of anthropological fieldwork did not provide such resources. It was impossible, for example, to reconstruct household labor time for the recent, much less the distant, past.

Given these limitations, I would like to address two possible weaknesses in the arguments above. The first involves a problem of statistical inference: Was there actually no relationship between household dependency ratio and length of the work day in Bola during 1975? Or was the lack of a Chayanovian relationship in figure 1 (p. 32) the result of a small and unrepresentative sample?

It is impossible now to add new information directly relevant to this question. Nevertheless, it would strengthen the possibility that figure 1 is accurate if it could be shown that Maale communities at other times or in other places showed a similar profile. This happens, in fact, to be the case.

In late 1982, I returned to Maale to carry out approximately a year and a half of additional fieldwork, both in Bola in region 1 and in a community called Bio in region 2 (see map 2, p. 160). In Bio, 30 households (out of approximately 130) were selected to represent geographical distribution and variation in wealth and dependency ratio within the area. The activities of household members were recorded for at least three days spaced at intervals from the clearing through planting and weeding seasons of 1983 (early February to early June). As figure 9 (overleaf) shows, there was no relationship between the average length of the work day

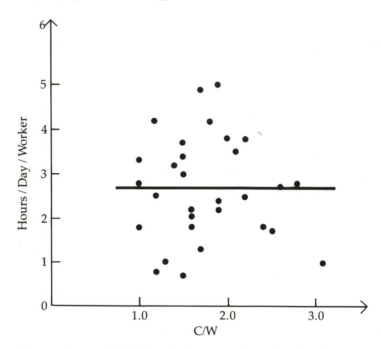

Figure 9: Hours of field labor per day per worker versus the dependency ratio of selected households in Bio during 1983

and household dependency ratio (the line shown represents the mean work day for all households).

Compared to figure 1, figure 9 shows more scatter. This is consistent with the fact that points in figure 9 represent the average of only 3 household work days, whereas those in figure 1 are based on the average of 21. Despite the fact that each point in figure 9, taken by itself, is a less reliable indication of household hours, the likelihood that the *selection* of households (30 compared to 9) biased the test of Chayanov's hypothesis is less. In short, both in Bola during 1975 and in Bio during 1983, households appear to have worked about the same number of hours compared to their neighbors, no matter their dependency ratio. (I shall not attempt to explain the Bio pattern here, except to say that the answer does not involve the transfer of dabo labor.)

The second issue I wish to address involves labor flows among households in Bola for 1975. On this issue, there is no problem of statistical interpretation; figure 2 (p. 44) was based on complete data for Bola. The issue, rather, is whether labor flows from low to high dependency households were in some sense traditional – the way things had always been done in Bola – or whether they were the result, as I have argued,

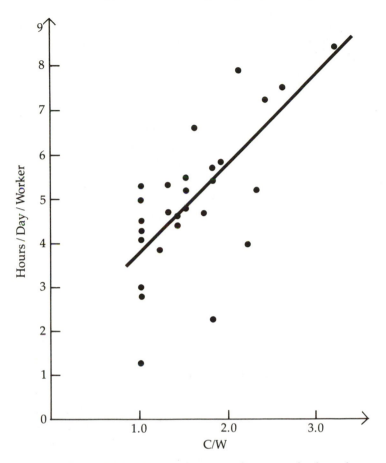

Figure 10: Hours of field labor per day per worker versus the dependency ratio of selected households in Bola during 1983

of factors specific to 1975. Otherwise put, were dabo labor flows epochal or historical?

The information one needs to answer this question involves, of course, the period before 1975. But such data are not available for Maale (nor indeed, as far as I am aware, are any similar data over a span of time for other cases). In its absence, information on labor time in Bola *after* 1975 is indirectly relevant. In 1983, 30 households (out of approximately 110) in Bola and the surrounding vicinity were chosen for intensive study according to the procedures described above. The results, shown in figure 10, are striking: By 1983, Bola households behaved as Chayanov predicted. Households with higher dependency ratios worked significantly longer hours, as the least squares regression in figure 10 shows.

The correlation coefficient, r, of length of the work day with household dependency ratio is 0.68, a result significant at the 0.001 level. Concomitant with figure 10, there was no net transfer of dabo labor from low to high dependency households in Bola during 1983.

I cannot present here an analysis of the wider social changes that took place in Bola from 1975 to 1983 – changes wrought principally by the Ethiopian revolution. Suffice it to say that the revolution came to Bola. It was not made there. By 1983, very little had changed in regard to local concepts of kinship or indeed in relation to the organization of household production. What *had* changed was local political organization. The Maale kingship had been abolished, and with it, the special position of Bola elders and influential market-villagers. By 1983, Bola elders were just like everyone else. They no longer had any special role to play, even ritually, nor any greater need for supporters. With the founding of socialist-oriented peasant cooperatives to take the place of the king and chiefs, the local political game was decisively changed.

Evidently, Bola patterns of labor time and dabo labor flows responded to the changed political environment. Old patterns of "working together" were disrupted, and households were thrown back upon themselves. But if the pattern changed after the revolution, there is no compelling reason to assume that political transformations before did not have similar effects on labor variables. To assume otherwise is to set up a putatively stable, traditional structure for 1975, which is then revolutionized by 1983. This would mistake, I argue, what was in fact historically determined for a change in epochal structures. From overall patterns in Maale society before and after the Ethiopian revolution, it is clear that "traditional" structures were not so stable, nor "revolutionary" changes so far-reaching.

In this sense, how a society responds at a later time may offer insight into how it worked at an earlier one. Disentangling historical from epochal patterns involves the complex process of piecing together insights to produce the best interpretation of empirical materials at hand.

Bibliography*

Abélès, Marc. *Le lieu du politique.* Paris: Société d'Ethnographie, 1983.

Abrams, Philip. *Historical Sociology.* Ithaca: Cornell University Press, 1982.

Adamson, Walter L. *Marx and the Disillusionment of Marxism.* Berkeley: University of California Press, 1985.

Anderson, Benedict. *Imagined Communities: Reflections on the Origin and Spread of Nationalism.* London: Verso, 1983.

Anderson, Perry. *Lineages of the Absolutist State.* London: Verso, 1974.

———. *Arguments within English Marxism.* London: Verso, 1980.

———. *In the Tracks of Historical Materialism.* Chicago: University of Chicago Press, 1984.

Appadurai, Arjun, ed. *The Social Life of Things: Commodities in Cultural Perspective.* Cambridge: Cambridge University Press, 1986.

———. "Putting Hierarchy in Its Place." *Cultural Anthropology* 3 (1988): 36–49.

Asad, Talal, ed. *Anthropology and the Colonial Encounter.* London: Ithaca Press, 1973.

———. "The Concept of Rationality in Economic Anthropology." *Economy and Society* 3 (1974): 211–8.

———. "Anthropological Conceptions of Religion: Reflections on Geertz." *Man* 18 (1983): 237–59.

Balibar, Étienne. "On the Basic Concepts of Historical Materialism." In Louis Althusser and Étienne Balibar. *Reading Capital.* Translated by Ben Brewster. New York: Pantheon, [1968] 1970.

Barlett, Peggy. *Agricultural Choice and Change: Decision Making in a Costa Rican Community.* New Brunswick, N.J.: Rutgers University Press, 1982.

Barrett, Michèle. *Women's Oppression Today.* London: Verso, 1980.

Barth, Fredrik. "Economic Spheres in Darfur." In Raymond Firth, ed. *Themes in Economic Anthropology.* London: Tavistock, 1967.

———. *Process and Form in Social Life: Selected Essays.* Vol. 1. London: Routledge & Kegan Paul, 1981.

Bendix, Reinhard. "Tradition and Modernity Reconsidered." *Comparative Studies in Society and History* 9 (1967): 292–346.

Benjamin, Walter. *Illuminations.* Edited by Hannah Arendt and translated by Harry Zohn. New York: Harcourt, Brace, & World, [1955] 1968.

*The following references include works, particularly recent ones, that are broadly relevant to basic theoretical issues in Marxism and anthropology. With the exception of the entries for Marx and Engels, not all references cited in the footnotes appear here, nor are all works listed here cited in the footnotes.

Bloch, Maurice, ed. *Marxist Analyses and Social Anthropology*. London: Malaby, 1975.

———. *Marxism and Anthropology: The History of a Relationship*. Oxford: Oxford University Press, 1985.

———. *From Blessing to Violence: History and Ideology in the Circumcision Ritual of the Merina of Madagascar*. Cambridge: Cambridge University Press, 1986.

Bourdieu, Pierre. *Outline of a Theory of Practice*. Translated by Richard Nice. Cambridge: Cambridge University Press, [1972] 1977.

Bourgois, Philippe. *Ethnicity at Work: Divided Labor on a Central American Banana Plantation*. Baltimore: Johns Hopkins University Press, 1989.

Brenner, Robert. "The Origins of Capitalist Development: A Critique of Neo-Smithian Marxism." *New Left Review* 104 (1977): 25–92.

Cancian, Frank A. *Economics and Prestige in a Maya Community: The Religious Cargo System in Zinacantan*. Stanford: Stanford University Press, 1965.

———. *Change and Uncertainty in a Peasant Economy: The Maya Corn Farmers of Zinacantan*. Stanford: Stanford University Press, 1972.

Chayanov, Alexander V. *The Theory of Peasant Economy*. Edited and translated by Daniel Thorner, Basile Kerblay, and R. E. F. Smith. Homewood, Ill.: Richard D. Irwin, [1925] 1966.

Clifford, James. *The Predicament of Culture: Twentieth-Century Ethnography, Literature, and Art*. Cambridge: Harvard University Press, 1988.

Clifford, James, and George E. Marcus, eds. *Writing Culture: The Poetics and Politics of Ethnography*. Berkeley: University of California Press, 1986.

Cohen, David William, and E. S. Atieno Odhiambo. *Siaya: The Historical Anthropology of an African Landscape*. Athens, Ohio: Ohio University Press, and London: James Currey.

Cohen, G. A. *Karl Marx's Theory of History: A Defence*. Oxford: Clarendon Press, 1978.

———. *History, Labour, and Freedom: Themes from Marx*. Oxford: Clarendon Press, 1988.

Cohn, Bernard S. "History and Anthropology: The State of Play." *Comparative Studies in Society and History* 22 (1980): 198–221.

Collier, George. *Socialists of Rural Andalusia: Unacknowledged Revolutionaries of the Second Republic*. Stanford: Stanford University Press, 1987.

Collier, Jane F. *Marriage and Inequality in Classless Societies*. Stanford: Stanford University Press, 1988.

Collier, Jane F., and Michelle Z. Rosaldo. "Politics and Gender in Simple Societies." In Sherry B. Ortner and Harriet Whitehead, eds. *Sexual Meanings: The Cultural Construction of Gender and Sexuality*. Cambridge: Cambridge University Press, 1981.

Collier, Jane F., and Sylvia J. Yanagisako, eds. *Gender and Kinship: Essays Toward a Unified Analysis*. Stanford: Stanford University Press, 1987.

Comaroff, Jean. *Body of Power Spirit of Resistance: The Culture and History of a South African People*. Chicago: University of Chicago Press, 1985.

Comaroff, John L. "Rules and Rulers: Political Processes in a Tswana Chiefdom." *Man* 13 (1978): 1–20.

———. "*Sui genderis*: Feminism, Kinship Theory, and Structural 'Domains.' "

In Jane F. Collier and Sylvia J. Yanagisako, eds. *Gender and Kinship: Essays Toward a Unified Analysis*. Stanford: Stanford University Press, 1987.

Comaroff, John L., and Simon Roberts. *Rules and Processes: The Cultural Logic of Dispute in an African Context*. Chicago: University of Chicago Press, 1981.

Cook, Scott. "Beyond the Formen: Towards a Revised Marxist Theory of Precapitalist Formations and the Transition to Capitalism," *Journal of Peasant Studies* 4 (1977): 360–89.

———. *Zapotec Stoneworkers: The Dynamics of Rural Simple Commodity Production in Modern Mexican Capitalism*. Washington, D.C.: University Press of America, 1982.

Corrigan, Philip, and Derek Sayer. *The Great Arch: English State Formation as Cultural Revolution*. Oxford: Basil Blackwell, 1985.

Cox, Oliver Cromwell. *Caste, Class and Race: A Study in Social Dynamics*. New York: Monthly Review Press, [1948] 1959.

Dahrendorf, Ralf. *Essays in the Theory of Society*. Stanford: Stanford University Press, 1968.

Deluz, Ariane, and Maurice Godelier. "A propos de deux textes d'anthropologie économique." *L'Homme* 7 (1967): 78–91.

D'Emilio, John. "Capitalism and Gay Identity." In Ann Snitow, Christine Stansell, and Sharon Thompson, eds. *Powers of Desire: The Politics of Sexuality*. New York: Monthly Review Press, 1983.

Diamond, Stanley. *In Search of the Primitive: A Critique of Civilization*. New Brunswick, N.J.: Transaction Books, 1974.

Dobb, Maurice. *Theories of Value and Distribution Since Adam Smith: Ideology and Economic Theory*. Cambridge: Cambridge University Press, 1973.

Donham, Donald L. *Work and Power in Maale, Ethiopia*. Ann Arbor: UMI Research Press, 1985.

Donham, Donald L., and Wendy James, eds. *The Southern Marches of Imperial Ethiopia: Essays in History and Social Anthropology*. Cambridge: Cambridge University Press, 1986.

Drake, St. Clair. *Black Folk Here and There: An Essay in History and Anthropology*. Los Angeles: Center for Afro-American Studies, University of California, 1987.

Elster, Jon. "Cohen on Marx's Theory of History." *Political Studies* 28 (1980): 121–8.

———. "Marxism, Functionalism and Game Theory." *Theory and Society* 11 (1982): 53–82.

———. *Making Sense of Marx*. Cambridge: Cambridge University Press, 1985.

Engels, Friedrich. *The Origin of the Family, Private Property, and the State*. London: Lawrence & Wishart, [1884] 1972.

———. "Friedrich Engels to Joseph Bloch." In Robert C. Tucker, ed. *The Marx-Engels Reader*. 2d ed. New York: W. W. Norton, [1890] 1978.

Errington, Shelly. *Meaning and Power in a Southeast Asian Realm*. Princeton: Princeton University Press, 1989.

Fabian, Johannes. *Time and the Other: How Anthropology Makes Its Object*. New York: Columbia University Press, 1983.

Firth, Raymond, ed. *Themes in Economic Anthropology*. London: Tavistock, 1967.

Foster-Carter, Aidan. "The Modes of Production Controversy." *New Left Review* 107 (1977): 47–77.

Foucault, Michel. *The History of Sexuality.* Vol. 1. Translated by Robert Hurley. New York: Pantheon, [1976] 1978.

———. *The Use of Pleasure.* Vol. 2 of *The History of Sexuality.* Translated by Robert Hurley. New York: Pantheon, [1984] 1985.

Fox, Richard G. *Lions of the Punjab: Culture in the Making.* Berkeley: University of California Press, 1985.

Fox-Genovese, Elizabeth, and Eugene D. Genovese. *The Fruits of Merchant Capital: Slavery and Bourgeois Property in the Rise and Expansion of Capitalism.* New York: Oxford University Press, 1983.

Friedman, Jonathan: "Tribes, States, and Transformations." In Maurice Bloch, ed. *Marxist Analyses and Social Anthropology.* London: Malaby, 1975.

———. "An Interview with Eric Wolf." *Current Anthropology* 28 (1987): 107–18.

Friedman, Jonathan, and M. J. Rowlands, eds. *The Evolution of Social Systems.* London: Duckworth, 1977.

Geertz, Clifford. *The Interpretation of Cultures.* New York: Basic Books, 1973.

———. *Works and Lives: The Anthropologist as Author.* Stanford: Stanford University Press, 1988.

Gellner, Ernest, ed. *Soviet and Western Anthropology.* London: Duckworth, 1980.

———. *Nations and Nationalism.* Oxford: Basil Blackwell, 1983.

Genovese, Eugene D. *Roll, Jordan, Roll: The World the Slaves Made.* New York: Pantheon, 1974.

Geras, Norman. *Marx and Human Nature: Refutation of a Legend.* London: New Left Books, 1983.

Geuss, Raymond. *The Idea of a Critical Theory: Habermas and the Frankfurt School.* Cambridge: Cambridge University Press, 1981.

Ghani, Ashraf. "A Conversation with Eric Wolf." *American Ethnologist* 14 (1987): 346–66.

Giddens, Anthony. *Central Problems in Social Theory: Action, Structure and Contradiction in Social Analysis.* Berkeley: University of California Press, 1979.

———. *A Contemporary Critique of Historical Materialism.* Berkeley: University of California Press, 1981.

Godelier, Maurice. *Rationality and Irrationality in Economics.* Translated by Brian Pearce. New York: Monthly Review Press, [1966] 1972.

———. *Perspectives in Marxist Anthropology.* Translated by Robert Brain. Cambridge: Cambridge University Press, [1973] 1977.

———. *The Making of Great Men: Male Domination and Power among the New Guinea Baruya.* Translated by Rupert Swyer. Cambridge: Cambridge University Press, [1982] 1986.

———. *The Mental and the Material: Thought Economy and Society.* Translated by Martin Thom. London: Verso, [1984] 1986.

Goody, Jack. *Technology, Tradition and the State in Africa.* Oxford: Oxford University Press, 1971.

———. *Production and Reproduction: A Comparative Study of the Domestic Domain.* Cambridge: Cambridge University Press, 1976.

————. *The Development of the Family and Marriage in Europe*. Cambridge: Cambridge University Press, 1983.

Gouldner, Alvin. *The Two Marxisms: Contradictions and Anomalies in the Development of Theory*. [New York: Seabury Press, 1980] New York: Oxford University Press, 1982.

Gramsci, Antonio. *Selections from the Prison Notebooks*. Edited and translated by Quintin Hoare and Geoffrey Nowell Smith. New York: International Publishers, [1948–1951] 1971.

Gudeman, Stephen. *The Demise of a Rural Economy: From Subsistence to Capitalism in a Latin American Village*. London: Routledge & Kegan Paul, 1978.

————. *Economics as Culture: Models and Metaphors of Livelihood*. London: Routledge & Kegan Paul, 1986.

Habermas, Jürgen. *Communication and the Evolution of Society*. Translated by Thomas McCarthy. Boston: Beacon Press, [1976] 1979.

Hakken, David, and Hanna Lessinger, eds. *Perspectives in U.S. Marxist Anthropology*. Boulder, Col.: Westview Press, 1987.

Harris, Olivia. "Households as Natural Units." In Kate Young, Carol Wolkowitz, and Roslyn McCullagh, eds. *Of Marriage and the Market: Women's Subordination Internationally and Its Lessons*. 2d ed. London: Routledge & Kegan Paul, 1984.

Harris, Olivia, and Kate Young. "Engendered Structures: Some Problems in the Analysis of Reproduction." In Joel S. Kahn and Josep R. Llobera, eds. *The Anthropology of Pre-Capitalist Societies*. London: Macmillan, 1981.

Hart, Keith. *The Political Economy of West African Agriculture*. Cambridge: Cambridge University Press, 1982.

Hartsock, Nancy C. M. *Money, Sex, and Power: Toward a Feminist Historical Materialism*. New York: Longman, 1983.

Hempel, Carl C. *Aspects of Scientific Explanation*. New York: Free Press, 1965.

Hobsbawm, E. J. *The Age of Capital, 1848–1875*. London: Weidenfeld & Nicolson, 1975.

Hymes, Dell, ed. *Reinventing Anthropology*. New York: Pantheon, 1969.

Jameson, Fredric. *Marxism and Form: Twentieth-Century Dialectical Theories of Literature*. Princeton: Princeton University Press, 1971.

————. *The Political Unconscious: Narrative as a Socially Symbolic Act*. Ithaca: Cornell University Press, 1981.

Kahn, Joel S. *Minangkabau Social Formations: Indonesian Peasants and the World-Economy*. Cambridge: Cambridge University Press, 1980.

Kahn, Joel S., and Josep R. Llobera, eds. *The Anthropology of Pre-Capitalist Societies*. London: Macmillan, 1981.

Kelly, Raymond C. *The Nuer Conquest: The Structure and Development of an Expansionist System*. Ann Arbor: University of Michigan Press, 1985.

Kirschoff, Paul. "The Principles of Clanship in Human Societies." In Morton Fried, ed. *Readings in Anthropology*. 2d ed. Vol. 2. New York: Thomas Y. Crowell, 1968.

Kołakowski, Leszek. *Main Currents of Marxism: Its Rise, Growth, and Dissolution*. 3 vols. Translated by P. S. Falla. Oxford: Clarendon Press, 1978.

Lange, Oskar. "Marxian Economics and Modern Economic Theory." *Review of Economic Studies* 2 (1934–35): 189–201.

Leach, Edmund R. *Political Systems of Highland Burma: A Study of Kachin Social Structure.* London: Athlone Press, 1954.

———. *Pul Eliya: A Village in Ceylon.* Cambridge: Cambridge University Press, 1961.

Leclerc, Gérard. *Anthropologie et colonialisme.* Paris: Fayard, 1972.

Lenin, Vladimir I. *The Development of Capitalism in Russia: The Process of the Formation of a Home Market for Large-Scale Industry.* Moscow: Progress Publishers, [1899] 1956.

Lenski, Gerhard. *Power and Privilege: A Theory of Social Stratification.* New York: McGraw-Hill, 1966.

Lewis, I. M., ed. *History and Social Anthropology.* London: Tavistock, 1968.

Löwy, Michael. "Naphta or Settembrini? Lukács and Romantic Anticapitalism." *New German Critique* 42 (1987): 17–31.

Lukács, Georg. *History and Class Consciousness: Studies in Marxist Dialectics.* Translated by Rodney Livingstone. Cambridge: MIT Press, [1923] 1971.

Lukes, Stephen. "Can the Base Be Distinguished From the Superstructure?" In David Miller and Larry Siedentop, eds. *The Nature of Political Theory.* Oxford: Clarendon Press, 1983.

———. *Marxism and Morality.* Oxford: Oxford University Press, 1985.

Marcus, George E., and Michael M. J. Fischer. *Anthropology as Cultural Critique: An Experimental Moment in the Human Sciences.* Chicago: University of Chicago Press, 1986.

Martinez-Alier [Stolcke], Verena. *Marriage, Class and Colour in Nineteenth-Century Cuba.* Cambridge: Cambridge University Press, 1974.

Marx, Karl. "The Poverty of Philosophy." In Marx and Engels. *Collected Works.* Vol. 6. London: Lawrence & Wishart, [1847] 1976.

———. "The Eighteenth Brumaire of Louis Bonaparte." In Marx and Engels. *Collected Works.* Vol. 11. London: Lawrence & Wishart, [1852] 1979.

———. *A Contribution to the Critique of Political Economy.* Translated by S. W. Ryazanskaya. Moscow: Progress Publishers, [1859] 1970.

———. *Capital.* Vols. 1 and 3. Translated by Ben Fowkes. New York: Vintage, [1867] 1976 and [1894] 1981.

———. *Theories of Surplus Value.* Part I. Translated by Emile Burns. Edited by S. Ryazanskaya. Moscow: Progress Publishers. [1905–10] 1963.

———. "Economic and Philosophical Manuscripts." In *Early Writings.* Translated by Rodney Livingstone and Gregor Benton. New York: Vintage, [1934] 1975.

———. *Grundrisse: Introduction to the Critique of Political Economy.* Translated by Martin Nicolaus. New York: Vintage Books, [1939] 1973.

Marx, Karl, and Friedrich Engels. "Manifesto of the Communist Party." In Marx and Engels. *Collected Works.* Vol. 6. London: Lawrence & Wishart, [1848] 1976.

———. "The German Ideology." In Marx and Engels. *Collected Works.* Vol. 5. London: Lawrence & Wishart, [1932] 1976.

McMurtry, John. *The Structure of Marx's World-View*. Princeton: Princeton University Press, 1978.

Medick, Hans, and David W. Sabean, eds. *Interest and Emotion: Essays on the Study of Family and Kinship*. Cambridge: Cambridge University Press, 1984.

Meillassoux, Claude. " 'The Economy' in Agricultural Self-Sustaining Societies: A Preliminary Analysis." In David Seddon, ed. *Relations of Production: Marxist Approaches to Economic Anthropology*. London: Frank Cass, [1960] 1978.

———. *Anthropologie économique des Gouro de Côte d'Ivoire*. Paris: Mouton, 1964.

———. "On the Mode of Production of the Hunting Band." In Pierre Alexandre, ed. *French Perspectives in African Studies*. London: Oxford University Press, [1967] 1973.

———. "From Reproduction to Production: A Marxist Approach to Economic Anthropology." *Economy and Society* 1 (1972): 93–105.

———. *Maidens, Meal and Money: Capitalism and the Domestic Community*. Cambridge: Cambridge University Press, [1975] 1981.

Merton, Robert K. *Social Theory and Social Structure*. New York: Free Press, 1949.

Miller, Richard W. *Analyzing Marx: Morality, Power and History*. Princeton: Princeton University Press, 1984.

Mintz, Sidney W. *Worker in the Cane: A Puerto Rican Life History*. New Haven: Yale University Press, 1960.

———, ed. *Slavery, Colonialism, and Racism*. New York: W. W. Norton, 1974.

———. "On the Concept of a Third World." *Dialectical Anthropology* 1 (1976): 377–82.

———. "American Anthropology in the Marxist Tradition." In Sidney Mintz et al., eds. *On Marxian Perspectives in Anthropology: Essays in Honor of Harry Hoijer, 1981*. Malibu, Calif.: Undena Publications, 1984.

———. *Sweetness and Power: The Place of Sugar in Modern History*. New York: Viking, 1985.

Moore, Stanley. *Marx on the Choice Between Socialism and Communism*. Cambridge: Harvard University Press, 1980.

O'Laughlin, Bridget. "Mediation of a Contradiction: Why Mbum Women Do Not Eat Chicken." In Michelle Z. Rosaldo and Louise Lamphere, eds. *Woman, Culture, and Society*. Stanford: Stanford University Press, 1974.

———. "Marxist Approaches to Anthropology." *Annual Reviews of Anthropology* 4 (1975): 341–70.

———. "Production and Reproduction: Meillassoux's 'Femmes, greniers et capitaux.' " *Critique of Anthropology* 8 (1977): 3–32.

Ollman, Bertell. *Alienation: Marx's Conception of Man in Capitalist Society*. 2d ed. Cambridge: Cambridge University Press, 1976.

Orans, Martin. "Surplus." *Human Organization* 25 (1966): 24–32.

———. "Maximizing in Jajmani Land: A Model of Caste Relations." *American Anthropologist* 70 (1968): 875–97.

———. "Domesticating the Functional Dragon: An Analysis of Piddocke's Potlatch." *American Anthropologist* 77 (1975): 312–28.

Ortner, Sherry B. "Theory in Anthropology Since the Sixties." *Comparative Studies in Society and History* 26 (1984): 126–66.

————. *High Religion: A Cultural and Political History of Sherpa Buddhism*. Princeton: Princeton University Press, 1989.

Ortner, Sherry B., and Harriet Whitehead, eds. *Sexual Meanings: The Cultural Construction of Gender and Sexuality*. Cambridge: Cambridge University Press, 1981.

Padgug, Robert A. "Sexual Matters: On Conceptualizing Sexuality in History." *Radical History Review* 20 (1979): 3–23.

Pearson, Harry W. "The Economy Has No Surplus: A Critique of a Theory of Development." In Karl Polanyi, Conrad Arensberg, and Harry W. Pearson, eds. *Trade and Market in the Early Empires*. Glencoe, Ill.: Free Press, 1957.

Plamenatz, John. *Karl Marx's Philosophy of Man*. Oxford: Clarendon Press, 1975.

Price, Richard. *First Time: The Historical Vision of an Afro-American People*. Baltimore: Johns Hopkins University Press, 1983.

Rapp [Reiter], Rayna. "Toward a Nuclear Freeze? The Gender Politics of Euro-American Kinship Analysis." In Jane F. Collier and Sylvia J. Yanagisako, eds. *Gender and Kinship: Essays Toward a Unified Analysis*. Stanford: Stanford University Press, 1987.

Reiter [Rapp], Rayna, ed. *Toward an Anthropology of Women*. New York: Monthly Review Press, 1975.

Rey, Pierre-Philippe. *Colonialisme, neo-colonialisme, et transition au capitalisme*. Paris: Maspero, 1971.

————. *Les alliances de classes*. Paris: Maspero, 1973.

————. "The Lineage Mode of Production." *Critique of Anthropology* 3 (1975): 27–79.

Roemer, John, ed. *Analytical Marxism*. Cambridge: Cambridge University Press, 1986.

Rosaldo, Michelle Z. "The Use and Abuse of Anthropology: Reflections on Feminism and Cross-Cultural Understanding." *Signs* 5 (1980): 389–417.

Rosaldo, Renato. *Ilongot Headhunting 1883–1974: A Study in Society and History*. Stanford: Stanford University Press, 1980.

————. *Culture and Truth: The Remaking of Social Analysis*. Boston: Beacon Press, 1989.

Roseberry, William. "Balinese Cockfights and the Seduction of Anthropology." *Social Research* 49 (1982): 1013–28.

————. *Coffee and Capitalism in the Venezuelan Andes*. Austin: University of Texas Press, 1983.

————. *Anthropologies and Histories: Essays in Culture, History, and Political Economy*. New Brunswick, N.J.: Rutgers University Press, 1989.

Rubin, Gayle. "The Traffic in Women: Notes on the 'Political Economy' of Sex." In Rayna R. Reiter, ed. *Toward an Anthropology of Women*. New York: Monthly Review Press, 1975.

Sacks, Karen. *Sisters and Wives: The Past and Future of Sexual Equality*. Westport, Conn.: Greenwood Press, 1979.

Sahlins, Marshall. *Tribesmen*. Englewood Cliffs, N.J.: Prentice-Hall, 1968.

————. "The Intensity of Domestic Production in Primitive Societies: Social Inflections of the Chayanov Slope." In George Dalton, ed. *Studies in Economic Anthropology*. Washington: American Anthropological Association, 1971.

————. *Stone Age Economics*. Chicago: Aldine-Atherton, 1972.

————. *Culture and Practical Reason*. Chicago: University of Chicago Press, 1976.

————. *Historical Metaphors and Mythical Realities: Structure in the Early History of the Sandwich Islands Kingdom*. Ann Arbor: University of Michigan Press, 1981.

————. *Islands of History*. Chicago: University of Chicago Press, 1985.

Said, Edward W. *Orientalism*. New York: Pantheon Books, 1978.

Salisbury, Richard F. *From Stone to Steel: Economic Consequences of a Technological Change in New Guinea*. London: Cambridge University Press for Melbourne University Press, 1962.

Samuel, Raphael. "British Marxist Historians, 1880–1980: Part I." *New Left Review* 120 (1980): 21–96.

Scheffler, Harold W. "The 'Meaning' of Kinship in American Culture: Another View." In Keith H. Basso and Henry A. Selby, eds. *Meaning in Anthropology*. Albuquerque: University of New Mexico Press, 1976.

Schneider, David. "Kinship, Nationality and Religion in American Culture: Toward a Definition of Kinship." In Robert F. Spencer, ed. *Forms of Symbolic Action*. Seattle: University of Washington Press for the American Ethnological Society, 1969.

————. "What is Kinship All About?" In Priscilla Reining, ed. *Kinship Studies in the Morgan Centennial Year*. Washington, D.C.: Washington Anthropological Society, 1972.

————. *American Kinship: A Cultural Account*. 2d ed. Chicago: University of Chicago Press, 1980.

————. *A Critique of the Study of Kinship*. Ann Arbor: University of Michigan Press, 1984.

Schneider, Jane, "Was There a Pre-Capitalist World System?" *Peasant Studies Newsletter* 6 (1977): 20–9.

————. "Peacocks and Penguins: The Political Economy of European Cloth and Colors." *American Ethnologist* 5 (1978): 43–37.

————. "European Expansion and Hand-Crafted Cloth: A Critique of Oppositional Use-Value vs. Exchange-Value Models." *Journal of Historical Sociology* 1 (1989): 431–8.

Schneider, Jane, and Peter Schneider. *Culture and Political Economy in Western Sicily*. New York: Academic Press, 1976.

Scott, James C. *The Moral Economy of the Peasant: Rebellion and Subsistence in Southeast Asia*. New Haven: Yale University Press, 1976.

————. *Weapons of the Weak: Everyday Forms of Peasant Resistance*. New Haven: Yale University Press, 1985.

Seddon, David, ed. *Relations of Production: Marxist Approaches to Economic Anthropology*. London: Frank Cass, 1978.

Semenov, Yuri I. "The Theory of Socio-Economic Formations and World History." In Ernest Gellner, ed. *Soviet and Western Anthropology*. London: Duckworth, 1980.

Shaw, William H. *Marx's Theory of History*. Stanford: Stanford University Press, 1978.

Sider, Gerald. *Culture and Class in Anthropology and History: A Newfoundland Illus-tration.* Cambridge: Cambridge University Press, 1986.

Skinner, G. William. "Chinese Peasants and the Closed Community: An Open and Shut Case." *Comparative Studies in Society and History* 13 (1971): 270–81.

———. "Mobility Strategies in Late Imperial China: A Regional Systems Analysis." In Carol A. Smith, ed. *Regional Analysis.* Vol. 1. New York: Academic Press, 1976.

———, ed. *The City in Late Imperial China.* Stanford: Stanford University Press, 1977.

———. "The Structure of Chinese History." *Journal of Asian Studies* 44 (1985): 271–92.

Smith, Carol A., ed. *Regional Analysis.* 2 vols. New York: Academic Press, 1976.

———. "Beyond Dependency Theory: National and Regional Patterns of Un-derdevelopment in Guatemala." *American Ethnologist* 5 (1978): 574–617.

———. "Culture and Community: The Language of Class in Guatemala." *The Year Left* 2 (1987): 197–217.

Snitow, Ann, Christine Stansell, and Sharon Thompson, eds. *Powers of Desire: The Politics of Sexuality.* New York: Monthly Review Press, 1983.

Stinchcombe, Arthur L. *Constructing Social Theories.* New York: Harcourt, Brace & World, 1968.

Stolcke [Martinez-Alier], Verena. "Women's Labours: The Naturalisation of So-cial Inequality and Women's Subordination." In Kate Young, Carol Wol-kowitz, and Roslyn McCullagh, eds. *Of Marriage and the Market: Women's Subordination Internationally and Its Lessons.* 2d ed. London: Routledge & Ke-gan Paul, 1984.

———. *Coffee Planters, Workers and Wives: Class Conflict and Gender Relations on São Paulo Plantations, 1850–1980.* New York: St. Martin's Press, 1988.

Stoler, Ann L. *Capitalism and Confrontation in Sumatra's Plantation Belt, 1870–1979.* New Haven: Yale University Press, 1985.

Strathern, Andrew, ed. *Inequality in New Guinea Highlands Societies.* Cambridge: Cambridge University Press, 1982.

Strathern, Marilyn. "Kinship and Economy: Constitutive Orders of a Provisional Kind." *American Ethnologist* 12 (1985): 191–209.

Taussig, Michael T. *The Devil and Commodity Fetishism in South America.* Chapel Hill: University of North Carolina Press, 1980.

———. *Shamanism, Colonialism, and the Wild Man: A Study in Terror and Healing.* Chicago: University of Chicago Press, 1987.

Terray, Emmanuel. *Marxism and "Primitive" Societies.* Translated by Mary Klop-per. New York: Monthly Review Press, [1969] 1972.

———. "Classes and Class Consciousness in the Abron Kingdom of Gya-man." In Maurice Bloch, ed. *Marxist Analyses and Social Anthropology.* Lon-don: Malaby, 1975.

———. "On Exploitation: Elements of an Autocritique." *Critique of Anthropol-ogy* 13/14 (1979): 29–39.

Therborn, Gören. *Science, Class, and Society: On the Formation of Sociology and His-torical Materialism.* London: New Left Books. 1976.

Thompson, E. P. *The Making of the English Working Class*. Harmondsworth: Penguin, 1968.
———. *Whigs and Hunters: The Origin of the Black Act*. Harmondsworth: Penguin, 1975.
———. *The Poverty of Theory and Other Essays*. New York: Monthly Review Press, 1978.
Trouillot, Michel-Rolph. *Peasants and Capital: Dominica in the World Economy*. Baltimore: Johns Hopkins University Press, 1988.
Turner, Terence. "Production, Exploitation and Social Consciousness in the 'Peripheral Situation.' " *Social Analysis* 19 (1986): 91–115.
Van Parijs, Philippe. "From Contradiction to Catastrophe." *New Left Review* 115 (1979): 87–96.
Vincent, Joan. *Teso in Transformation: The Political Economy of Peasant and Class in Eastern Africa*. Berkeley: University of California Press, 1982.
———. "Anthropology and Marxism: Past and Present." *American Ethnologist* 12 (1985): 137–47.
Wallerstein, Immanuel. *The Modern World-System: Capitalist Agriculture and the Origins of the European World-Economy in the Sixteenth Century*. New York: Academic Press, 1974.
Weber, Max. *Roscher and Knies: The Logical Problems of Historical Economics*. Translated by G. Oakes. New York: Free Press, [1903–1906] 1975.
———. *The Protestant Ethic and the Spirit of Capitalism*. Translated by Talcott Parsons. New York: Charles Scribner's Sons, [1904–1905] 1958.
Wessell, Leonard P., Jr. *Karl Marx, Romantic Irony, and the Proletariat: The Mythopoetic Origins of Marxism*. Baton Rouge: Louisiana State University Press, 1979.
Wessman, James W. *Anthropology and Marxism*. Cambridge: Schenkman, 1981.
White, Hayden. *Metahistory: The Historical Imagination in Nineteenth-Century Europe*. Baltimore: Johns Hopkins University Press, 1973.
Williams, Raymond. *The Country and the City*. New York: Oxford University Press, 1973.
———. *Marxism and Literature*. Oxford: Oxford University Press, 1977.
———. *Problems in Materialism and Culture*. London: Verso, 1980.
———. *Keywords: A Vocabulary of Culture and Society*. Rev. ed. New York: Oxford University Press, 1985.
Wolf, Eric R. *Sons of the Shaking Earth*. Chicago: University of Chicago Press, 1959.
———. *Peasants*. Englewood Cliffs, N.J.: Prentice-Hall, 1966.
———. *Peasant Wars of the Twentieth Century*. New York: Harper & Row, 1969.
———. "American Anthropologists and American Society." In Dell Hymes, ed. *Reinventing Anthropology*. New York: Pantheon, 1969.
———. *Europe and the People Without History*. Berkeley: University of California Press, 1982.
———. "Ideas and Power." In Thomas Harding and David Kaplan, eds. *Festschrift for Elman R. Service*. Forthcoming.

Wolpe, Harold, ed. *The Articulation of Modes of Production.* London: Routledge & Kegan Paul, 1980.

Wood, Allen W. *Karl Marx.* London: Routledge & Kegan Paul, 1981.

Wright, Eric Olin. "Giddens's Critique of Marxism." *New Left Review* 138 (1983): 11–35.

Yanagisako, Sylvia J. *Transforming the Past: Tradition and Kinship Among Japanese Americans.* Stanford: Stanford University Press, 1985.

Young, Kate, Carol Wolkowitz, and Roslyn McCullagh, eds. *Of Marriage and the Market: Women's Subordination Internationally and Its Lessons.* 2d ed. London: Routledge & Kegan Paul.

Index